Britain in Agony

BRITAIN IN AGONY

The Growth of Political Violence

Richard Clutterbuck

FABER AND FABER

LONDON AND BOSTON

*First published in 1978
by Faber and Faber Limited
3 Queen Square London WC1
Printed in Great Britain by
Latimer Trend & Company Ltd Plymouth
All rights reserved*

To
NIKKI

British Library Cataloguing in Publication Data
Clutterbuck, Richard
  Britain in agony.
    1. Violence—Great Britain 2. Great Britain
    —Politics and government—1964—
    I. Title
  322.4'2   JN231

  ISBN 0-571-11188-2

Contents

Contents

PART III—DISRUPTION, REACTION AND REFORM

Contents

Abbreviations

ACAS	Advisory, Conciliation and Arbitration Service.
APEX	Association of Professional, Executive and Computer Staff.
ASLEF	Amalgamated Society of Locomotive Engineers and Firemen.
ASTMS	Association of Scientific, Technical and Managerial Staffs.
AUEW	Amalgamated Union of Engineering Workers.
BBC	British Broadcasting Corporation.
BP	British Petroleum.
CAC	Central Arbitration Committee.
CBI	Confederation of British Industry.
CEGB	Central Electricity Generating Board.
CIR	Council on Industrial Relations.
CPBML	Communist Party of Britain, Marxist-Leninist.
CPEML	Communist Party of England, Marxist-Leninist.
CPGB	Communist Party of Great Britain.
CPSA	Civil and Public Services Association.
DEP	Department of Employment and Productivity.
DPP	Director of Public Prosecutions.
EEC	European Economic Community.
EEPTU	Electrical, Electronic, Plumbers' & Telecommunications Union.
EPA	Employment Protection Act, 1975.
EPEA	Electrical Power Engineers' Association.
FT Index	Financial Times Index.
FTAT	Furniture, Timber and Allied Trade Unions.

GMWU   General and Municipal Workers' Union.

IMF   International Monetary Fund.
IMG   International Marxist Group.
IRA   Irish Republican Army.
IS   International Socialists.
ITV   Independent Television.
IRIS   Industrial Research and Information Services.

LAW   Loyalist Association of Workers.

MORI   Market and Opinion Research International.

NAFF   National Association for Freedom.
NALGO   National Association of Local Government
                Officers.
NCB   National Coal Board.
NCCL   National Council for Civil Liberties.
NEB   National Enterprise Board.
NEC   National Executive Committee.
NEDC   National Economic Development Council.
NF   National Front.
NFBTE   National Federation of Building Trade Em-
                ployers.
NIRC   National Industrial Relations Court.
NJCBI   National Joint Council for the Building Industry.
NP   National Party.
NUJ   National Union of Journalists.
NUM   National Union of Mineworkers.
NUT   National Union of Teachers.

OAPEC   Organization of Arab Petroleum-Exporting
                Countries.
OPEC   Organization of Petroleum-Exporting Countries.
ORC   Opinion Research Centre.

PIB   Prices and Incomes Board.
PLP   Parliamentary Labour Party.
PP   Posted price (of oil).
PR   Proportional Representation.

RHC	Red Hand Commando.
RPI	Retail Price Index.
RUC	Royal Ulster Constabulary.
SDLP	Social Democratic and Labour Party.
SLL	Socialist Labour League.
SNP	Scottish Nationalist Party.
SWP	Socialist Workers' Party.
TGWU	Transport and General Workers' Union.
TRUEMID	Movement for True Industrial Democracy.
TUC	Trades Union Congress.
TULRA	Trade Union and Labour Relations Act, 1974.
TULR(A)A	Trade Union and Labour Relations (Amendment) Act, 1976.
UCATT	Union of Construction and Allied Trades and Technicians.
UDA	Ulster Defence Association.
UPW	Union of Post Office Workers.
USCA	Ulster Special Constabulary Association.
USDAW	Union of Shop, Distributive and Allied Workers.
UVF	Ulster Volunteer Force.
UWC	Ulster Workers' Council.
WRP	Workers' Revolutionary Party.
WSL	Workers' Socialist League.

Preface

Most of the research for this book was done in 1976–7 with the support of a grant from the Wolfson Foundation which provided me with a research assistant; the book also incorporates some earlier research done on the incidents at Saltley, Shrewsbury and Red Lion Square in 1974–5 under a Social Science Research Council grant.

Our primary source of information was from interviews with people who witnessed or took part in the events described, supplemented by a study of their plans, their reports and (where applicable) their journals before and afterwards; secondary sources are acknowledged in the notes.

We interviewed people of all points of view—trade unionists, employers, pickets, demonstrators, victims of violence, journalists and police officers. They included members of political parties and pressure groups across the political spectrum, from extreme Left to extreme Right. Only very rarely (twice, I think) did anyone refuse to talk to us. Almost without exception they were frank and forthcoming and prepared to argue and discuss their views. They all knew that I was writing a book. Many of them asked me not to quote them by name, so I have thought it best to name none, except for well-known public figures, such as Sir Derrick Capper or Arthur Scargill, whose views in general are already on record. I am immensely grateful for their frankness, which highlighted at least one encouraging feature of British society which still survived amongst so many bleak ones. Trying to strike a balance between such wide ranging views has been a fascinating experience, and there can be none of my conclusions with which all of them would agree.

I must pay a tribute to our much maligned press. In reports compiled against the clock and printed overnight, the facts reported by journalists on the spot have generally proved accurate and their interpretations have stood the test of time. Looking back at the morning papers as a source of information three years later, I am filled with wonder and admiration. The same goes for radio and television reports; notes I made while watching the TV on the night have usually been confirmed.

I want to clarify one word which appears a lot—'Marxist'. I use it in its literal sense. The word 'Left' is so imprecise that I have avoided it where possible. There are as many Marxist sects as there are Christian sects, and they are as different in their interpretation as Catholics and Jehovah's Witnesses. There are, for example, two totally different sects represented within the Labour Party, though both are in a small minority in the Party. I argued with members of many of these sects and I agreed with much and disagreed with much of what they said. They would disagree no less with each other. But, though they differ in interpretation and method, they all aim at the same kind of society as Karl Marx described. I use the word 'Marxist' to mean that, not (as it is sometimes used) as a term either of approval or abuse.

I have been remarkably lucky with my research assistants, Nicola Ratcliffe, Penelope Wellburn and Louise Perry. With their varied disciplines (political sociology, history and law) and with their even more varied political views, their opinions will differ on my conclusions; but they all contributed richly to the book as interviewers, researchers and critics—and as stimulating comrades in arms. I am most grateful both to them and to the Wolfson Foundation which made their employment possible.

EXETER
December 1977   Richard Clutterbuck

Introduction

The seven years from 1971 to 1977 must surely be amongst the most agonizing in British history. They were by British standards exceptionally violent years: our economic performance was dismal; and our society, instead of drawing together as it normally does in a crisis, seemed to become more cantankerous, less generous and less compassionate.

In so far as the blame rests upon the Governments it must be shared, for the Conservatives were in power for the first period and Labour for the second. The two periods were, in their very different ways, equally disastrous. The malaise lies deeper than party politics.

The first four years, 1971-4, were the most violent for over sixty years (since 1911) in terms of internal political violence: in strikes, demonstrations and terrorism. The second three, 1975-7, saw unprecedented inflation, a collapse of the pound and the worst unemployment since the 1930s; and in 1976-7 there began a fresh wave of violence, both on the picket lines and in demonstrations, in which parties or pressure groups of the Right and Left were in conflict with each other or with the police. This violence was openly advocated, orchestrated and provoked in a way which has been rare in British history. It had the effect of poisoning not only industrial relations but also political, social and racial harmony; and this seemed to be its intention, both on the Left and on the Right.

Throughout the seven years there was a ground swell of fear. Up until 1974 the fear was that the complex structure of our industrial society, whereby we earn our livelihood, would break apart in chaos. After 1974 the fear was that our economy was galloping towards collapse. For an island which can only grow 50 per cent of its food and has to buy the rest by selling exports for which 80 per cent of the raw materials have to be imported, a collapse either of the structure of industry and commerce or of the economy could literally mean starvation.

In this context, it was not easy to remember that we are still a very rich country. Around the middle of the period—late 1974— I was discussing the agony of Britain with a mature and intelligent Labour Party constituency worker, a history graduate, and she reminded me that, despite the almost permanent atmosphere of economic crisis, Britain was at that moment more prosperous in real terms than ever before in our history and that the majority of us, especially at working level, had the highest standard of living we had ever had.

She was, of course, quite right. The opulent Edwardian era had been opulent only for a few. It is true that our balance of payments had been healthier in those days; so had our prospects, and so had our economic growth rate; but our production was far lower then and so was our average standard of living.

She reminded me that, year by year, with very few exceptions, our Gross National Product per head had been climbing steadily for over two centuries. So had real earnings, which had consistently outstripped prices. Wages had doubled in purchasing power in the previous fifty years and had for many manual workers quadrupled.

That was in 1974. Despite the crisis, neither of us knew that we were in fact going over the peak and turning downwards—at any rate as far as real earnings were concerned. From 1975 the average standard of living, for all workers, professional, managerial, technical, clerical and manual, began to fall—and unemployment began to rise.

After two centuries of constantly rising expectations, from a seventy-hour to a forty-hour week, from walking to cycling to motorcycling to driving to work, from no holidays to holidays in Blackpool to holidays in Spain, the strain of going into reverse was a severe one, perhaps even exceeding the strains of the peak of internal political violence in 1972–4.

These years of confrontation and violence had played their part. So had the world economic decline, accelerated by the quadrupling of oil prices in 1974. But other industrial countries— especially Germany and Japan—have coped with the same world crisis, and with their own internal strains, far more successfully. Their economic growth has been checked but not to the extent that their people's living standards have fallen, as ours have.

Perhaps we have other compensations. Ralf Dahrendorf said, in 1977:

> I would almost assume—it sounds a terrible thing to say for a German who lives in Britain—that the British version of somewhat lower economic performance and individual income, but higher social equilibrium, as you call it, may well be preferable.[1]

How stable is this 'social equilibrium'? We do have an unrivalled record of non-violence in our society, and we have an unarmed police force. It is over 900 years since we were last overrun by foreign troops and nearly 300 years since we had a violent or unconstitutional change in our system of government. We may be low in many other league tables, but we are unquestionably top in non-violence and constitutional stability. Many would also claim that we are top of the league in personal freedom. Yet the majority of British people envy the Germans their success and are frustrated at our own apparent inability to do as well as they do. Our commonest topic of discussion is about who is to blame.

It is true that we live on an overcrowded island—but so do the Japanese, and their import-export problem is almost more intractable than our own. They were certainly more vulnerable than we were to the rocketing oil prices which so devastated us in 1974. It is true that we led the world in industrialization so that our factories, shipyards and mines are the oldest—but the Germans industrialized very soon after us, and their output per man is now double our own. So is their standard of living.

So what *did* go wrong? Can we recoup? Can we ever have a revival? Can we avoid repeating our mistakes?

How far are our troubles due to our industrial relations system? To the exploitation of industrial disputes for political ends? To inadequate investment and the diversion of capital to the wrong things? To too much, or too little state control? To the handling of our economy? Or to economic factors beyond our control?

Is our tradition of minimum force and non-violence in resolving our social and political problems breaking down? Is respect for the rule of law declining? Or is the community losing the will to enforce its laws? Have we become more vulnerable to

the use of violence or disruption—or the threat of it—as a means
of bringing about change?

Or is our political system to blame? Is our kind of parliamentary democracy, so long the envy of the world, no longer
adequate for modern conditions?

Michael Moran[2] has suggested that parliamentary representation has now been overtaken by functional representation; and
that the power of Parliament and of the electorate has been overtaken by the power of the Trade Unions, the Confederation of
British Industry and other corporate interests exerting extraparliamentary pressure or direct action. He also suggests that an
individual member of the public will act in accordance with one
view as a voter and with a quite contrary view as a member of a
corporate body such as a trade union or professional association.
He believes that failure to appreciate this paradox was a major
factor in the fall of the Heath Government.

If this is true, it is an apparent denial of parliamentary democracy, but some would argue that it has always been so—with
the power of, for example, the newspapers and the financial
establishment of the City of London dictating policy in past
years as much as the Trade Unions do now. Perhaps the problem
is that, in the past, pluralist interests tended to push in the same
direction whereas now they more often conflict. Is this a satisfactory situation? Or should we find some way of restoring democracy in its literal sense—'power to the people'? This has now
become the war cry of both the Left and the Right.

It is axiomatic that in parliamentary elections people vote
against one party rather than *for* another. 'Let's get rid of the Tory
government' or 'Don't let the Socialists in.' They vote from fear.

Since 1970, their fears have become more clearly focused.
People who fear a Conservative government fear industrial confrontation and a society disrupted by unrest. People who fear a
Labour government fear bureaucracy and economic collapse.
These fears are now more influential than the traditional fears
of the manual workers that the Tories will help the bosses to
keep them down and of professional, managerial and skilled
workers that Labour will grab their savings and take away the
rewards for their skills—though these traditional fears do also
still apply.

My theme is the violence and the agony, which began with
the Industrial Relations Act of 1971. My first task was to find

out how this Act came into being. It proved immensely unpopular with both trade unions and employers and resulted in the largest ever number of days lost in strikes which it was specifically aimed to avoid. Yet it was in line with what the public, including a majority of trade union members, had been demanding for the previous five years.

The disaster of the 1971 Act had its element of personal tragedy. Even his political opponents would not question the sincerity and moral courage of Edward Heath, and trade union leaders respected him as the most straightforward of contemporary prime ministers in negotiation. But both the electorate and the Conservative Party were unforgiving when the legislation they had demanded proved a failure. Amongst the most generous in Heath's final rejection and humiliation was Harold Wilson, who had himself tried to introduce similar legislation in 1969, but had had the political instinct to drop it when he realized that it would blow up in his face.

So the Industrial Relations Act set the high tragedy in motion, leading inexorably to personal and national disaster. As well as disasters it produced its heroes, like Arthur Scargill, and its martyrs, like the Shrewsbury Pickets. And—as if violence was a contagious disease—the months after Mr Heath's fall produced peaks of other kinds of violence in England, in political demonstrations and in IRA terrorism. As this wave of violence subsided, the economic collapse gathered momentum—and led to more violence.

My second task was to find out what actually happened in these violent incidents; at the Saltley Coke Depot where thirty policemen and strikers were injured; at Shrewsbury; in Red Lion Square, where Kevin Gately became the first man to die in an English riot for over half a century; at Grunwick, where violent demonstrators injured over a hundred policemen in a day; at Hendon; at Lewisham; and at the Ladywood by-election, where one in every seven policemen on duty was injured in a single evening.

From this strictly practical examination, I have tried to discover why the response to these conflicts, industrial and political, was so violent. I have gone on to look at the effect all this had on our society and on its prospects; to assess our chances of repairing the damage; and to examine some of the alternatives we might consider for ordering our affairs rather better in the future.

PART I
Up to 1974

1 In Place of Strife

Moderates and militants

The fear that the election of a Conservative Government would lead to industrial confrontation and disruption is quite new, and peculiar to the 1970s. In 1958–63, the last six of the thirteen-year Conservative Government, the number of days lost in strikes was well below average and fell to an annual level never since rivalled (1·7 million) in 1963, the last year before the General Election; yet in 1964 a Labour Government was elected. In 1969, the last year of that Labour Government, the number of days lost by strikes (6·8 million) was the highest for 12 years; yet in 1970 a Conservative Government was elected.

It was after 1970 that the change came. The number of days lost rose in 1971 to 10·8 and in 1972 to 23·8 million, the highest in our history.[1]

The thing that most forcibly impresses the historian studying industrial relations is that almost every measure suggested in the 1950s, 1960s or 1970s has been tried before. Attempts have been made to enforce cooling off periods and strike ballots. Strikes have been banned on various grounds, if for example, their purpose was judged to be to coerce the government, or if they caused hardship to the community. Strikes and lockouts were made illegal in the Second World War and remained so—surprisingly—throughout the subsequent Labour administration of 1945–51. Up till 1906, trade unions and pickets were legally liable for civil damages. Arbitration has at times been made compulsory. Yet again and again British governments, usually encouraged by industrialists themselves, have conceded greater rights to unions and pickets before their frustration exploded into violence, with the result that (except for associated traffic accidents) no one has been killed in an industrial confrontation between strikers and blacklegs or strikers and police in Britain since 1911.

During the nineteenth century, when first the right to com-
bine and then the right to picket were fought for and won with
so little bloodshed, two very different 'families' grew up in the
trade unions, still clearly recognizable in the so-called 'moderates'
and 'militants' of today. The 'moderate' family grew out of the
Co-operative and Non-Conformist philosophies of the early
socialists such as Owen, Lovett and Place, to provide for mutual
assistance in hard times, to gain reasonable working conditions,
to get a fair share of the profits for manual workers, extending
their say in management, with the aim (still enshrined in Clause
IV of the Labour Party's Constitution) of public ownership of the
means of production, distribution and exchange. It is noteworthy
that in Britain, in contrast to other countries, the laws facilitating
the extension of trade unionism and the right to picket were
passed by Parliament (in 1871 and 1875) *before* any significant
numbers of industrial workers had a parliamentary vote[2] (which
was not until 1884). The attitude of the main stream of the
'moderate' trade union family was that higher production meant
higher earnings, so they did not aim generally to disrupt the
system.

By contrast, the 'militant' family, following the philosophies
of Marx and Engels, aimed at revolutionary change, to be brought
about by causing a collapse of industry and of the existing structure of society. The two families, therefore, might alternatively
be described as 'industrial' and 'political'.

1889 saw the first British 'political' strike, in the London
docks, of which the leaders (Tom Mann and John Burns) were
not dockers, and were members of the embryonic Communist
Party. This was followed by growing violence, resulting in 1893
in the first two fatal casualties in an industrial dispute in Britain
since 1842. This violence continued despite the 1906 Trades
Disputes Act, which gave trade unions and peaceful pickets the
legal immunities they sought. The most violent strikes in the
whole period of 1842–1977 occurred in 1910–11, when four
people were killed.

The First World War and the 1920s saw a decline in public
esteem for the trade unions, arising initially from a 'political'
strike by munition workers on Clydeside at the height of the
fighting on the Western Front in 1916. The adverse public
reaction to this led to a split between the Communist Party and
the Independent Labour Party. The post-war economic reces-

sion (one of the relatively few periods during which real wages fell) and the abortive General Strike led to tougher legislation and a decline in trade union membership. Unemployment rose to two million, and a bitter and frustrated British work-force developed a deep-seated preoccupation with defending jobs and spinning out the work. By contrast, the German work-force, hit even harder by inflation than by unemployment, developed a preoccupation with production and high wages. Although the German trade unions were dismantled by Hitler from 1933 onwards, this outlook survived, and was reinforced by the desperate determination to reconstruct after the war. So the British and German traditions born in the 1920s and 1930s have continued.

Reaction to post-war prosperity

In 1942, with a life-time trade unionist (Ernest Bevin) as Minister of Labour, strikes and lockouts were outlawed and remained so until the 1951 Industrial Disputes Order restored the right to strike, though with provision for compulsory arbitration. This was followed by a period of industrial expansion and full employment and—generally—of industrial harmony.

Nevertheless, the number of strikes began to increase in the middle 1950s[3] and there was much public criticism of 'demarcation' strikes—such as the 1955 strikes in the docks, newspaper industry and railways, all of which arose partly or wholly from inter-union disputes. Though these three strikes were official, 90 per cent of the strikes were unofficial.[4] Public hostility to trade unions, as reflected by Gallup Polls, increased sharply between 1954 and 1959.[5] Many people felt that, with much of industry nationalized and most of the rest operating under government controls in a planned economy, strikes were largely outdated and trade union power excessive. Strong arguments were put forward in Parliament for legislation to reform the trade unions and curb strikes, including proposals to enforce secret ballots and cooling-off periods before strikes could legally be called, and the stopping of income tax refunds to strikers and public assistance to their families. These proposals were firmly resisted by Tory Prime Minister Harold Macmillan,[6] who gave higher priority to maintaining a harmonious society. Taking as his slogan a comment by a constituent, 'We've never had it so good!', he won re-election in 1959, the third successive Conservative victory, unique in British political history in that, as a government winning and retaining power, they increased their number of seats in three successive elections.

This very harmony, however, had its reaction. The official trade unions, co-operating with management and the government to achieve a steady rise in production and in the standard of living, were behaving typically in the 'moderate' or 'industrial' tradition of unionism. The 'political' trade unionists, who saw industrial disputes as a vehicle for social change, had to seek other means. In 1961 the unmasking (by Frank Chapple and others) of an attempt by Communist Party trade union officials in the Electrical Trades Union to rig union elections by recording fraudulent votes, led to overturning of the election in Court and the substitution of independently conducted postal ballots in that union and some others. There was also a growth in the number of 'wildcat' strikes, organized in defiance of trade unions by militant shop stewards and other unofficial leaders. These, though they only involved small numbers, directly resulted in the laying off of thousands of other workers.[7] Wildcat strikes increasingly became headline news so that, although the number of days lost in 1963 was very low, the Labour Government elected in 1964 was under strong pressure both from public opinion and official trade union leadership to 'do something'.

The Donovan Commission

What they did was to appoint in early 1965 a Royal Commission, chaired by Lord Donovan, with terms of reference

> . . . to consider relations between managements and employees and the role of trade unions and employers' associations in promoting the interests of their members and in accelerating the social and economic advance of the nation, with particular reference to the law affecting the activities of these bodies, and to report.

The Donovan Commission, like most, had a wide-ranging membership[8] including trade unionists, employers, lawyers, academics and others. This meant that it had to choose between a compromise report or a split with one or more minority reports.[9] It chose the compromise and produced a unanimous report in June 1968.[10]

The report focused on strikes as a major sign of disruption in industrial relations, and especially the high percentage of un-official strikes—the problem, as they put it, of the 'short spon-taneous outburst lasting an average of two and a half days'. The basic finding was that two systems[11] of collective bargaining co-existed in British industry. One, the formal system, embodied the official institutions. The other, the informal system, was 'created by the actual behaviour of trade unions and employees' associations, of managers, shop stewards and workers'. These loose, informal arrangements at plant level produced conflict and should be replaced by new and comprehensive collective bar-gaining arrangements—still at plant level—to deal with the dis-putes over rates, working conditions and personnel problems which would inevitably arise.

The Report's recommendations were based upon voluntary reforms, to be instigated by the boards of companies who had, of course, a very real incentive to find ways of resolving disputes without sacrificing production. Like every previous commission of inquiry in the previous hundred years, Donovan's rejected most of the proposals for legislative restrictions on trade unions and strikes, and summed up the problem of enforcing such agreements on industrial relations by law as follows:

> Those who would be bound by the agreements (unions) do not break them in any case and those who are in the habit of breaking them (members) would not be bound.[12]

He differentiated, however, between the enforcement of agree-ments of this type (over wages, conditions, etc.) and the use of legal sanctions to endorse agreed *procedures*, but he added:

> ... sanctions will remain unworkable until a fundamental change in our system of industrial relations has led to a situa-tion in which employers may be able and willing to use such rights as the law gives them ...

and he concluded that

... at the present time legislation making procedure agreements legally enforceable would not in fact be enforced, and
like all legislation that is not enforced would bring the law
into disrepute.[13]

Prophetic words!

Donovan also considered the feasibility of conciliation pauses
and the use of strike ballots, but decided that neither were useful
ways of controlling strikes. He did, however, recommend an
Industrial Relations Act to assist in the process of reformation
of collective bargaining at plant level. Companies above a certain
size would be required to register their collective agreements
with the Department of Employment and Productivity. This
would establish that the board of directors was responsible for
industrial relations and would enable such agreements to be subject to official overview to see whether they were 'clear and firm'.
Sanctions, in the form of a 'monetary penalty', would be imposed
if companies failed to register.[14]

The Report recommended that a statutory Industrial Relations Commission should be set up 'to investigate and report
upon cases and problems arising out of registration' and other
matters in industrial relations, but that there should for this
body be no penalties for refusing to carry out its recommendations. On the other hand, the Report did propose that a public
tribunal should be set up to hear 'recognition disputes' and make
recommendations for their settlement, and that when disputes
were referred to this tribunal there should be an embargo on
strikes and lockouts by parties to the dispute, backed by financial
penalties.

The Donovan Report was accepted with certain reservations
by the TUC, but was rejected by the left of the Labour Party,
as well as by the CBI and the Conservative Party—Iain Macleod
describing it as 'a programme for inaction'. Public response was
also lukewarm: the solutions were too gradual and long-term to
satisfy public expectations, and the yearning for a firm legal
approach was not fulfilled.

Harold Wilson and the Communists

While the Donovan Commission had been sitting, the Government had been fighting a continuing battle on two fronts: not only against disruptive strikes but also against inflation. They had inherited a serious balance of payments deficit from the Conservatives, arising out of a consumer-led boom with its inevitable import bonanza.

Mr Wilson's answer was to establish a new Department of Economic Affairs under the deputy leader of the Labour Party, Mr George Brown. The aim was to arrive at a more positive approach by offsetting the supposedly negative influence of the Treasury on economic policy.

George Brown set to work with characteristic vigour and with a mixture of charm, emotion and bullying, but he was unable to persuade either the TUC or the CBI to commit themselves to anything concrete. The most he could get was their signature to a Declaration of Intent on Prices, Productivity and Incomes.

He also set up a Prices and Incomes Board (PIB) under the Chairmanship of a former Conservative Minister, Aubrey Jones, working to a norm of 3–3½ per cent for annual pay increases. The PIB was, however, authorized to make exceptions where there was a direct contribution to higher productivity, or where certain pay rates had fallen out of line with others for similar work, or where these rates were too low for a reasonable standard of living, or where a higher increase was essential to bring about a redistribution of manpower.[15] The PIB, which made a bold attempt to introduce an element of job evaluation into its recommendations, was one of the successes of the 1964–70 administration, at any rate until 1969, when its very success in keeping down wages may have contributed to the force of the wage explosion when it came. The Department of Economic Affairs, however, was less successful. It was disbanded in 1967, and its functions combined with those of the Ministry of Labour in a new Department of Employment and Productivity under Mrs Barbara Castle.

Meanwhile, strikes had continued to bedevil Mr Wilson's efforts to restore the balance of payments, and the pound had to be devalued in 1967. This was generally ascribed to the crippling strike of the National Union of Seamen in 1966. Mr Wilson became convinced that this strike was being directed by people who, along with a genuine desire to improve the pay and conditions of seamen, wanted the British economy to fail as a means

B

of bringing about radical political change. In the most forthright attack on the Communist Party's industrial organization ever made by a Prime Minister of any party, he said on 20 June 1966:

> It is difficult for us to appreciate the pressures which are being put on men I know to be realistic and reasonable, not only in their executive capacity but in strike committees in individual ports, by this tightly knit group of politically motivated men who, as the last General Election showed, utterly failed to secure acceptance of their views by the British electorate but who are now determined to exercise back-stage pressures, forcing great hardship on the members of the Union and their families, and endangering the security of the industry and the economic welfare of the nation . . .[16]

and in a further debate on 28 June he added

> The House will be aware that the Communist Party, unlike the major political parties, has at its disposal an efficient and disciplined industrial apparatus controlled from Communist Party headquarters. No major strike occurs anywhere in this country in which that apparatus fails to concern itself.[17]

He named Bert Ramelson, the head of this organization, three others on his full-time staff, and a number of other Communists who, though small in number, were working with great dedication and ruthlessness to extend their control of the seamen's union and of the strike, with the aim of securing

> . . . what is at present the main political and industrial objective of the Communist Party: the destruction of the Government's prices and incomes policy.[18]

He went on to describe how they did this, with a number of quotations from non-Communist officials in the union.

The public appeared to support him. Public opinion polls showed that 58 per cent agreed with him in blaming the Communists and 54 per cent thought that Communist Party members should be barred from becoming trade union officials.[19] In 1967 public attitudes hardened still further. 72 per cent wanted to ban unofficial strikes, and no less than 82 per cent thought that

Communists either planned (24 per cent) or exploited (58 per cent) industrial troubles.[20]

Public disenchantment

In 1968 these views continued to gather momentum, even amongst trade unionists themselves. A National Opinion Poll Survey conducted in August 1968 found 58 per cent of trade union members in favour of making arrangements between management and unions legally enforceable, 60 per cent in favour of outlawing unofficial strikes, 77 per cent in favour of a secret ballot before unofficial strikes could be held, and 65 per cent in favour of a cooling-off period of 60 days.

Meanwhile, the Conservative Party had published their own proposals for the reform of industrial relations—in April 1968, a few weeks before the publication of the Donovan Report. Their paper, entitled *A Fair Deal at Work*, reaffirmed five earlier pledges: to make collective agreements legally enforceable; to set up a register of trade unions; to ensure corporate legal status for registered trade unions; to establish a new system of industrial courts; and to set up a code of good industrial practices. It also included a number of new proposals: to redefine trade disputes so as to exclude sympathetic strikes, inter-union disputes and action to force men to join a closed shop; to protect individual workers against discrimination if they declined to join a union or a closed shop; and to enforce a cooling-off period and a secret ballot.[21]

The tide of public opinion was now running strongly against Labour. Their incomes policy was highly unpopular,[22] the pound had been devalued and the number of industrial disputes was rising rapidly. In October 1968 *The Times* headlined 'The Year of the Strike', pointing out that in the previous five years there had never been as many as 3 million days lost in strikes whereas $3\frac{1}{2}$ million had already been lost in the first eight months of 1968.[23] The regular monthly public opinion polls from December 1967 to July 1969 showed a continuing Conservative lead, seldom under 15 per cent and usually around 20 per cent.[24]

A Fair Deal at Work clearly matched the public mood, so the Government realized the urgent necessity of industrial relations legislation, if only to pre-empt the Conservatives. Moreover, since the incomes policy was provoking industrial unrest and perhaps even fanning the inflation it sought to curb, there was a strong case for abandoning it; but if this were done a substitute would be necessary, not only to satisfy public demand but also to reassure the international banking community that the Government had the will to tackle inflation effectively in some other way.

Barbara Castle and In Place of Strife

The Minister responsible was Mrs Barbara Castle, Secretary of State for Employment and Productivity. Despite her reputation as a doctrinal left-winger, she was a pragmatic political animal and a very dynamic one: she accepted the urgency of catching the tide of public opinion and had, by January 1969, issued her legislative proposals in the Draft White Paper—*In Place of Strife*.[25] Some of her proposals would have made even previous Tory Governments blench. She threw down the gauntlet to the unions in forthright terms:

> In certain situations today, strikes by groups in key positions can damage the interests of other people so seriously that they should only be resorted to when all other alternatives have failed.

The 'typical British strike', she said, was unofficial and normally in breach of agreed procedures; it came with little warning and could have serious disruptive effects. She followed Donovan in rejecting legally binding collective agreements, but proposed altering the 1871 Act so that collective agreements could be made legally enforceable if desired. She also accepted Donovan's recommendation for a Commission on Industrial Relations (CIR) without legal sanctions, to be concerned with ways of improving and extending procedural agreements.

But she went a long way further than Donovan in other ways. She proposed certain penal clauses in relation to recognition, registration, compulsory ballots and conciliation pauses. Trade unions were to register with a new Registrar of Trade Unions and Employers' Associations, and failure to do so would lay them open to financial penalties. The Secretary of State was to have discretionary powers to secure a conciliation pause of up to 28 days in unconstitutional strikes or where adequate joint discussions had not taken place; to require a union or unions to hold a ballot before calling an unofficial strike which would involve a serious threat to the economy or to public interest and where there was a serious doubt as to whether it commanded the support of a majority of those concerned; and to make orders to enforce recommendations on inter-union recognition disputes. Fines for non-compliance could be imposed through a new Industrial Board.

These proposals were warmly welcomed by the press and the public, whose disenchantment with the unions was intensified by a number of unpopular strikes.[26] There was, however, bitter opposition from the TUC and from sections of the Labour Party, both inside and outside Parliament. There were two separate and in some ways conflicting streams of objection, embracing both the 'industrial' and 'political' outlooks mentioned earlier. Moderate trade union leaders saw the proposals as weakening the bargaining power of the trade unions, and eroding their own power as leaders. In this they were supported by a number of Labour MPs normally regarded as right-wing. On the other hand, left-wing Labour MPs and militant trade unionists who saw industrial disputes in the Leninist sense, as being the best means of changing society, also saw *In Place of Strife* as prejudicing their power. Opposition by both of these streams was focused on the three penal clauses, over which Mrs Castle had gone further than had been recommended by Donovan.

On 3 March in Parliament, fifty-seven Labour MPs voted against the Government and approximately thirty others abstained. On 26 March the Labour Party's National Executive Committee repudiated *In Place of Strife*. Amongst those who repudiated it was a Cabinet Minister, James Callaghan, then Home Secretary and later to succeed Harold Wilson as Prime Minister. In view of his own lack of sympathy with the left wing of the Labour Party, it is probable that his motives were not so much concerned with power as with order and social stability, and he may be regarded as one of the first to perceive that *In Place of Strife* (like its close relation, the Industrial Relations Act of 1971) would blow up in the Government's face.

Be that as it may, the Government announced on 15 April that a shortened version of *In Place of Strife* would be introduced in Parliament. On 7 May the Labour Party Chairman, Douglas Houghton, warned the Government at a Parliamentary Labour Party meeting that it risked the disintegration of the Party if it persisted with the legislation.

Vic Feather, General Secretary of the TUC, called a special Congress on 5 June, which adopted by an overwhelming majority[27] (8,252,000 to 359,000) a motion declaring 'unalterable opposition' to the imposition of financial penalties on trade unions and work-people, while endorsing the General Council's own alternative, its *Programme for Action*. This proposed to strengthen the TUC rules so that a union would have to take 'immediate and energetic steps' to stop strikes arising from inter-union disputes, and gave the General Council the right to intervene in unofficial strikes.

Harold Wilson continued to argue that legislation was essential but he and Barbara Castle were increasingly isolated, even within the Cabinet. On 18 June Wilson was left with no option but to accept defeat and save what face he could; in return for dropping the penal clauses, he was given a 'solemn and binding undertaking' from the TUC General Council that it would intervene in unofficial and unconstitutional strikes.

Mr Wilson's intention had been to introduce a revised Bill in the autumn, with only interim legislation embodying the shortened version of *In Place of Strife* for the time being. The new Bill would establish the right of every worker to belong to a union, empower the Government to enforce recommendations by the Council on Industrial Relations (CIR) for trade union recognition, and remove existing restrictions debarring workers from receiving unemployment benefits when they were laid off due to a strike in which they were not directly involved. The Government would also have the power to impose a settlement on inter-union disputes where the TUC and the CIR had failed to secure a return to work; also to impose a conciliation pause if necessary.

In the event, the Government did not proceed with either the interim legislation or the Bill, and was left with just the TUC's undertaking.[28]

Labour's election strategy, 1969–70

Harold Wilson must have been well aware that no 'solemn and binding undertaking' to take 'immediate and energetic steps' would have any appreciable effect in holding back the flood of wage demands after four years of wage restraint, nor the flood of strikes which would greet any attempt to do so by a government so humiliated and demoralized. Garland's cartoon in the *Daily Telegraph* on 19 June 1969 perhaps best summed up public scepticism with two pictures: the first showed Harold Wilson and Vic Feather glaring at each other, carrying placards marked 'In Place of Strife' and 'Programme for Action'; the second showed them shaking hands with the words changed to 'In Place of Action' and 'Programme for Strife'.[29]

In a valiant attempt to honour his 'solemn and binding undertaking', Vic Feather did, to be fair, take the most 'immediate and energetic steps' in trying to settle disputes, but to little avail. If 1968 had been a bad year with 4,672,000 man-days lost in strikes, 1969 was worse with 6,799,000. Strikes continued to be front-page news, and public opinion polls continued to show the electorate's dissatisfaction with the Labour Government's inability to check unofficial strikes, and a growing yearning for the Tory alternative.

At this point Harold Wilson took what was seen by many as a cynical decision to cut his losses and let wage demands rip, in the hope of regaining enough popularity to face an election without the certainty of political annihilation. In fact, this interpretation may be unjust, as there was probably no way in which the wages explosion could have been contained. Be that as it may, the price, in national terms, was a heavy one. The inflationary spiral was given a powerful twist and gathered a momentum which not only Heath's Government but also Wilson's next one, when he returned to power in 1974, proved quite unable to check.

The pressure had built up in the first half of 1969, during which real earnings had fallen (by 0·4 per cent), meaning that in four of the six half-yearly periods between Labour's re-election in 1966 and the summer of 1969, workers had suffered a decline in real pre-tax incomes. Coupled with this was Labour's failure to control prices. As a result, shop-floor militancy had built up, and the trade union officials, so far from leading it, were either trying to control it or running to keep up.

To an unusual extent this militancy was joined and in some cases led by low-paid, traditionally non-militant workers, whose relative positions had not improved under the incomes policy. In the second half of 1969 there were militant wage demands by dustmen, teachers, firemen and nurses. The Government's incomes 'norm' stood at zero, with a ceiling of $3\frac{1}{2}$ per cent, but wage settlements in the last quarter of 1969 involved average increases of 7–8 per cent.[30] The number of days lost by strikes rose to record levels in 1969 and further still in the first half of 1970.[31] Wages began to overtake prices again: the overall rise in real earnings in Labour's last twelve months was just over 5 per cent, almost double the average annual increase of the previous four years.[32]

There was an important element of election strategy here. Both sides realized that the result of the election would depend on the timing of the trade cycle and of the public opinion cycle which followed it. Economic expansion brought increased wages which brought increased prices which in turn reduced the benefits of the wage rises and eventually hit the balance of payments. The relative speeds of these movements were decisive. If the public opinion cycle could be made to move faster, Labour could conceivably gain the lead before inflation got out of hand, which seemed (early in 1970) almost certain to happen by the autumn or winter of 1970. Realizing that a summer election gave him his only chance, Wilson made little attempt to check the rise in wages. In January and February 1970 there were major settlements in the public sector averaging 12 per cent.[33]

The public opinion polls reflected the success of Wilson's political strategy. In July 1969 the Conservatives had a lead of 19 per cent. By the end of the year this had fallen to 7 per cent. Though the alarming wage rises in the public sector caused a temporary reversal to $10\frac{1}{2}$ per cent early in 1970, by the middle of May all public opinion polls showed a Labour lead in voting intentions.[34]

Even more striking was the upsurge in public expectation of a Labour victory. A series of Marplan polls between January and June asked 'Which party do you think will win the general election?' The answers were:[35]

1970	Cons. %	Lab. %	Don't know %	Majority expecting Conservative win
January	57	27	16	+30
April	47	36	17	+11
Mid-May	21	64	15	−33
Mid-June	14	67	19	−53

In the event they were wrong, and so were all the immediate pre-election public opinion polls.[36] Harold Wilson's political gamble had very nearly come off, but not quite. Whether it was a cynical attempt to buy the electorate before the economic consequences became clear or whether the pressure was beyond his power to control, he had unleashed both a wages explosion and an encouragement of industrial militancy which were to launch Britain into six years of agony and strife, of which he himself was to endure the second half.

On 18 June 1970 the Conservatives gained sixty-six seats from Labour in the biggest swing against a government in power since 1945. Edward Heath took office with an absolute majority of thirty and what seemed to be the clearest possible mandate for industrial legislation.

2 The Industrial Relations Act

Edward Heath faces the unions

The General Election of June 1970 was fought largely on the failure of the Labour Party in its overall economic management, within which the failure to control the trade unions was paramount. The Conservative Manifesto, *A Better Tomorrow*, had the reform of industrial relations as one of its major planks:

> There were more strikes in 1969 than ever before in our history. Already in the first three months of 1970 there were 1,134 strikes compared with 718 in the same period last year, when the Labour Government said that the position was so serious that legislation was essential in the national interest. This rapid and serious deterioration directly stems from Labour's failure to carry through its own policy of reform of industrial relations.

The Manifesto went on to promise that, if returned to power, the Conservatives would introduce a new industrial relations bill based on *A Fair Deal at Work*, 'to provide a proper framework of law within which improved relationships between management, men and unions can develop'.

On the evidence of five years of public opinion polls, of the support for Labour's *In Place of Strife* and the public dismay at its withdrawal, and of the 4·8 per cent swing from Labour in the General Election, Edward Heath could assume that he had a popular mandate to implement the proposals in *A Fair Deal at Work*, and Robert Carr, the new Secretary of State for Employment, immediately started planning how to do this.

Meanwhile, public support was strengthened by a continued rise in the number of industrial disputes and stoppages, particularly in the public sector, which caused much personal suffering and resulted in what were regarded in the context of the times as highly inflationary wage settlements. A national dock strike began in July, a few weeks after the election, and a Court of Inquiry recommended increases in earnings ranging from £2 to £10 per week. Council workers struck at the end of September, demanding rises of up to £15, and returned to work in November after an inquiry headed by Sir Jack Scamp had recommended, much to Heath's displeasure, increases of £2 to £10 a week. In November 100,000 miners went on strike with a demand for £5 a week and, although they eventually voted to accept £3, more than a million working days had by then been lost.[1]

But perhaps the most traumatic of the 1970 disputes was in the electrical supply industry. Barred by law from a total stoppage (because of the hazard to life) the power workers on 7 December began a work-to-rule and overtime ban in support of a 25 per cent claim, their case being that they had co-operated in increasing output to the extent that the need for systematic overtime had become rare, and manpower had been reduced by nearly 20 per cent in three years. The effect on the public in mid-winter was severe. A State of Emergency was declared and a rota system of power cuts was enforced all over the country, most homes facing a total blackout several evenings each week. As they waited in the bus queues, clutching hard-won candles and spare torch batteries, heading for cheerless evenings in cold rooms, their comments on the need for legislation to 'thump the unions' were predictable, and the public opinion polls recorded an all-time record in unpopularity of trade unions and strikes.

The settlement, however, was a severe blow to the Government. Management and the unions jointly requested a Court of Inquiry. The Government agreed on condition that the terms of reference should include 'consideration of the public interest'. The unions protested in vain and Treasury officials presented evidence about the state of the economy. The Court, under Lord Wilberforce, took note of this evidence but made a massive award, which the Government claimed was 10·9 per cent, but was generally estimated at 15 per cent or more, the *Economist* calculating its real worth to be 18 or 19 per cent[2] and angrily predicting that the Wilberforce settlement would open the floodgates.

In the early months of 1971, however, the Government had its first significant victory over a major trade union. On 20 January the Union of Post Office Workers (UPW) called out some

180,000 members in support of a demand for increases of 15–20 per cent. The Post Office Corporation had offered 8 per cent, the target figure for annual rises declared by the Government. Postal services were severely disrupted, but postmen are not by nature militant and their work brings them into close personal contact with the public. Many of them were very unhappy with the personal suffering caused to small businesses (the 'corner shops'), to families and to young couples trying to keep in touch. In March the Union accepted a settlement of 9 per cent, to the humiliation of their leaders but to the relief of most postal workers.

All the same, the Post Office strike had cost 6,250,000 man-days—the largest number lost in a single strike since the 1920s.[3] Added to the loss of 10,908,000 during 1970 (4 million more than in 1969), this still gave cause for public alarm.

The humiliation of the postal workers' leaders, however, made other unions more cautious about forcing the pace and the actual number of strikes* in the first six months of 1971 was half the number of those in the first six months of 1970 under the Labour Government.[4] Employers, as well as the Government, gained confidence in resisting wage demands.

The Industrial Relations Bill

Meanwhile, the Industrial Relations Bill had been presented to the House of Commons in December 1970. Robert Carr had earlier produced a consultative document outlining his proposals and he invited the TUC to discuss it, but they refused because he had declared that it was based upon 'eight central pillars' which the Government did not intend to remove. They complained of 'wilful denial of the facilities for consultation that have been accorded to the TUC by every government for at least the past thirty years' on the grounds that, as the eight pillars had been firmly fixed without discussion, nothing else was worth discussing.

The Industrial Relations Bill was fought through Parliament during the first half of 1971, strenuously opposed at all stages by the Labour Party, and 'Kill the Bill' demonstrations were or-

* Not to be confused with the number of working days lost which was, of course, enormous due to the loss of 6·25 million in a single strike.

ganized all over the country by the trade union movement, confident that it could be killed as easily as *In Place of Strife*. Opinion polls, however, continued to show consistent support for it by the public, including the majority of trade union members, and the Government refused to give way. The Bill reached the Statute Book as the Industrial Relations Act in August 1971.

The eight pillars—the kernel of the Act—were as follows:

1. *The statutory right to belong or not to belong to a trade union:* this linking together of the positive and negative rights, placing the two on an equal footing, was something with which Donovan had strongly disagreed. It led logically to the voiding of the pre-entry closed shop and the non-operability of the post-entry closed shop. However, an alternative was allowed in 'agency shops' in which under certain conditions every employee would have to join a union, or pay regular contributions to it or, if a conscientious objector to membership, to a charity.

2. *Registration of unions and employers' associations:* as a condition of registration, unions would have to satisfy a new Registrar of Trade Unions and Employers' Associations that their rules contained minimum safeguards for members' rights. If the Registrar did not approve of the rules presented he would have the power to withhold or cancel registration. Unregistered unions would be liable for unlimited damages, have no immunity against tort liability for inducing breaches of any contract, and lose certain valuable tax rebates.

3. *The enforceability of collective agreements,* which were to be assumed legal contracts unless a written provision by the parties stated otherwise. Where such agreements were legally enforceable, a breach of agreement or the absence of 'all such steps as are reasonably practicable' to prevent one on the part of the union(s) involved would constitute an 'unfair industrial practice'.

4. *The limitation of legal immunities:* it would be an unfair industrial practice for any person 'in contemplation or furtherance of a trade dispute, knowingly to induce another person to break a contract to which that other person is a party' unless the person so doing was either a trade union or was acting within the scope of his authority on behalf of such a person. Unregistered unions would not enjoy this legal immunity. A number of other activities were defined as 'unfair industrial practices', thereby curtailing the freedom to strike. These included certain forms of

secondary boycotts and sympathetic action, and strikes in support of closed shops or union recognition.

The definition of legal picketing was also narrowed. According to the Trade Disputes Act of 1906, with which Donovan and *In Place of Strife* had concurred, 'it shall be lawful in contemplation or furtherance of a trade dispute' to attend at or near a house or place 'merely for the purpose of peacefully persuading any person to work or abstain from working'. The 1971 Act narrowed this immunity by redefining 'industrial dispute' (in place of the former 'trade dispute') and by removing the protection from picketing at or near a person's place of residence.

5. *The right of a union to be recognized:* this worried the large unions because it opened the way to erosion of their strength by disgruntled members, especially those with special skills, seeking others to handle their interests.

6. *Machinery to define bargaining units* and say which unions should represent the workers within those units.

7. *The selective enforcement of procedure agreements.*

8. *Emergency provisions:* the Secretary of State was empowered to apply to a new Industrial Court for a *cooling-off period* of 60 days where industrial action was likely to injure the national economy, imperil national security or create a serious public disorder. He could also apply for a *strike ballot* for the same reasons, or where the livelihood of a substantial number of workers in the industry was endangered.

Several agencies were set up or extended in scope to implement the Bill: a new National Industrial Relations Court, with the status of a High Court, to deal with matters relating to collective issues and as a court of appeal from the existing Industrial Tribunals; these latter, broadened in scope to deal with cases involving individuals infringing the provisions of the Bill; the Commission on Industrial Relations, given a statutory basis; and a new Registrar of Trade Unions and Employers' Associations.

Those offending against the provisions of the Act would be guilty of 'unfair industrial practices'—civil offences only, as the Conservatives insisted—and legal enforcement took the form of fines and compensation to the injured party. The 1971 Act repealed and replaced the Acts of 1906 and 1967 and the new immunities applied only to registered organizations and those with authority under union rules. By these means the Government hoped to foster 'responsible' unions, which would control their members and thus curb unofficial strikes. What was viewed as 'irresponsible' shop-floor power was under attack. In the parliamentary debate on the Bill, Tom Normanton for the Conservatives argued that:

> A divorce of actual power from actual responsibility ... has enabled many irresponsible and disruptive individuals to acquire shop-floor power—to shelter under the immunity clauses of trade union legislation passed by governments under circumstances which no longer prevail ... It seemed to me, therefore, that one of the essentials now is to restore this balance of power and responsibility.[5]

The unions refuse to register

The first major attack on the Act after it came into force was the decision of the TUC Annual Congress in September 1971 to instruct its member unions not to register. This motion, moved by the Amalgamated Union of Engineering Workers (AUEW) was passed by a fairly small majority—5,625,000 to 4,500,000, but it was to prove decisive. In October, seventy-two unions, with 4,960,000 members, had deregistered;[6] nine others, with 2,120,000, were taking steps to do so; twenty-four more, with 2,480,000 members, had postponed their policy decision; while only twenty-two, with a total membership of 400,000, had declared their intention to register.[7]

Many unions had been initially reluctant to commit themselves until they saw what the others were going to do, for the incentives to register were very strong. Liability to be sued for unlimited damages by firms or by individuals, and the loss of other legal immunities, could potentially have ruinous results, and the loss of tax relief on provident funds could be very expensive: the loss was estimated at £750,000 a year to the Transport and General Workers' Union (TGWU).[8] After their initial caution, however, as reflected by the first vote, the great majority of unions recognized the strength they would gain by standing together, because it would give rise to continual challenges to employers and government to invoke the law by suing for damages (a cause of bitter conflict before the Act of 1906 gave unions immunity) or back down.

The attitude of the trade unions to the law in general was equivocal and was perhaps best summed up by Hugh Scanlon, President of the AUEW:

> Let us . . . make it perfectly clear that generally speaking the trade union movement accepts, operates and conforms with the law of the land. Our opposition and determination is quite specific. It is to this law and to this Act and to the courts set up thereunder. The courts which are active under this act, particularly the NIRC (National Industrial Relations Court) are brazenly political and do not appear to operate under the ordinary rules applying to other courts.[9]

Thereafter, the industrial challenge to the Conservative Government took a variety of forms. There were two major national strikes involving violent picketing: the miners' and building workers' strikes. There was the enforcement of a compulsory secret ballot in a threatened railway strike which resulted in an overwhelming rebuff for the Government. There was a series of trials of strength in the NIRC resulting in the imprisonment of strike leaders for contempt of court, which had far-reaching effects on the attitude of other trade unions. And there were a number of sensational appeals to the NIRC against the trade unions, two by individuals (James Goad and Joseph Langston) and one by a small firm (Con-Mech) which, although 'successful', finally convinced most employers that the Act exacerbated rather than eased their problems, and that it was not in their interest to invoke it.

The miners' strike of January–February 1972, violent by British standards, had probably more long-term significance than any of the others, but the Industrial Relations Act played very little part in it, so it will be examined in a later chapter. So will the building workers' strike, which resulted in some vicious violence and intimidation at Shrewsbury and Telford and the imprisonment of some of the strike leaders; but they were convicted by a criminal court and not by the NIRC.

A compulsory ballot

The Government's first serious attempt to use the emergency

provisions of the Act was in averting a national railway strike. The provisions worked perfectly, but the result was a humiliating reverse for the Government. The railway unions submitted a pay demand far in excess of the government 8 per cent ceiling. The Government applied to the NIRC for a conciliation pause. This was ordered by the Court and the unions reluctantly obeyed. When this expired, the Court was asked to order a ballot of all railwaymen on whether to accept an offer advised by an outside arbitrator. Again, the unions obeyed, by now scenting victory, because the union leaders had recommended rejecting the offer and they were confident that the men would support their call to continue industrial action. This they did, overwhelmingly, by five to one.[10]

After the massive publicity surrounding the ballot, the Government felt itself unable to do other than settle for a much higher award (13 per cent), claiming somewhat lamely that this was a good example of the Act in operation, and that a potentially damaging dispute had been resolved by the process of law instead of by a strike. Trade unionists, however, interpreted it differently; they had only to vote more pay for themselves, it seemed, and they would get it. The Government, presumably, learned the same lesson, for they never again applied to the Court to enforce a secret ballot.

The dockers challenge the courts

The shortcomings of using the law to resolve industrial disputes were, however, even more convincingly demonstrated in a series of dockers' disputes taken to the NIRC during the spring and summer of 1972.

The disputes were, in fact, no more than a continuation of the running battle between the dockers and the port authorities over the loss of jobs due to mechanization. British ports had for years been losing trade to their continental competitors because of a Luddite determination to retain labour-intensive methods of loading and unloading rather than use modern cargo-handling equipment. As late as 1965, the stevedores in the Dickensian Hay's Wharf were still using Dickensian porters' barrows to wheel sides of bacon off the ships. Only when the Transport and General Workers' Union (TGWU) was able to convince the dockers that the resulting loss of port usage (especially to Dutch and German ports) would inevitably mean fewer jobs and lower earnings was the new equipment accepted at each stage.

The stage reached in 1972 concerned the loading and un-loading of containers—'stuffing and stripping'. In the case of many items, such as refrigerated food, double handling could best be avoided by doing it in the container depots or cold stores outside the docks. The dockers demanded that this work should be the prerogative of members of the dock workers' section of the TGWU wherever it was done, and this brought them into con-flict with members of other unions, especially the Union of Shop, Distributive and Allied Workers (USDAW). There was then a four-cornered battle: dockers demanding the work; other work-ers resisting the demand; employers willing to pay more because of higher productivity, and to keep the peace; and the Govern-ment restraining them to stem the flood of wage demands.

In March 1972, dockers in Hull, Liverpool and London began to black lorries delivering goods from container firms. On 24 March the NIRC granted an order to a Lancashire firm, Heatons, requiring the TGWU to restrain its members from blacking their container lorries at Liverpool. The TGWU, following TUC instructions not to recognize the NIRC, refused to be represented at the hearing, and six days later was fined £5,000 for contempt of court in failing to comply with the order. On 14 April a similar order was granted to another firm and, with neither order being obeyed, the two firms again applied to the Court. The TGWU was fined a further £50,000 and warned that, if it did not purge its contempt, all its assets might be frozen. At the beginning of May, the TGWU Committee decided by a small majority to pay the fines, but, claiming that it was fighting the battle for the whole trade union movement, it threatened to withhold its affiliation fees unless it was recompensed by the TUC, which had until 23 April maintained its advice to unions to boycott the NIRC.

The TGWU representative then did appear before the Court to plead that the union could not comply with the orders because it had no power to force its members to co-operate, as the strike was unofficial. The President of the Court, Sir John Donaldson, rejected this plea, arguing that the shop stewards were officers of the union, and if they did not co-operate their credentials should be withdrawn. The Court of Appeal, however, under the Master of the Rolls, Lord Denning, quashed the fines on the grounds that under the union rules the TGWU did not in fact have power to order its shop stewards (who are voluntary unpaid representatives elected by their own men) to comply, and that the Court's action, if any, must be against the individuals themselves. This, of course, was just what the Government had hoped to avoid.

Sir John Donaldson acted at once in accordance with the Appeal Court's judgement, notwithstanding notice of appeal to the House of Lords. He ordered the shop stewards blacking a container firm at the Pool of London to appear before the NIRC and they refused, some of them expressing delight at the prospect of going to prison,[11] in the hope of making the legislation look as oppressive as possible.

On 17 June, the day the men were due for imprisonment, the Official Solicitor stepped in.[12] Appearing before the Appeal Court on the men's behalf (but without their permission) he had the order for contempt quashed on the grounds of insufficient evidence.

The shop stewards, however, were determined to go to prison and continued their blacking. Some of the same men, including a charismatic Communist Party member, Bernie Steer, refused to obey a further court order to cease blacking another London cold storage depot and five of them—all shop stewards—were committed to Pentonville Prison on 21 July. The results confirmed the Government's worst fears. By that evening the ports of London, Liverpool and Hull were all at a standstill, and lorry drivers who had up till then been counter-picketing to save their own jobs, withdrew in sympathy with the 'Pentonville five'. The strikes spread. For five days there were no newspapers, and the TUC General Council voted to call a one-day national strike unless the men were released. This was fortuitously avoided as a result of a judgement on 26 July on an appeal to the House of Lords over the original Heatons' case. The Law Lords ruled that trade unions *were*, after all, responsible for the actions of their shop stewards. The TGWU was ordered to pay the previously quashed fines of £55,000 plus the costs of the appeal, a further £25,000.[13] This was a severe blow to the trade union movement, but it did enable Sir John Donaldson to order the release of the five stewards from Pentonville, stating that the grounds on which they had been imprisoned had now changed. The Government and the country breathed again.[14]

This case also had a decisive effect on most of the unions which

had been putting off their decision about registration. Frank
Chapple's EEPTU, Clive Jenkins' ASTMS and USDAW all
deregistered, and eventually only thirty-four unions held out,
most of them very small ones, and these were suspended by the
TUC in September. Thus virtually the entire trade union movement was now openly defying the Act and neither the Government, nor most of the employers, were anxious to challenge them
again.

Individual attempts to use the Act

The final proof of the futility of the Act came with attempts to
invoke it by two individuals and a small firm. Late in 1972 the
AUEW refused to readmit an ex-member, James Goad, who had
a most irregular history in the union, having previously allowed
his membership to lapse three times. Goad applied to the NIRC
for an injunction that the AUEW permit him to attend branch
meetings, from which he was being excluded. The Court ruled
that he was indeed a member of the union, and ordered the
union to admit him. They refused to attend the Court or to
comply, and were fined £5,000 for contempt. They refused to
pay, so the Court ordered their bank to hand over the money.
They still refused to admit Goad, so the Court sequestered their
assets to extract a further fine of £50,000.[15]

Goad's employers were embarrassed, as other employees struck
in protest. So were the Government, who were just beginning to
make some progress in pay policy discussions with the CBI and
TUC. Goad had little sympathy, and retained still less when he
offered to withdraw his action for a payment in cash.[16]

The other individual 'Hampden' was a Chrysler employee,
Joseph Langston, who resigned from the AUEW, which had a
closed shop in the plant in which he worked. Chrysler suspended
him on full pay, but he came in for some abuse when he went (with
much television publicity) to collect his pay. He tried to sue the
AUEW, but the NIRC held that this was not covered under the
Act. He had initiated an appeal against this ruling when Chrysler
dismissed him. He then sued Chrysler for compensation for
unfair dismissal, which they promptly paid to end the affair.
The NIRC declined to order his reinstatement.[17]

The third case arose in September 1973. A small engineering

firm, Con-Mech, obtained an NIRC order against the AUEW concerning a recognition dispute. As usual, the union boycotted the Court and refused to comply. The Court sequestered £100,000 of the union's assets and announced that Con-Mech could apply for compensation for losses arising from the strike. The Court eventually awarded them £47,000 in April 1974—much to the embarrassment of the Labour Government which was by then in office, and in the process of repealing the Act and dissolving the NIRC. Nevertheless, until the repeal was on the Statute Book the award was legal. The AUEW called a national strike, which was only called off when an anonymous donor (believed to be the Newspaper Proprietors' Association) paid all the money owed by the AUEW into the Court.[18] By this time it had long been evident that, even if a Conservative Government had still been in power, most employers would themselves have been clamouring for the repeal of the Act.

Industrial relations and the law

The failure of this legislation, which had been so consistently demanded by the public, was one of the major causes of the fall of Edward Heath, as is discussed in Chapter 9—just as the failure to introduce such legislation had been a major cause for the defeat of the Wilson Government in 1970.

Much more lasting damage, however, was done to public respect for the law. Winston Churchill had warned against this as early as 1911, in the debate on the Trade Union No. 2 Bill:

> It is not good for trade unions that they should be brought in contact with the courts, and it is not good for the courts. The courts hold justly a high and, I think, unequalled prominence in respect of the world in criminal cases, and in civil cases between man and man, no doubt, they deserve and command the respect and admiration of all classes in the community, but where class issues are involved, and where party issues are involved, it is impossible to pretend that the courts command the same degree of general confidence. On the contrary, they do not, and a very large number of our population have been led to the opinion that they are, unconsciously, no doubt, biased.[19]

Churchill made this comment in the wake of a long series of cases which had aroused great resentment in the trade union movement; the 'Trilogy' cases (1892, 1895 and 1901) concerning conspiracy; *Lyons* v. *Wilkins* (1899) about picketing; *Temperton* v. *Russell* (1893) about boycotting; and the *Taff Vale Railway* case (1901) in which a union was successfully sued for damages to the company by a strike. Many of the inequities in the law were removed by the Trade Disputes Act of 1906 but the bitterness and suspicion remained, and the question of liability for breach of contract reared its head again in *Rookes* v. *Barnard* as recently as 1964.[20]

This has caused the judiciary to be most reluctant to extend the involvement of the courts in industrial disputes, because defiance of the courts, particularly if successful, is dangerously infectious. It was no doubt with this in mind that Sir John Donaldson (who was a High Court Judge) decided that in the NIRC he would dispense with all formalities, such as wigs, robes, bench and witness-box.[21] He presumably foresaw that cases would arise, such as those described, in which the application of trade union muscle would result in humiliation of the court and of the laws on which it made its judgements. Though most of its work was constructive and uncontroversial, concerning such things as redundancy payments and unfair dismissals,[22] it was the small number of controversial ones, such as the bizarre intervention of the Official Solicitor, apparently to save the state from the consequences of its own laws, which brought the law into disrepute, and encouraged people to defy the courts. Despite Donaldson's attempt to make the NIRC bear as little resemblance as possible to the High and Criminal Courts, this contempt undoubtedly rubbed off on to the courts as a whole. The full extent of the damage to the fabric of British society cannot yet be judged.

Nevertheless, it was another form of defiance and contempt which accounted even more than this for the downfall of the Conservative Government: the defiance expressed in the form of violence by strikers against non-strikers and police in the miners' and building workers' strikes in 1972. These are discussed in the chapters immediately following.

3 Arthur Scargill and the Flying Pickets

Background to the 1972 miners' strike

The 1972 miners' strike will have a place in British history, along with the dock strike of 1889 and the General Strike of 1926, as having had a major influence on British politics and society. It was, by British standards, unusually violent: one picket was killed (albeit in a traffic accident), and in a single incident, at the Saltley Coke Depot, thirty were injured, sixteen of them policemen. 'Mass picketing', that is physical obstruction by, in many cases, thousands of demonstrators as well as strikers, largely supplanted 'peaceful persuasion' as envisaged in the picketing laws; though in the long term the influence of its success may have been outweighed by the adverse public reaction to it. The strike proved the effectiveness of the massed 'flying picket' in which hundreds of men were shunted about the country by coach, not only to picket their own places of work (the collieries) but also to prevent the operation of other installations to try to bring industry as a whole to a halt. The strike was also, for many of its leaders, avowedly political in its aims.

Nevertheless, it has created some myths which need exploding. The first myth is that this strike was a challenge to the Industrial Relations Act; the second myth is that it was 'Communist-inspired'.

When the strike began in January 1972, the emergency clauses of the Industrial Relations Act had not yet come into force.[1] Nor would most of them have been relevant, because the constitution of the National Union of Mineworkers (NUM) already required a ballot of all members before calling a national strike; and such a ballot was held without any Government prompting on this occasion. The strike was an attack not on the Act, but on the Government's incomes policy.

For the overwhelming majority of individual miners it was a

straightforward strike for higher pay, even though a number of
their leaders saw from the start its potential for achieving political
ends. There is nothing particularly unusual about this; amongst
those trade union officials interviewed by the author who would
describe their own philosophy as Marxist, the majority made it
clear that the underlying object of *all* their strikes was political.[2]
The issues on which their strikes were called—wages or conditions—were to them secondary ones.

The NUM and the mining community as a whole are amongst
the most politicized of trade unionists. The NUM (having grown
out of a loose federation of mining unions) also delegates far
more power than most unions to its Area Councils. Some of these
(e.g. Scotland, Wales and Kent) have a long Communist tradition. Of the twenty-seven members of the National Executive
itself in 1972, six were members of the Communist Party of
Great Britain (CPGB). Five others were Labour Party members
who would describe themselves as Marxist and, on almost any
motion with political implications, would vote with the six Communist members. These eleven had only to persuade three others
to vote with them to have a fourteen to thirteen majority.

Nevertheless, in the 1972 strike it was *not* the Communists
who made the running; in fact it was they who were running to
keep up.[3] The pressure for a pay rise came from the miners
themselves. The hazards and hardships of their work had traditionally entitled them, in the eyes of the public and of themselves,
to be amongst the most highly paid manual workers. During the
previous ten years they had dropped behind, under a policy of
wage restraint imposed by Lord Robens, who had just completed his 'Ten-year stint'[4] as Chairman of the National Coal
Board (NCB). This was a period of rising productivity but also
of retrenchment in the pits, with cheap oil fast eroding the position of coal as Britain's prime source of energy. During the 1960s
about 400 pits were closed and 400,000 jobs lost in the mining
industry. Robens, supported by NUM leader Will Paynter (himself a CPGB member) had persuaded the miners that, if wages
rose too high, many more pits would become uneconomical, and
particularly those in areas where there was no alternative employment, such as South Wales. This would have meant the destruction and dispersal of tightly knit mining communities, and it was
out of loyalty to them that the miners responded to Lord Robens'
lead. When he retired, the NCB was unable to contain the pres-

sure within the ranks of the miners to catch up to their normal position at the top of the wage table. Just as they were about to launch a major collective bargaining offensive to bring this about, the Government forestalled them by imposing an anti-inflation policy restricting wage rises to an 8 per cent annual ceiling.

The Wilberforce settlement of the 1970 power strike breached this limit, but the Government had thereafter successfully stemmed the predicted avalanche of claims by standing firm in the postal workers' strike in January–March 1971. The miners, having themselves settled for only a modest rise at the end of 1970, were determined in 1971 to get what they regarded as their due.

The strike begins

On 1 November 1971, the NUM instituted an overtime ban in support of claims of up to £9 per week, the NCB having offered a maximum of £1·80. The miners' case was that the cost of living had risen by 11 per cent in the previous year and that the Government ceiling of an 8 per cent rise in reality meant a cut of 3–4 per cent in real wages.[5] Their demand was that the basic pay of underground workers should rise from £19 (take-home £14) to £28 and of surfacemen from £18 (take-home £13) to £26.

When the NCB declared that it could not raise their offer because of the Government's 8 per cent ceiling, the NUM Executive decided upon a ballot on whether or not to call a general strike. This was obligatory under the NUM constitution and the majority required before a general strike could be called was 55 per cent (reduced in 1971 from 66 per cent). In the event, of 271,000 eligible, 92 per cent recorded their votes at the pithead, 145,482 for the strike and 101,910 against—a majority of 58·8 per cent. So the first national coal strike since 1926 was called on 9 January 1972.

Coal stocks had been high but the ten-week overtime ban had run them down fast, so the NUM felt confident that the strike would be effective. The Government, however, felt no less confident that the coal stocks would hold out for longer than the miners, and did not take any decisive action to limit consumption for over a month. By this time, however, a new factor had begun to take effect, far more effectively than the actual stoppage of coal production and of collection of coal from the pitheads: the use by the miners of massed flying pickets to prevent stocks of fuel of all kinds, and other essential commodities, from entering the power stations, and to prevent the import of fuel from overseas into British ports.

Arthur Scargill

The idea of flying pickets was not itself new, and it had been tried with success in the unofficial Yorkshire miners' strike in 1969, when buses were used to send parties of Yorkshire miners to picket the mines in Nottinghamshire and Derby and persuade their men to join the strike. They had only limited success and failed to carry the official union leadership with them, but many lessons were learned. Amongst the unofficial leaders in Yorkshire at that time was Arthur Scargill, a young militant at odds with the official union leadership. Three years later he was to make his name at Saltley and soon after that to become President of the Yorkshire Area of the NUM at the age of thirty-four.

Arthur Scargill joined the Young Communist League in 1953, at the age of fifteen, when the Secretary was Jimmy Reid. The two have a great deal in common, both in philosophy and in power of organization and leadership. Both achieved great successes in 1972, while still in their thirties: Reid in reversing the Government's decision to close the Upper Clyde shipyards, and Scargill, as will be described, at Saltley.

Scargill, who had started work in the mines at fifteen, became convinced at eighteen that the route to real power lay in the trade union movement rather than in any political party. He remains a member of the Labour Party but his main role in life has always been as a trade union activist, at first as an unofficial strike leader and later as a full-time union official.[6]

He is dedicated to revolutionary change to a Marxist society. He believes that this will best be achieved by industrial conflict, because this gets the rank and file aroused and involved, and will lead to control of the trade unions by people who have his views and aims. Since the card vote of the unions dominates the Labour Party Conference, he sees this as the route to control of the Labour Party, which would include a change of rules to give more power to the Conference. Having secured this control, the next stage would be to draw into the Labour Party, or into alliance with it, all movements now to the left of it, including the Communist Party and the Trotskyists. In this respect his aim is similar to that outlined in the Communist Party Manifesto, *The British Road to Socialism*, except that the Communists have more reservations about the ultra-left.

His philosophies are probably best expressed in the following quotations from the interview he gave to Robin Blackburn, of the *New Left Review*, in June 1975:[7]

> The biggest mistake we could make is that of suggesting that a wage battle is not a political battle. Of course it is . . . once we begin to divorce wages from politics, then we lose our perspectives . . . you will not get real control of the society in which we live unless you commit and convince the working class of *the need to struggle*.
>
> We could take over all the means of production, distribution and exchange more or less immediately. I believe we can do it . . . The issue is a very simple one: it is *them* and it is *us*. I will never accept that it is anything else because it is a class battle, it is a class war. While it is them and us my position is perfectly clear: I want to take *from* them *for* us.

In specific references to the 1972 coal strike he said:

> You see we took the view that we were in a class war. We were not playing cricket on the village green like they did in '26. We were out to defeat Heath and Heath's policies because we were fighting a government. Anyone who thinks otherwise was living in cloud-cuckoo land. We had to declare *war* on them and the only way you could declare war was to attack the vulnerable points. They were the points of *energy*; the power stations, the coke depots, the coal depots, the points of supply. And this is what we did.
>
> Well, the miners' union was not opposed to the distribution of coal. We were only opposed to the distribution of coal to industry because we wished to paralyse the nation's economy. It's as simple as that.

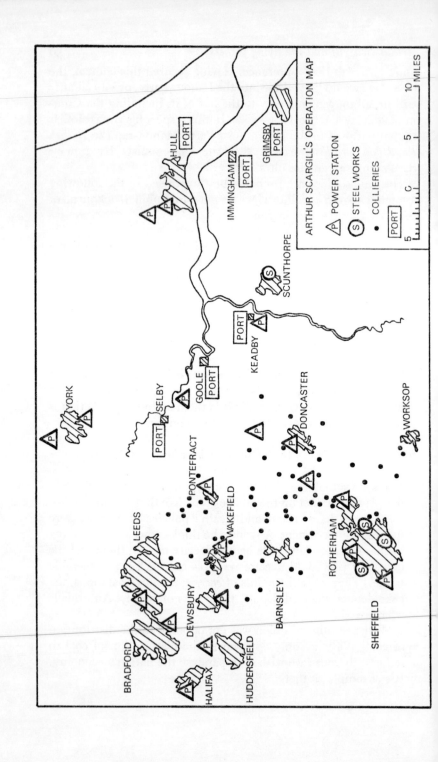

ARTHUR SCARGILL'S OPERATION MAP

△ POWER STATION
Ⓢ STEEL WORKS
• COLLIERIES

PORT

|5 | | C | | 5 | | 10 |
MILES

YORK
BRADFORD
HALIFAX
HUDDERSFIELD
LEEDS
DEWSBURY
WAKEFIELD
PONTEFRACT
SELBY PORT
GOOLE PORT
BARNSLEY
DONCASTER
KEADBY PORT
SCUNTHORPE
IMMINGHAM PORT
HULL PORT
GRIMSBY PORT
ROTHERHAM
SHEFFIELD
WORKSOP

The flying pickets

When the strike began in January 1971, Arthur Scargill was a member of the Barnsley Area Strike Committee and was in charge of picketing in the Barnsley District. There was at once an argument between the moderate and militant factions over picketing the ports and power stations, and he prevailed. He did not confine himself to the Barnsley District or to the area covered by the Yorkshire NUM, but sent flying pickets, at strengths of up to 1,000, to ports and power stations as far away as Ipswich, Great Yarmouth and Bedford. At Ipswich, for example, he concentrated 1,000 pickets to close the port and then moved on to the power station, leaving only a token picket to keep it closed.

He had a good intelligence organization and made full use of the ready offers of help from student organizations at Essex University. Students acted as lookouts so that pickets could be switched to best advantage, and 1,000 miners were accommodated in the university. There was a rare degree of solidarity:

> We showed to the university students a degree of discipline and organization which they had probably read about in their Marxist books, but had not seen for themselves. The first thing that we did was to tell them that we were in charge and that we would determine what we did ... they agreed. We had the International Marxist Group, the International Socialists, the Workers' Revolutionary Party and all the other organizations ... agreeing with us that they would have to sink their differences: that we would have to fight one common enemy and that we had no time to discuss whether Trotsky said X, Y or Z in 1873.[8]

He seized his chances. He quotes one example with relish. The miners had deployed 400 pickets to prevent the loading of a queue of 300 lorries at a local coke depot. At a discussion with the manager and the Police Superintendent he offered to reduce the pickets if the depot would agree to issue coke only on permits supplied by the NUM, for delivery to hospitals, schools, old people, etc, but not to power stations or factories. They refused. At that point a harassed official broke in and said 'They're turning back the oil.' The manager looked alarmed and the police officer asked him why he needed oil in a coking plant. He replied that without it the plant cooling system would fail, with probable damage worth £3 million. Scargill who, up till then, had no idea of this, said that they were indeed stopping the oil, but agreed to allow it through in exchange for an agreement to operate the permit system—which was promptly signed.

In the area served by the Yorkshire Area of the NUM, Scargill had the plan organized in more detail. He ran it from an Operations Room which would have brought credit to an Army Headquarters in war. He had an operations map showing all the six ports, nineteen power stations, four steelworks and seventy coal mines (see Map). He maintained a log-book showing where all the men available for picketing were located from hour to hour. He paid a retainer fee to four bus companies who undertook to provide coaches at immediate notice to transport them. He ran a two-tier system: large coaches to transport the pickets to a central point and minibuses to distribute them to the gates, etc., to be picketed. His plans ensured that the large coaches always picked up a full load at a single point, because of the uncertain delays involved in a 'milk-round' pick-up.

By early February, he claimed that virtually all the ports and power stations in Yorkshire and East Anglia were closed.

Whether or not this claim was exaggerated, the energy situation was giving the Government cause for alarm, and so was the growing use of mass picketing, culminating in the incident at the Saltley Coke Depot from 4–10 February described in the next chapter. On 10 February the Government declared a State of Emergency. Power cuts were imposed on almost every home on a rota system. Factories were told not to use power on specified days or to reduce their demands, and thousands of workers were laid off.[9]

Violence

Meanwhile, some of the picketing was becoming increasingly violent. It had begun on 21 January at the NCB's Yorkshire Regional Headquarters in Doncaster, where pickets attempted to prevent clerical staff from entering. Most of these belonged to unions unaffected by the strike and many of them were women.

They had to run the gauntlet for some 200 yards between pickets standing three or four deep on either side. According to one eyewitness, 'They were kicked, punched and spat upon. This treatment was given to all irrespective of age, sex or any apparent union membership.' Three days later, a number of girls were injured in a similar attack at the NCB's Scottish Area Headquarters at Alloa and at the West Wales Headquarters at Tondu.

Using violence against women, however, was repugnant to the majority of miners and was immediately condemned by Mr Joe Gormley, President of the NUM, and by the miners generally. It was alleged that most of those taking part were not miners at all and that the violence had been instigated by members of the Socialist Labour League (a Trotskyist movement which later renamed itself as the Workers' Revolutionary Party). Be that as it may, the incidents drew much adverse publicity and damaged the miners' case.

On 4 February there occurred the only fatal casualty of the strike—an accidental one. At Keadby Power Station, one of those whose gates were manned by Scargill's flying pickets, a miner was run over by the rear wheel of a long articulated lorry. The miner had earlier been on picket duty and had spent his off-duty period in a pub. He had just returned to the scene and misjudged the sweep of the rear wheel of a long articulated lorry.

This was the day that the incident at the Saltley Coke Depot began and, though it was generally understood to have been an accident, there is no doubt that it heightened the emotions of the men picketing the depot. For it was on the following day, 5 February, that Arthur Scargill received an urgent telephone call asking him to despatch the maximum possible number of flying pickets to Saltley, and the decisive battle in his war began.

4 The Battle of Saltley

The mountain of coke

The Saltley Coke Depot in Nechells Place, Birmingham, contained a huge pile of coke estimated at 100,000 tons. Its normal outflow was about 400 lorries a day, mainly to power stations. On 17, 18 and 19 January, twenty-six members of the South Derbyshire branch of the NUM picketed Nechells power station nearby, trying to build up information about how widespread was the effect of the Saltley Coke Depot.[1]

By the end of January, the number of lorries being served daily had risen to 650–700. On 3 February, the *Birmingham Mail* ran a story about a traffic jam a mile long as 'lorries from all over the country waited at Saltley, Britain's last major gas coke stockpile'. By 5 pm that evening seven pickets had been established outside the depot, and the NUM representative was discussing with the police the number of pickets to be allowed. The police agreed to sixteen.

Meanwhile, the *Birmingham Mail* story was taken up by the national press and television, and the Saltley 'mountain of coke', which the Gas Board admitted had been depleted by 30,000 tons since the strike began, took on a symbolic significance to miners all over the country. The photographs of queues of lorries, when the TGWU had long ago announced that their members would move no stocks of coal or coke during the strike, aroused great resentment.

Thus far, the pickets had been organized by Jack Lalley, of the Staffordshire NUM Executive. They were not very effective, and only about one in a hundred drivers were voluntarily turning back. On 4 February, 596 vehicles were loaded. Lalley had meanwhile called for reinforcements, and a small contingent arrived from Hemheath Colliery, Stoke-on-Trent. Nevertheless, drivers who had travelled from all over the country and had been waiting in the queue for more than an hour refused to turn back, and Lalley warned that he would call for 300 pickets from Yorkshire if this continued.

On Saturday 5 February, scuffles began between police and pickets, and two arrests were made. A police spokesman was reported in the press as saying 'If the lorries wish to go in we have given instructions that the entrance must be cleared. If the pickets bar the way they are causing an obstruction.'

The Yorkshire miners answer the call

At 4 pm that afternoon Arthur Scargill received a telephone call in Barnsley calling for pickets to go to Birmingham as soon as possible. The caller explained: 'There's a coke depot there, lorries are going in, *hundreds of them*!' Although it was a Saturday afternoon, Scargill had 200 pickets on their way in coaches within three hours and another 200 more were following. Scargill himself drove through the night and arrived in Birmingham at 3 am on Sunday 6 February. Here, close to Nechells Green, he ran into a concentration of police. 'I'd never seen so many police in my life, hundreds and hundreds of police, at three o'clock in the morning, in coaches.' He asked the way of one, who said, 'Sorry, sir, I'm a stranger here.' He went on into the centre of Birmingham where he found his pickets being accommodated in the Communist Party Headquarters by the Party's District Organizer, Frank Woddis, who was an ex-miner from Scotland and an old friend of Scargill's. Others were accommodated in the TGWU hall and the Labour Party Headquarters. The local Secretary of the Labour Party, Moira Simmons, took charge of accommodation along with one of Scargill's companions from Yorkshire, Alvin Phillips. Word was sent around through party and union channels and offers poured in from families offering to accommodate a picket. By the second night nearly all of them had beds in people's homes, and the beds in the clubs and Headquarters were used as transit accommodation for fresh pickets coming in. Labour MP Denis Howell organized hot meals for them in the Labour Party Headquarters.

Meanwhile, a Strike Headquarters was set up at the Labour Club and plans made to get massed pickets to the Coke Depot by 6 am when the gates were due to open.

C

On Sunday 6 February, police were on duty from 4 am at the depot and by 7 am 200 pickets had arrived. Most of these were still local miners. The police made a gentlemen's agreement with the NUM and the Gas Board to use only one of the two gates into the depot and to keep the other closed. It is an indication of the underlying reasonableness of all sides that it was taken for granted that this agreement would be honoured, and it was.

Several lorries were turned away, and the pickets were jubilant. Other drivers, however, mainly self-employed, were determined to go on, and one had an Alsatian dog in the cab. Feelings began to rise, and before the end of the morning the Gas Board staff closed the gates and announced that they would remain closed until 10 am next morning.

The violence begins

At 4 am on Monday 7 February police began to man the gates, and 220 were on duty by 6 am. Lorries were already queuing and pickets began to assemble shortly before 7 am. By 9.50 am, ten minutes before the gates were due to open, the number of pickets had swollen to 800, including Arthur Scargill's reinforcements from Yorkshire. At 10 am the gates opened and disorder immediately broke out. By 11.30 nine arrests had been made and the number of pickets had increased to 2,000. They had been joined by 150 building workers to demonstrate solidarity. Some of the pickets were crossing and recrossing the Saltley Road in an attempt to disrupt the traffic. During the day only forty-seven lorries were loaded and forty-four turned away.

On Tuesday 8 February, further pickets arrived from South Wales, Yorkshire, Derbyshire and the North Midlands. By 7.30 am there were 100 pickets, and 800 by 9 am. Up till this point, feeling between the pickets and the police had remained reasonable, both being well aware of the dangers of crowds surging forward in the path of oncoming lorries. There was a good liaison between the police and the local NUM headquarters, and with Jack Lalley in particular, in the hope of avoiding injury.

Arthur Scargill introduced a more forceful physical approach. He was clearly enjoying himself. Perched on top of a public urinal, he exercised command like a tug-of-war coach. He would first exhort his men to launch a concerted push, heads down, frontally against the cordon, so that the police would rush men in from the flanks to hold it. He would then switch the pressure suddenly at right angles, so that the flank of the cordon would break and miners would pour out into the road. The others responded with the roar that greets a goal at Wembley. Police reserves would rush in to reopen the road, and in the mêlée fists would fly and arrests would be made.

At 10.20 am the first serious injury occurred. After some altercation, an eight-ton lorry began to move. There was a shout of 'He's going in, lads!' and the crowd began to surge forward. The driver, fearing that he was going to be pulled from his cab, put his foot down just as the crowd forced back the police cordon, keeping the road open in front of him. Three policemen and two pickets were injured. One of these, Chief Inspector Shelley, had a fractured thigh. Immediately it was clear that a man had been seriously injured, all activity stopped and everyone co-operated in helping the ambulance get through to get him to hospital.

As soon as another lorry appeared, however, fighting broke out again with full fury. The atmosphere was not unlike that when a man is injured in a rugby scrum; once he has been carried away, the referee blows his whistle and battle is resumed.

There was, in fact, little depth of hatred between the miners and most of the police—especially local Birmingham police and police reinforcements from mining areas. There were exceptions, and in a physical battle between policemen battling to keep the public highway open and miners determined to force them back, few on either side would have expected the day to pass without some robust exchanges. The police were heavily outnumbered[2] but changed over every hour or so. Scargill tried to rile them by calling out: 'We've got them on the run, lads, they can only last half an hour now'—again the atmosphere of the football terraces. He said that after the injury of Chief Inspector Shelley the police attitude changed to one of greater sympathy for the miners and less for the lorry drivers.

The real hatred, undoubtedly, was between the miners and the drivers, few of whom were members of the TGWU—though the pickets found one who was and had him expelled from his union; he was out of work within four hours. Most of the drivers, however, were self-employed, many owning just one lorry, on which they were paying a mortgage, and they were determined to get their loads through. Scargill believed that many were

earning £50 or £60 a day, some industrial firms paying them a
bonus of £50 a load. For miners fighting for an increase of £9 a
week on a £19 basic wage, their belief that this was so (whether
true or not) added bitterness to the normal hatred of a striker for
a blackleg.

During this day, Tuesday, the police had to fight every lorry
through individually. Eighteen arrests were made and eighteen
people were injured, six of them police. The police were persuading most of the drivers not to attempt the passage and, of
the fifty which did attempt it, only thirty-nine got through.

Mobilizing reinforcement by other unions

On Tuesday evening, Scargill made energetic attempts to get
other unions in Birmingham involved. He decided that Thursday
must be made the day of decision. At a special District meeting
of the AUEW on the Tuesday evening he made an emotional
appeal: 'We don't just want your pound notes. Will you go down
in history as the working class of Birmingham who stood by
while the miners were battered, or will you become immortal?
I do not ask you—I demand that you come out on strike.' There
was an immediate response from moderates and militants alike,
and the next two days were spent on rallying support for a
massive sympathy strike and demonstration.

On Wednesday 9 February the police cordon was established
to keep the road open before the first lorries were due. Five
hundred pickets were also there, and they grew to 2,000 during
the day. By 10.30 am ten arrests had been made. At 11 am a two-
minute silence was called for the miner killed at Keadby, and a
collection made for his dependants, to which police officers on
duty contributed. Arthur Scargill made an emotional speech to
the crowd: 'See he hasn't died in vain!' During the day, twenty-
five arrests were made and there were four injuries, two of them
police. Once again, every lorry had to be forced through individually, and only forty-three were loaded.

Closing the gates

During that day, the police had heard the news that the TGWU and AUEW were going to call sympathy strikes next day (Thursday 10 February). This was clearly going to be a rough day, and by 7 am 400 pickets had arrived in militant mood, some wearing helmets. By 10 am there were 800 police on duty. Coach loads of sympathy strikers were converging from all directions. Soon after 10 am Nechells Place and the main road passing it were completely blocked to traffic by a crowd of 15,000. The Chief Constable, Sir Derrick Capper, decided at 10.45 that there would be risk of death or serious injury if the police tried to force a passage for lorries through this crowd and asked the manager of the depot to close the gates. At 11 am he announced that the gates would be closed for the rest of the day. The crowd was jubilant. Arthur Scargill agreed to disperse the crowd on condition that he could use the police public address equipment and make a speech. To use his own words, 'I gave a political speech to that mass of people and told them that it was the greatest victory of the working class, certainly in my lifetime. The lads who were there were overcome with emotion, emotion in the best possible way . . . here was the living proof that the working class had only to flex its muscles and it could bring Government, employers, society to a total standstill.'[3]

Perhaps the emotion of that final hour was best captured by Alan Law, Midlands Regional Secretary of the TGWU:

By this time the police line at the top of Nechells Place had moved a hundred yards down the hill and the marchers had followed them, so that the police ring was no longer a ring of steel keeping back the pickets, but the jam in the layer-cake—in other words, the police were entirely surrounded by pickets—hopelessly outnumbered.

The tables had been turned with a vengeance.

And there was more to come. The whole length of both footpaths along Saltley Road were blocked with the lads from the factories, men from different unions, welded together by their burning urge to show their miner friends what Birmingham workers could do to help when the call went out.

And along Saltley Road, over the Viaduct, striding down the centre of the road came another column of marchers approaching the scene from the opposite direction, and headed by the small figure of a Scottish piper, his kilt swirling, the plaintive tune on the air over the heads of the thousands of madly cheering Birmingham workers who by now were shouting and singing, filled the air with wild delight.

Through the pickets and through the ranks of police, who parted for him like the Red Sea parted for those other marchers so many centuries ago—on he strode, followed immediately behind by his bodyguard of Scotsmen proudly smiling as they acknowledged the cheers.

And behind them came the column of his mates, through the police cordon, into the centre of the masses, their banners held high—more and still more of them until the whole area was full of working people standing shoulder to shoulder—surely there was no room left for more?

But the police lines parted again, and into the arena stepped the crowning glory—a single line of girls and women, their faces wreathed in smiles, taking up their places on the inner ring of pickets, waving to the cheers and claps of their menfolk, and fully conscious of the admiring glances of our friends on the police line, whose mood seemed to have changed overnight.

What price a baton charge now?

And so we all stood and moved towards the Saltley Gate. Ten thousand voices took up the cheer: 'Close the gate, close the gate, close the gate.'

The roar became tumultuous, it stopped the traffic in Saltley Road, which by now was full of shouting workers moving steadily forward towards the gate. It had to close, it had become a fixation, that gate was the object of so much feeling on the part of the multitude, including, I suspect the hundreds of policemen, that if the chanting had lasted much longer the gate would have run out of patience and closed itself.

At 10.45 am a Gas Board official walked out from his office inside the yard, and taking a key from his pocket, inserted it into the lock, and closed the gate of Saltley Gas Works.

I looked up into the sky and right at that minute the sun broke through the clouds and shone on the 10,000 workers as they stood cheering and singing and on full-grown Yorkshire miners openly weeping.[4]

By 12.15, only a hundred pickets were left and by 2 pm there was no one in Nechells Place except two policemen guarding the closed gate—once again an indication of the underlying confidence in the police, even after feelings had been running so high for the past six days. Later that day, it was agreed by all concerned that the depot would admit only vehicles carrying trade union permits to collect coke for hospitals, schools, old people etc. Next day, only a token picket of twenty-four appeared on the scene.

The effects of Saltley

During the six days, thirty people had been injured, sixteen of them police. Seventy-six arrests had been made, the great majority of whom were miners. The figures were:

Arrests	Age breakdown	
61 miners	16–20 years:	22
3 drivers	21–25 years:	17
2 motor workers	26–30 years:	10
1 insurance agent	31–35 years:	6
2 unemployed	36–40 years:	6
5 students	41–45 years:	5
1 academic	46–50 years:	6
	51 and over:	4

The factor which made the Saltley incident the most violent in British industrial history for sixty years was the symbolism of the 'coke mountain', which seemed to the miners to provide an enormous leak in their blockade of industry and the power stations. Arthur Scargill's first impressions on seeing it were: 'I have never seen anything like it in my life. It was like the most gigantic stack of any colliery that I had ever seen. It was esti-mated that there were a million tons; it was like a mountain . . . it was an El Dorado of coke. There were a thousand lorries a day going in and you can imagine the reaction of our boys, fresh from the successes in East Anglia, fresh from the successes in Yorkshire.' Or, as one of pickets shouted to a *Birmingham Post* journalist, 'It's our blood on that coke!'

Another factor was that it presented Arthur Scargill, who had the bit between his teeth after his triumphs in closing the ports in East Anglia, with an opportunity to become a national figure, with the television cameras trained on him and the Chief Con-stable bowing down before him. He proved a colourful and effective leader. Initially, according to one reporter who covered the whole incident, he had an inflammatory effect on the crowd, but when the number of injuries began to rise he tried to moderate the mood.

Another factor was that this strike was the first since 1926 in which not only the whole of the coal industry, but also all the trade unions concerned, transport, dock, railways etc., stood together. The strike was in its fifth week and the struggle seemed to be evenly balanced. Lorry drivers of the TGWU, like train drivers, had generally respected the NUM pickets at power stations and depots.

The Saltley incident also drew attention to some interesting aspects of the law, for example the point at which 'peaceful persuasion' becomes obstruction, the right to stop people who want to go to work, unlawful assembly, and the legality of picketing places not directly connected with the dispute, such as depots, power stations and ports. All of these had their effect in the drafting of the Labour Government's legislation in 1974–5. They are discussed in Chapters 10 and 19.

The incident underlined the political element in the strikes of that period. This was partly brought about by the increased Government intervention and the attempt to substitute court proceedings for collective bargaining under the 1971 Industrial Relations Act; also by the avowedly political aims, in this strike, of left-wing trade union leaders. The Saltley incident, in particular, also aroused the beginnings of a right-wing backlash, whose effects began to be felt politically in the winter of 1973–4, and in the subsequent formation of private 'vigilante' and 'Essential Services' organizations by General Sir Walter Walker and others. These aspects are discussed in Chapters 10 and 18.

Finally, the incident highlighted some of the elements of industrial confrontation, such as the nature of political and industrial militancy; the actions and relationship of the Government and employers; the interrelation of rival groups of workers; the political exploitation of violence and the reaction to it; the attitude of the police and their interaction with other participants; and the influence of the media.

The results were highly satisfactory to the miners. The original NUM demand was for an increase of £9 a week for underground workers, and the NCB offer which was rejected and brought about the strike was £1·80. On 9 February, the day before the gates were closed at Saltley, the NUM (with Government agreement) offered £3·50, nearly double the Government's ceiling of 8 per cent. The NUM rejected this, but modified their original demand to £7. In the wake of Saltley, the Government appointed a Court of Inquiry under Lord Wilberforce 'to inquire into the causes and circumstances of the present dispute' and 'to report'. In fact, the Government and the NCB had agreed in advance to accept the Court's recommendations, and it seems likely that Lord Wilberforce was instructed to go as far as was necessary to end the strike. He recommended £6 a week rise for underground workers and this, after some adjustment of fringe benefits and equivalent agreements for surface workers, was accepted. The strike ended on 25 February.

This settlement represented a rise of 27 per cent. It smashed the Government's anti-inflation policy, and did much to destroy the credibility of its declared aim to subject industrial relations to the rule of law.

The reaction to violence

On the other hand, the response to the violence, even more than the response to the very real threat of collapse of the economy, aroused a powerful adverse public reaction which alarmed both trade union leaders and the Labour opposition in Parliament. In the next miners' strike in the winter of 1973-4, NUM leaders at national and local level went to great lengths to restrain their pickets and to make them keep within the law and to avoid violence. There were no serious incidents of violence at all in that strike. The cardinal fact is that industrial violence—even on this relatively mild scale, compared with that which is normal in other countries—was deplored by the public, and led to increased sympathy for the police.

The most interesting—and perhaps, in the long run, the most significant—effect of Saltley lay in the actions and attitudes of the police and, in particular, those of the Chief Constable, Sir Derrick Capper. The restraint they showed was in their normal tradition. So was the underlying goodwill despite the feelings aroused by violence in close contact. The police could, without question, have kept the road open, and strictly it was their duty to do so. They could have done this by deploying, say, 3,000 constables instead of 800 (by comparison, 9,000 were mobilized for the 1968 Grosvenor Square demonstration) and, if necessary,

by using water cannon, tear-gas or rubber bullets as soldiers have
in Northern Ireland. Any of these things, however, would have
unleashed far greater violence and sacrificed public sympathy.
The question is whether giving way rather than doing these
things will have the greater or the lesser long-term effect.

In discussion some years after the event,[5] Arthur Scargill said
that, had the police brought in massive reinforcements and used
water cannon or tear-gas to blast a passage through the crowd on
10 February, the resulting violence would have got beyond their
control, not only at Saltley but at many other sites where miners
were picketing. If he were a Trotskyist seeking a revolutionary
situation, he said, this would have suited him—but he was not.
If his leadership had resulted in such an event, in which large
numbers of miners, other workers and police had been killed
or wounded, his men would not have forgiven him and would
not have followed his leadership again.

Few policemen would have wished to see such a situation
develop either. Nevertheless some, both those who were on the
spot and those who witnessed other picketing elsewhere in the
country, believe that Sir Derrick Capper was wrong in closing
the gates. He himself would probably agree with Scargill, however, that the alternative was a massive escalation of force at a
heavy cost in injuries and fatalities, leading to greater breaching
of the law, and to far greater violence later.

A number of Conservative politicians, however, were openly
critical of Sir Derrick's surrender, and considered that it was
this which not only brought down the Government, but opened
the way for the inflation which threatened to destroy the British
economy in 1974–5. Be that as it may, the Chief Constable is
legally not responsible to Ministers, and has the duty to make his
own interpretation of the law and to enforce it. There is a long
tradition of allowing considerable latitude in this interpretation,
and most police officers would prefer this to be so.

There were gloomy predictions that, the police having given
way to mob rule, mob rule would hereafter become the norm in
picketing situations. The five years following Saltley, including
the 1973–4 strikes, proved this prediction false. The police restraint and eventual submission brought them public sympathy
and support, and this influenced trade union leaders and shop
stewards to restrain violence and avoid mass confrontations
during these five years—until Grunwick in 1977 (see Chapter 16).

5 The Shrewsbury Pickets

The 1972 building strike

A very different kind of violence was used in the other great
national strike of 1972: the building workers' strike. Though
there were no really serious casualties (one man lost the sight of
an eye) there were many minor injuries. More importantly, there
was some very ugly intimidation, and an underlying viciousness
about some of the incidents which was rare in the miners' strike.
This may have been caused partly by the fact that the building
strike reached its peak just after the long and unedifying saga in
the docks had ended in the imprisonment and release of the five
London shop stewards (see Chapter 2). The 'long hot summer'
of industrial strife had undoubtedly raised the temperature of
confrontations. And the hatred between regular building workers
and the 'lump' workers, of whom more later, was particularly
bitter. There were also many more building workers ignoring
the strike call than there were 'cowboy' truck drivers trying to
break through the miners' picket lines.

The violence was much more diffuse. Building sites have no
focus like the gate of a power station or a coke depot. Strike-
breaking bricklayers, carpenters or painters were generally to be
found in twos or threes, or even alone on top of a ladder, feeling
very vulnerable to scores or even hundreds of flying pickets
rampaging across the site, picking up iron bars as they went and
shouting murderous slogans about blacklegs. The sum of human
fear at Shrewsbury was vastly greater than at Saltley.

The violence in the building strike—and especially at Shrewsbury and Telford—did raise some very important points of law.
The legal drama was set not in the National Industrial Relations
Court, but in the Criminal Courts. Two of the organizers were
sentenced to long terms of imprisonment (three years and two
years) and the choice of offences for which they were convicted

caused controversy and resentment. This contributed further to
the deterioration of relations between the Government and the
unions. Moderate trade union leaders found themselves—often
with evident distaste and embarrassment—supporting men who
had been convicted by a jury for their part in events in which
singularly nasty violence and intimidation had been used by one
group of workers against others. (The police were scarcely involved in the violence at all.)

Background to the strike

The strike began on 26 June 1972 and lasted for twelve weeks.
Most of the violence occurred in the last four weeks, between 11
August and 6 September.[1]

Like the miners, many building workers felt that their restraint
and moderation had caused them to be overtaken by the others
in the wages race. There had, until 1970, been a very large number of unions (see below) and they felt that the employers had
played off one against the other. Even though there had been a
merger of several of them into the Union of Construction and
Allied Trades and Technicians (UCATT), many building
workers still felt their unions were weak and ineffective. The
leaders of the new UCATT were at the same time anxious to
discount this impression, and prove that the merger of its com-
ponent unions was going to pay. There was also some competition for leading positions in the union.

Building work is very different from work in a factory or a
mine. It is mainly casual, often seasonal, and there is no job
security; for many there are no welfare services or pension
schemes; and, because sites are temporary and the labour fluid,
site facilities such as canteens, WCs and drying rooms are mini-
mal.

When the strike began, the basic rate for a building tradesman
averaged £25 for a 40-hour week. There was a bonus system
whereby, for example, a bricklayer was required to lay 30 bricks
an hour, or 240 in an 8-hour day to get his basic rate, but if he
laid more than that (as most of them did) he received a bonus for
the extra bricks he had laid even though he had worked only 8
hours. If he worked for more than the 8 hours, he was paid for
the bricks he laid at the same bonus rate. Being, in effect, piece-

work, there was a temptation to skimp it, but many bricklayers regularly earned between £40 and £50 a week. Nevertheless, it was argued by the union that they had to work unreasonable hours to get a living wage, and under much tougher conditions than, say, neighbouring workers in the motor industry, who had a basic rate of £40 to £50.

The demand, whose rejection caused the strike, was for a basic rate of £30 for a 35-hour week.

An abrasive factor during the strike was the existence of the 'Lump'. This was a collective term used for 'labour-only sub-contract workers', who did a job for a lump sum. There were, in fact, three kinds of Lump worker. First, there were the specialists, such as refrigeration mechanics, who were called in to install cold storage machinery, and these caused no problems or ill feeling. Second, there were groups of normal tradesmen, such as bricklayers, carpenters, painters, etc., who could be brought in to reinforce or even displace regular workers in the same trade and earn a lot more money, causing obvious resentment. Third, were large bodies of unskilled labour, usually employed by a sub-contractor for such tasks as pipe-laying, for which he would receive a lump sum and pay his labourers whatever he chose from it. Such contractors often took on dubious labour (men on the run, working on the quiet while drawing the dole, etc.) and paid them a good deal less than the rate on which his estimate for the job was based, with the result that he was able to make a very large profit. When there are pickings of this kind to be made, rackets creep in and strong-arm methods are used. There is also much scope for tax evasion, of which there have been some notorious cases. The Lump, in all, included over one-third of the million workers in the construction industry. Although many of the employers in the building trade dislike the Lump system, they found it hard to break away from it.

Employers and trade unions

The National Federation of Building Trade Employers (NFBTE) comprises about 80,000 employers, ranging from huge construction firms like Wimpeys to small builders employing a handful of men. It is not easy for the NFBTE to control the rates which the employers pay; some may give in to pressure to pay more rather

than be bankrupted by a stoppage (and there was plenty of scope
for doing this on the quiet under the bonus scheme); others
would undercut the big firms and then use Lump labour and
unscrupulously low standards to make the job pay.

Until 1970, there were twenty-three trade unions operating in
the construction industry. Then a number of them merged to
form UCATT, and thereafter there were four main unions
involved (UCATT, TGWU, GMWU, FTAT).

Wages and conditions were fixed by the National Joint Council for the Building Industry (NJCBI), made up of employers'
and unions' representatives. Under the main Council there were
ten Regional Councils, and on nine of these the trade union
representative was the UCATT man (generally representing the
more skilled workers), the TGWU man (representing the less
skilled) being on the tenth.

In every Region there were Regional Conciliation Panels,
comprised of equal numbers of employers and trade union
representatives, with the regional secretaries of the NFBTE and
the union (usually UCATT) as joint secretaries. These panels
were remarkably effective in solving routine disputes, and it
was recorded by the joint secretary of the biggest region (London)
that, despite the equal balance of members of management and
labour, they were able to agree on a judgement in 90 per cent of the
cases.

The building industry is generally tough but not militant.
Because employment is casual, men who make a name as
'troublemakers' are likely to be laid off, and sometimes black-
listed. At the time the strike began, only 25 per cent of building
workers were members of unions at all.

Operating in parallel with the trade unions was the Building
Workers' Charter Group. This was trying to use the strike to
attract the loyalty of building workers from the official union
leadership, which they regarded as 'soft'. 'Charter' (as it was
usually known) was formed in April 1970, mainly organized by
Communist Party members. At the first meeting there were 288
delegates. Over half of these (159) represented building sites,
and the remainder represented branch committees of the then
much fragmented trade unions. The pattern of delegates (e.g.
eighty-seven from branches of the Amalgamated Society of
Woodworkers and only two from Plumbers' Trade Union branches) clearly indicates that attendance was based more on shared

ideas of politics or militancy rather than on any even representation of the industry.

Their aims included:

1. £1 per hour for a 35-hour week.
2. Comprehensive regulations for holidays, safety, welfare, pensions and de-casualization.
3. A single trade union for the building industry, requiring 100 per cent membership, and banning of the Lump.
4. Full nationalization of the building industry.

The group published a monthly paper, *Charter*, under the slogan of 'Agitator Educator Organizer'. The first issue came out in July 1970, and by the fourth issue it had sales of 10,000. One of its main aims was to co-ordinate industrial activity and weld it into a national force, on the basis that 54 per cent of Britain's national investment was in construction.

Its second conference was in April 1971, and 500 delegates attended. In April 1972 there were 900 delegates, claiming to represent 250,000 men—that is 25 per cent of the workers in the industry (though it is hard to say how many of these knew or approved of their 'representation').

Charter members played an active part in the 1972 strike, though they became so involved that they did not find time to continue to publish their paper. This was a reflection of the fact that they had little formal organization, and the small group who ran it preferred to devote their energies and their funds to the strike—though this may well have been a mistake.

After the strike, which was generally regarded as a failure, and the violence from it, which caused adverse public reaction, Charter began to decline. The 1973 conference attracted 600 delegates and the 1974 one fewer still. The paper also began to decline and, despite putting some of their most dynamic members on to organizing it, it ceased publication at the end of 1975 (though it was later revived).

Charter never advocated violence or played any part in it. The same is generally true of the CPGB. Charter was really a pressure group, and its paper devoted as much space to the denunciation of 'moderate' trade union leaders as of employers. Generally, in fact, where the Communists were strongest the violence was at its least. In London, for example, the Regional Council of UCATT had twenty-one members of whom sixteen were Communists; they in turn appointed a Regional Committee of six members of whom five were Communists. London is the largest region, but had far fewer cases of violence during the 1972 strike than the Midlands or Yorkshire.

Sequence of events

For the first six weeks of the strike (i.e. until early August), the policy was to harass employers with 'guerrilla strikes' by sending flying pickets to different sites each day, urging the workers to strike. There was no alternative but to use flying pickets because a building site has no perimeter and no gates, and the labour force changes weekly or even daily. When called out on strike, the men were not too keen to volunteer for picket duty as they knew they could go and get a job on a site somewhere else, and most of them did. Much of the flying picket work was therefore done by the Strike Committees themselves, sometimes supported by a 'heavy mob' of men with a taste for a punch-up. Generally, however, there was little violence during the first six weeks.

The fluid labour force made these guerrilla strikes ineffective, so the Strike Committees began to concentrate more on the big firms where they hoped to make more of an impact and get more publicity. This too, however, was ineffective, because the big firms were usually the best employers, for whom men were happy to work, and a high percentage of their labour force had been with them for some years; these men would return to work as soon as they could. In any case, the big firms could take the stoppage in their stride, invoke the time clause in their contract and pass on the cost to the client at the end.

After six weeks, therefore, some Strike Committees were beginning to become exasperated by the lack of support from the building workers and the prospect of failure of the strike. That was the climate in which violence began.

Initially, there were few injuries and the violence took the form of intimidation, frequently by smashing machinery and indicating clearly that if the men did not stop work they would be next. Between 11 and 21 August about six men were attacked on four different sites, though their injuries were slight. On 24 and 25 August two policemen were kicked in the mouth, and on 28 August three building workers were shaken off scaffolding.

The most serious injuries occurred in Shrewsbury and Telford on 6 September. One man was pulled down from the scaffolding and a stone or brick dropped on his head, leaving him blind in one eye; and a number of other men were injured. In these incidents, which spread to several sites, there was mass intimidation by a 'flying picket' of some 250 men. These Shrewsbury incidents are dealt with more fully below.

The only other serious injury was the result of an attack on one of the more active members of the Birmingham Strike Action Committee, Mike Shilvock, who was also a member of the CPGB. The attack was presumably made by or on behalf of a Lump sub-contractor who was exasperated with the flying pickets. The men who carried it out were clearly well practised in the art of beating-up. They picked a night when his wife was out at a choir practice, and knocked on Mr Shilvock's door. Being suspicious, he kept the chain on the door. Through the gap, a knife was flashed at him; he drew back to keep out of range, and the men tore the chain out of the wall with a shoulder charge on the door. They 'did him over' for two minutes in absolute silence, and then broke his arm at the elbow and left him.

Ironically, it was on this day that the unions accepted the employers offer of a guaranteed £5 a week bonus (which most men earned anyway) with the basic remaining at £25, so that both sides could claim a victory and the strike was over.

Shrewsbury: the background

The events at Shrewsbury and Telford on 6 September marked the peak of the strike.

Just as the violence at Saltley was caused mainly by men from Yorkshire and elsewhere, so the violence at Shrewsbury was caused not by local men, but by men from the areas to the west in Cheshire and North Wales. These areas had particularly militant Strike Action Committees and had achieved a much greater degree of success than elsewhere: work on many sites had been stopped, mainly by flying pickets formed from the members of the Strike Action Committees, often in their own cars, though sometimes in coaches. Nevertheless, the flying pickets were becoming more and more exasperated with the Lump workers who chose to ignore them. The pattern of operation of the flying

pickets was generally on these lines: a picket—perhaps just a few
members of the Strike Action Committee in their private cars—
would go to a site during the lunch break and warn the men that
tomorrow the site would be black. Next day they would return
with one or two coach loads of pickets and the site would be
clear except for, say, four Lump workers up on the scaffolding
putting in the windows. This enraged the pickets, because they
could see the effect of their strike being eroded. On the other
hand, the four Lump workers were getting, perhaps, £400 for
putting in these windows, and if they could finish the job within
a week they would have £100 each and go on next week to another
job, so they were not interested in stopping work. Nor were they
interested in whether the regular workers got a basic £25 or £30
—their view was that they were mugs not to join the Lump themselves. Both sides therefore felt that right was on their side.

Nevertheless, all the ingredients for violence are present on a
building site. If the Lump workers would not come down from
the scaffolding, the pickets would give it a shake. The men above
would drop something, which would probably be thrown back.
With crowbars and sledgehammers close at hand, the surprising
thing is that the injuries were not more serious considering the
passions aroused.

Each week, eight Strike Action Committees used to meet at
Chester. One of these was from Oswestry, and they had become
disturbed at the reports of work continuing on building sites in
Shrewsbury, and particularly in the New Town being built at
Telford nearby. Shrewsbury and Telford were, in fact, in the
Birmingham area, but UCATT in Birmingham had said they
were unable to picket them as they had too many sites of their
own to deal with. The Oswestry men had therefore sent down a
few pickets, but without effect. Shrewsbury had only a very small
and ineffective Strike Action Committee of its own, so work was
clearly going to continue. The matter was raised by the Chairman
of the Oswestry Strike Action Committee at Chester on 31
August and a unanimous vote was taken that as many members
as possible from the eight Committees represented would attend
at Oswestry on Wednesday 6 September to go to Shrewsbury
and 'stop the sites'.

Shrewsbury: 6 September 1972

Between 9 and 10 am on Wednesday 6 September 1972, about 250 pickets met at the Oswestry Labour Club, where they were joined by six coaches booked by the various Strike Action Committees. At about 11 am, the six coaches were entering Shrewsbury when they saw road works in progress at Shelton Road on the outskirts, and at the Kingswood housing estate nearby. They turned the coaches into a pub car park and swarmed across the site, as one witness described it, 'like Apache Indians'. There was no question of peaceful persuasion. Doors and windows were smashed, pipes torn up, brickwork pushed over, and men working were bombarded with stones and other missiles. The workers ran off in all directions in terror, a number of them asking a resident nearby to lock them in his garage for safety. After considerable damage had been done, the foreman of a plant hire contractor produced a shotgun from his car and confronted the pickets. He later put it back in his car, from which it was taken by the pickets and smashed while he himself was attempting to leave the site. The broken gun was taken back to the coaches.

The pickets then turned back to the Shelton Road site which they had passed in their coaches. Once again, there was no attempt at persuasion. They overturned a dumper, a roller, a compressor and a van, smashed windows and tore up kerbing, and sent the workers running off the site.

By this time, the police had received a 999 call, describing the scene and saying that the pickets had a gun. Six policemen under a Chief Inspector sped to the scene and confronted the 250 pickets returning to their coaches from the Shelton Road. They called for the strike leaders and ten men came forward, including Desmond Warren (a member of the CPGB) and Eric Tomlinson. The police officers advised the strikers about the laws of peaceful picketing, and the strikers ascribed all the disorder to the shotgun incident. The police demanded the return of the gun and Tomlinson fetched it from one of the coaches.

The pickets then moved on to the Mount site just the other side of the pub, the coaches coming with them. On the way, there is evidence that Tomlinson urged them to 'cool it off' and that Warren said 'The police are here, you had better keep it down.'

The policemen, still about six strong, reached the Mount site

ahead of them. The pickets came on to the site chanting 'Kill the
Lump!' About twenty of them began to range over the site while
the remainder sat on the bank chanting 'Kill, kill, kill!' They
were met by the site agent, who called for the leaders. About
twenty of them went into his office where, he claims, he was
threatened with violence and that Warren said 'This is a revolution, not a strike!' The agent offered to collect the work-force
into the site canteen. Here they were addressed by a number of
the pickets, including Warren, and six of the men later gave
evidence that they had been threatened with such phrases as 'If
you want a fight we will give you one' and 'You can work if
you want, but you will be carried home in a pine box!'

Some damage was done on this site but there was less violence
than on the others, possibly owing to the presence of the police.

From the Mount site the pickets moved in their coaches to the
other end of Shrewsbury where they debouched on to the Severn
Meadows site, where once again they streamed across the site
shouting 'Kill the bastards! Get the bastards off!' There had
been a tip-off that there was a plan to keep the police occupied
on the Severn Meadows site while the main body of pickets
went on through it to the Weir site nearby. Again, there was
widespread intimidation on both sites, the workmen scattering
and running for their lives. A press photographer was threatened
and took refuge with the police.

The Shrewsbury police had undoubtedly been taken by surprise as the picketing in Shrewsbury had previously been peaceful. Their impression in retrospect was that the pickets had
probably intended to go direct to Severn Meadows but had been
incensed when they saw the work going on in the Shelton Road
and Kingswood sites and turned into the pub car park on the
spur of the moment. There were no police present on either of
the first two sites, and the maximum number on the scene before
the pickets left Shrewsbury was never more than eleven. The
actions were so dispersed that the constables themselves seldom
witnessed any violence—indeed, violence tended not to occur
when they were present. They could undoubtedly have made
arrests, however, for such offences as 'conduct likely to cause a
breach of the peace', but if they had done so, the violence would
almost certainly have increased.

After the action on the Severn Meadows and Weir sites, some
of the pickets dispersed into pubs and into a fish-and-chip shop

as it was about lunchtime. One of the coaches had to return empty to Chester as it had a school pick-up. The remainder then piled into the other five coaches and headed twelve miles down the road to Telford. They went first to a large new housing estate at Brookside, an oval-shaped site about three-quarters of a mile by half a mile wide, with a perimeter road running round it. The local police had had a message from Shrewsbury that the coaches were heading in the Telford direction, but there were so many building sites in the New Town that they found difficulty in keeping track of them. The coaches stopped on the perimeter road at Brookside, and the pickets, it was said, 'literally disgorged into the nearest buildings'. There was extensive violence and damage, and this time a bricklayer was pulled off the scaffolding and seriously injured. Seven other men were injured, mainly by stones thrown at them while they were up on the scaffolding.

Since Brookside was a large estate mainly of small houses, most of the men working on it were alone or in groups of two or three. Ten or twenty pickets would rampage into the house, and initially start smashing equipment, knocking down brickwork and tearing off doors, indicating that they would turn on the tradesmen next if they did not stop work. In most cases the tradesmen ran off in terror. One of the most active of the pickets was a giant of a man, who walked around tearing the young trees out by the roots; painters, carpenters and bricklayers watched him with some alarm, and he then swung round like King Kong and advanced towards them. They jumped from their ladders and ran.

By the time the police arrived on the Brookside site, most of the workers had left, apart from a handful who were addressed by Warren in the open. A photograph by a news cameraman of this meeting shows the bricklayer who had already received injuries which were to result in the loss of the sight of an eye standing at the back of the crowd, and it was said later that he was still in a state of concussion, not thinking to run away and wandering about in a daze. Nevertheless, the photograph is proof that the scale of violence was certainly not high by international standards. The real point at issue was the degree of intimidation; this certainly was high, and appeared to be the aim of the operation, and it was on these grounds that the pickets were convicted.

From Brookside, after a brief call at a private development site, the pickets travelled in coaches one and a half miles to another New Town scheme at Woodside. The police on this occasion had got there before them, but not in sufficient numbers to prevent them from doing damage. The pickets debouched from the coaches and spread out in groups amongst the houses, pulling men from their work and smashing windows as before. News of what had happened at Brookside had already reached the site, and most of the men had already left for home, but again there was a small meeting, addressed by Warren and Tomlinson.

Altogether, on the five sites in Shrewsbury and two sites in Telford, the damage was estimated at £3,000 and a total of eleven men were injured. None of those injured were either pickets or policemen; all were building workers who had remained at work.

Shrewsbury: the trial

Immediately after these events, a police inquiry was begun by the West Mercia Constabulary. In view of the very large number of witnesses on the seven sites, and the fact that all of the 250 pickets came from distant places ranging from Oswestry to North Wales, this inquiry took three months, and was considered by the Director of Public Prosecutions (DPP) in January 1973. A total of 214 charges were made against twenty-four of the pickets, and magistrates' hearings were held in May. The main trial did not take place until the closing months of 1973. Warren and Tomlinson were sentenced to three years and two years in prison respectively and one other man, Jones, to nine months. The others received only suspended sentences.

The trial was in two parts: six of the leaders on more serious charges and the other eighteen on lesser charges.

Of the eighteen on lesser charges, all were charged with unlawful assembly and affray; in addition each was originally charged with a number of individual offences of assault, intimidation or damage, bringing the total number of charges to 122. The DPP and counsel decided that it was impractical to ask a jury to return verdicts on 122 charges, so the eighteen were eventually charged only with unlawful assembly and affray. Four of them pleaded guilty to unlawful assembly and the charges of affray against these were dropped. None of these eighteen re-

ceived anything other than suspended sentences, so none of them
went to prison.

The six leaders were charged with conspiracy as well as unlawful assembly and affray. They too were also charged with
additional individual offences, such as intimidation, assault occasioning actual bodily harm, common assault and damage, bringing the total number of charges against the six to ninety-two.
Once again, the DPP and counsel decided to proceed only with
the three main charges against each and to leave the others on
the file. There were, for example, twenty-eight charges in all
against Warren: the three main ones and twenty-five of assault,
intimidation, damage, etc.; against Tomlinson there were
twenty-one: the three main charges and eighteen individual
charges.

Of the six leaders, three (Warren, Tomlinson and Jones) were
found guilty on all three of the main charges and were sentenced
respectively to three years, two years, and nine months on each
charge, to run concurrently. Later, on appeal, the convictions on
affray were quashed, but this did not affect the length of sentence
they served, as the sentences were concurrent. By the time the
appeals were over, Jones had already completed his sentence.
Warren and Tomlinson continued to serve theirs, and became
the centre of a widespread campaign for their release. The convictions for conspiracy were particularly criticized and were later
to lead to a change in the law.

Many people felt that, if they were guilty at all, they should
have been convicted of the individual charges of assault and
intimidation rather than on these blanket charges. It has been
suggested that the reason for this was that the Court could give
a bigger sentence on the general charges whereas (with the exception of assault occasioning actual bodily harm) the maximum
sentence would have been about three months. This argument,
however, is invalid since the sentences could have been con-
secutive. If, for example, Warren had been sentenced to three
months' imprisonment on each of twenty charges he could have
spent five years in prison.

The real reason was a practical one, which reveals a weakness
in the legal system which would be hard to cure. Even when the
number of charges was reduced, the jury had to return verdicts
on three charges against each of the six accused, that is, eighteen
verdicts in all. As it was, the trial lasted twelve weeks. If the

Court had proceeded on all the individual counts, the jury would have had to return ninety-two verdicts which would clearly have been an impossible task for a single jury. If, on the other hand, the accused had been tried separately, the trials would in all have lasted even longer, and there would have been a serious risk of them prejudicing each other.

The fact that the convictions for affray were quashed came about for a similar reason. An 'affray' is a 'continuous riot'. There were, in fact, seven 'affrays', one on each site. To have charged each of the accused with each of these would again have presented the jury with an impossible number of verdicts to return. Counsel therefore decided to prefer a single charge of affray covering all seven sites, both in Shrewsbury and Telford. On appeal, however, the defence counsel said that it could only be an affray if the rioting had continued in the buses on the way between Shrewsbury and Telford. On these grounds, the convictions were quashed.

With hindsight it would seem that it would have been better to have tried the accused on charges of unlawful assembly and on, say, two or three charges each of individual assault and intimidation, selecting charges which were serious (such as the assault on the bricklayer who lost the sight of an eye) and which the evidence suggested were most likely to be proved. If they had been convicted on specific charges of violence and intimidation, the convictions and sentences would have seemed fairer to the public, and to other trade unionists in particular. Those witnesses and victims to whom we spoke left us in no doubt as to the viciousness of the violence and the extreme degree of terror which they felt, and the judge left no doubt of his own feelings on this in passing sentence. It would have been better if this had been unequivocally reflected in the verdict given by the jury, so that justice was seen to have been done.

The effects of Shrewsbury

The questions raised about the law are discussed again in Chapter 19, and these had considerable influence on subsequent legislation in 1974 and 1975. Of more immediate effect, however, was the public revulsion against the violence and intimidation, and this revulsion (like that against the much less vicious mass violence at Saltley) undoubtedly had a restraining effect on industrial disputes during the next three years. No one, not even those convicted, denied that violence and intimidation had occurred; the only question in Court was whether those accused were responsible for it.

As at Saltley, the media were criticized for magnifying the violence but, in the event, the better public understanding of what it felt like for an isolated building worker to be in fear of his life from flying pickets probably had a beneficial effect in restoring and sustaining the British tradition of non-violence.

6 Days of Hope

The steam goes out of the strikes

As the building strike came to an end in September 1972 the sky began to clear, almost imperceptibly at first, and for the next fourteen months (that is, until the Arab–Israeli war brought about the quadrupling of oil prices) it seemed that Britain might be emerging from her agony. On almost every front things seemed to be over the worst.

The dock strike had ended on 16 August. The building trade unions, the majority of whose members were already disregarding the strike, settled for a bonus consolation prize with no change in the basic rate of £25 per week. Communist Party shop stewards and the Charter Group lost ground and militancy took a knock all round.

This was reflected in strike figures. Contrasting with the loss of $12\frac{1}{2}$ million working days in the first quarter of 1972 (miners' strike) and $6\frac{3}{4}$ million in the third quarter (building strike) the loss in the fourth quarter was down to $1\frac{1}{2}$ million, and remained at around this level for the following year.[1]

Contributing to this was the tacit abandonment of the Industrial Relations Act by all three sides—Government, employers and unions—for solving any but minor disputes over such things as bargaining structures and unfair dismissals.[2] All the major unions, being unregistered, were technically deprived of their privileges and immunities under the law and could be sued for damages caused by strikes, but no one cared to sue them. The Government (after the 1972 railway strike) did not demand strike ballots. Employers generally did not resist closed shops and fought shy of cases like those of Goad, Langston and Con-Mech.[3]

Stage 1: A freeze on pay and prices

The miners' strike, however, had destroyed the Government's attempts to hold pay rises down to 8 per cent. The failure of the building strike had to some extent been misleading, as it had failed because of the nature of construction work. Individual building workers, conscious of their lack of job security, preferred not to get branded as troublemakers, and many of them had been shaken by the stark demonstration of their vulnerability to violence and intimidation by flying pickets. Other settlements in the autumn of 1972, however, were averaging 15–17 per cent and average weekly earnings had risen by 12 per cent since the previous autumn. The Retail Price Index was rising at little more than half that rate, so the real value of earnings, even after tax, was rising fairly fast; too fast, in fact, for the rise in production, which had been very slight and was only just starting to pick up. Moreover, world commodity prices rose very sharply in 1972, so the outlook for both inflation and the balance of payments was disturbing.[4]

On 26 September 1972, after the settlement of the building strike, the Government made proposals for an incomes policy and invited the CBI and the TUC for discussions in the hope of reaching a voluntary agreement in the more conciliatory climate. With the TUC themselves alarmed about the prospects of unemployment, there were some hopeful signs. A relationship had begun to develop between Heath and the TUC General Secretary Vic Feather. The trade unions found Heath a straightforward man to deal with, and respected him for this. Nevertheless, the economic price demanded by the TUC was too great for Heath (or his Treasury advisers) to accept, and so were the differences over industrial relations, and the talks broke down.[5] On 6 November the Government announced a three-month freeze on pay and prices as Stage 1 of a new counter-inflation policy, during which a Stage 2 for pay and price restraint would be worked out for introduction early in 1973.

The freeze produced protest demonstrations and some industrial action, particularly in the public sector. Some unions managed to rush settlements through before the deadline and this inevitably annoyed others who were left behind. The industrial action, however, was not on a large scale, most unions preferring to hold their fire until they saw what the Government intended in Stage 2.

Stage 2: the Counter-Inflation Act

On 17 January 1973 the Government published a White Paper and draft Bill, which later became the Counter-Inflation Act. This Act gave them power to control pay and prices for three years. Pay rises were to be calculated on a group basis, the negotiators being free to decide how the rise was to be distributed within the group (a foretaste of the 'kitty bargaining' procedure which became fashionable later). Annual rises were not to exceed £1 a week plus 4 per cent on the current pay bill of the group (excluding overtime), with a maximum of £250 a year for any individual—manager, technician or labourer. No increase could take effect until twelve months after the previous one. The freeze was to be extended until the end of March for pay and the end of April for prices.

To administer the Act, the Government set up a Pay Board and a Prices Commission. These were to examine anomalies arising from the freeze (e.g. between similar groups where one had settled just before it and the other had missed the bus). These anomalies would then be adjusted in Stage 3, which was to begin in the autumn. After that, the Pay Board was to prepare a Report on Relativities (which was in the event to play a crucial role in the miners' strike and General Election at the beginning of 1974).

The publication of the White Paper was a signal for many groups which had been holding their fire to take action. Gas workers began stoppages and overtime bans and extracted concessions over redundancies and pensions. The civil service unions called their first ever one-day national strike. 126,000 stopped work for a day and followed this with a work-to-rule and overtime ban. Civil servants, however, seldom attract much public sympathy, and there was an even more adverse reaction to selective stoppages by 50,000 ancillary hospital staff—so much so that the TUC asked the Government to treat hospital workers (whom most people agreed were badly underpaid) as a special case, with the promise that the TUC would not quote the settlement in justification of other claims.

As in 1967–9, the public were beginning to show exasperation with strikes in nationalized public services, in which the 'employers' being squeezed and made to suffer were the people themselves.

It was probably this which broke the resistance to Stage 2. Once again the miners' action proved decisive but, whereas in February 1972 it was they who had smashed the Government's previous attempt to restrain inflation, this time it was they who saved it. The NUM executive was split. The Marxist element, led by the Vice-President Mick McGahey, demanded a strike, but the majority of the executive advised acceptance of a settlement under Stage 2. They were conscious that the 1972 strike, though successful, had alienated much of the normally deep-rooted public sympathy for the miners, and that a further strike within little over a year would arouse hostility. In view of the split, however, the NUM called a strike ballot on 13 April. The miners voted by a large majority (143,006 to 82,631) against striking, and the NUM executive therefore settled within Stage 2.

This took the steam out of a 'day of national protest and stoppage' called by the TUC for May 1. Only 1,600,000 workers turned out. The TUC had by then already expressed its 'resentful and reluctant acquiescence' to Stage 2. Other unions followed the miners' lead and during the seven months of Stage 2 (2 April to 31 October 1973) the Pay Board approved or screened 6,544 settlements covering 15,951,000 workers, refusing only 44.[7]

Vic Feather leaves the TUC

In September 1973 Vic Feather was succeeded as General Secretary of the TUC by Len Murray. This marked a significant change in the complexion of trade unionism in Britain—a change which was perhaps inevitable and may have come to stay. Murray was not a product of the shop floor but a university economics graduate who had worked his way up through the TUC bureaucracy. He could not bring the same earthy humour and feel for the man on the assembly line which Vic Feather had brought into negotiations; on the other hand, Murray (who was fifty-one) had had many years of experience of Whitehall negotiation, and understood the workings of the minds of Ministers and their Permanent Secretaries a good deal better than most of his predecessors did. Whether this kind of understanding was of more value than the feel for the shop floor is arguable. It is the same as the age-old argument for and against the professional army General Staff—the Whitehall warrior or the soldiers' general. Perhaps a soldiers' general who has also learned the Whitehall game is the ideal, but few people can adequately cram two life-times into one. For good or ill, Murray introduced a new style into high-level negotiations. At the same time he had to gain the confidence of the men on the ground and was clearly vulnerable if he ever appeared to be seeing things too much through bureaucratic eyes at their expense.

He took over at a time when the country really seemed to be on the road to recovery; when the Government appeared to be regaining control of the economy; when the threat of mass disorder on the picket lines seemed to have passed. Perhaps there were already signs of danger ahead: the OPEC states had discovered the power of unity and oil prices were rising. So were other commodity prices. But within Britain strikes remained at a far lower level than in 1972. The prices and incomes policies appeared to be working, and seemed to be generally accepted by the work-force.

Stage 3—a child to be strangled at birth

Inflation was still running at 10–12 per cent per annum (see figures under Note 4 above). In theory, rises of £1 a week plus 4 per cent would not keep pace with this, but in practice the rises in *earnings* did roughly keep up. The Government had argued that Stage 2 would add $7\frac{1}{4}$ per cent to the wage and salary bill, thereby halving the wage-inflation rate. *The Economist* had been nearer the mark in predicting that, when settlements made in November 1972 came into effect in April 1973 (involving a million workers) and when overtime loopholes were taken into account, the wage bill would rise by 10–$10\frac{1}{2}$ per cent; but their forecast of an 8 per cent rise in prices was also, like the Government's forecast, an underestimate.[8] In retrospect, *The Economist* blamed the unexpectedly large rise in commodity prices.[9] They claimed in November 1973 that Britain had 'beaten the world in controlling domestic inflation' but that this success had been obscured by the effects of higher import costs, which had accounted for nearly two-thirds of the price increases. In the twelve months up to November 1973, for example, the prices of industry's basic raw materials and fuels had risen by 42 per cent whereas shop prices had risen by just under 10 per cent.[10] This was because wage rises had been successfully restrained while productivity boomed.

Nevertheless, the next stage had clearly to be more flexible than Stage 2 if pay was to continue to keep ahead of prices. On 8 October 1973 the Government published its White Paper out-lining Stage 3, to run from 7 November 1973 to July 1974. It confirmed that the economy was still on course for a 5 per cent growth rate between mid-1972 and mid-1974 and that during 1974 the growth rate would be continued at $3\frac{1}{2}$ per cent, 'broadly in line with the long-term rate of growth of the economy's productive potential'.

Stage 3 allowed for a norm of £2·25 a week or 7 per cent, whichever was the larger, plus a 1 per cent flexibility margin, with an individual maximum annual rise of £350. Two new features were the provisions for extra pay for those who had to work 'unsocial hours' and for 'threshold payments' when the Retail Price Index (RPI) rose by more than 6 per cent. The threshold payments were to be 40p per week increase for every 1 per cent rise in the RPI above 6 per cent. Taken together, these measures were expected to produce average increases in earnings of 10–11 per cent.

Hopes of public acceptance of Stage 3 were high. The TUC's reception—'unacceptable and probably unworkable'—was criti-cal but hardly a call to arms. Some economists were sounding warnings that all was not as well as it seemed, pointing out that the labour market was too tight; that the rise in production of the first half of the year had stopped;[11] that industry had reached capacity levels in production before industrial investment had begun to increase; and that consumption and imports had surged while industrial expansion was levelling off, resulting in a rapid rise in the balance of payments deficit.[12]

Not all economists, however, were gloomy. *The Economist* published an optimistic article, predicting a fall in commodity prices, an improvement in the terms of trade, and increased productivity which would result in only 8 per cent of the 11 per cent wage bill being reflected in wage costs.[13] The Government's plan depended for success on two things: a general acceptance of the prices and incomes policy, and a steadying of commodity prices.

The hopes of acceptance seemed to be justified. Wages were still ahead of prices and, above all, unemployment was at an almost record low level, having fallen from 4 per cent in January 1972 to $2\frac{1}{2}$ per cent in October 1973. Even if import prices did rise more than expected, wage-earners should be protected from the effects by the threshold payments scheme.

There were, however, two time-bombs already ticking, which were to destroy all these hopes, to bring down the Government and to sentence the country to far worse agonies than in 1972— record inflation, a falling standard of living and unemployment at levels unheard of since the 1930s—and all under a Labour Government.

One time-bomb was in the NUM, where the National Executive was delicately balanced between the moderates, led by the President Joe Gormley, and the Marxist element led by the Vice President, Mick McGahey. Gormley was convinced that the miners' interests lay in a continuation of stability and full employment, and was confident that he could negotiate a pay rise within Stage 3 which, because of the flexibility allowed, would be generous enough to be accepted. The Marxist wing, however, remained determined to use industrial action to bring about wider political change. McGahey succeeded in getting his own Scottish miners' demand for increases of £8 to £13 in the basic wage accepted as NUM policy. This was equivalent to a rise of over 40 per cent and it was clear that the Government could not accept it. McGahey therefore issued a call to arms at the NUM Annual Conference in July: 'It is not negotiation in Downing Street, but it is agitation in the streets of this country to remove the Government that is required.'[14]

The second time-bomb was the Arab–Israeli war, which had begun on 6 October 1973, just two days before the Government announced Stage 3 and four days before the NCB made a generous offer to the miners—so generous, in fact, that it defeated its own object, as will be seen. No one at the time foresaw that a war in Palestine and Sinai would result in the quadrupling of the price of the most vital commodity of all—oil—throwing Britain (and the whole Western world) into a desperate energy crisis within five weeks.

Whether the Marxist faction would have carried the executive and the miners into a strike without the opportunity offered by the energy crisis will be debated for years to come. They did carry it, and thereby achieved their political aim of bringing down the Government—a milestone in British political history.

D

7 Oil and the Arab-Israeli War

The rising price of oil

The low cost of producing and transporting oil had always been the enemy of the miners' bargaining power and had resulted in widespread pit closures in the 1960s. On 1 January 1973 the posted price of oil was $2·40 per barrel. By October 1973 it had risen to $3·01 and an additional element of revenue for the producing countries had been introduced by transfer of part-ownership of assets under participation. To apply pressure on the West to withhold support from Israel during the Yom Kippur War, it was raised rapidly, first to $5·11 and finally on 23 December (to take effect on 1 January 1974) to $11·65.

The 'posted price' is a notional figure used to fix the royalty (60 per cent). Its relationship to the cost of oil coming from the Gulf to the UK was as follows:

Price of oil from Gulf per barrel	*1 Jan 73*	*1 Jan 74*
A. Posted price (PP)	$2·40	$11·65
B. Producing countries' royalty (60% of PP)	1·45	7·00
C. 'Participation' revenue (variable), say	—	2·00
D. Revenue for oil companies	0·25	0·90
E. Production cost	0·10	0·10
F. Market price at Gulf loading point (B + C + D + E)	1·80	10·00
G. Transport from Gulf to UK	80	1·30
H. Price of Gulf oil in UK (F + G)	2·40	11·30

It is noteworthy that the actual cost of production in the desert in 1973 was a very small part of the price (10c). The royalty was far greater: even in January 1973 it was fourteen and a half times the production cost and by January 1974 it was seventy times.

By comparison, the oil companies' revenue was also small (25–90c) and much of this was committed to exploration for new fields. For the owners of the deserts, therefore, oil has aptly been described as 'black gold in the bank'; there is no particular hurry about drawing it out and spending it, and what is not spent does not depreciate—in fact it gains in value. Moreover, if some has already been converted into money in an actual bank balance, the producing country can at will reduce production of oil or even stop it altogether. It had thus, by 1973, become the most powerful weapon in the world for diplomatic bargaining.

Up till 1972, the Organization of Petroleum Exporting Countries (OPEC) had been disunited. If one country tried to raise its royalty the oil companies could usually persuade another one to undercut it. A royalty of fourteen and a half times the production cost (or four times the total receipt of the oil companies for production, exploration, overheads and profit) was regarded by both sides as generous enough. The Shah of Iran, however, unlike most of the others, had many millions of mouths to feed, so he had a real incentive to seek the most he could get for his black gold while it lasted. It was he who convinced the others of the enormous power they could wield if only they could form a price cartel.

The first precipitating factor was the devaluation of the dollar in February 1973. OPEC members felt that the oil price should be raised to compensate for the loss of purchasing power of their royalties. During 1972 it had already been agreed that the posted price of crude oil should be raised by 5·8 per cent on 1 April 1973 and at a meeting in Geneva in June, eight of the eleven OPEC states reached an agreement with the oil companies to raise it a further 6·1 per cent, making an aggregate increase of nearly 12 per cent.

At their meeting in Vienna on 15 and 16 September, OPEC decided to ask for further increases and on 8 October negotiations began between the oil companies and the six Gulf states. The Yom Kippur War, however, had begun on 6 October and the talks broke up in deadlock on 12 October.

The fortunes of war

On 10 October the Russians began to airlift military equipment to Egypt and Syria and on 13 October the USA responded with deliveries to Israel. On 17 October, at Kuwait, the ten Arab members of OPEC (OAPEC) decided to reduce production of petroleum by at least 5 per cent progressively each month, until Israeli forces had withdrawn completely from the territories occupied in the 1967 war and legal rights for Palestinians had been restored.

By that time the war, which has started with exhilarating successes for the Arabs on both the Syrian and Egyptian fronts, had begun to turn sour. On 16 October the Israelis had driven the Syrians back to within 18 miles of Damascus. In Sinai the fighting had bogged down into a war of attrition between 10 and 15 October, and that night General Arik Sharon cut through between the Egyptian armies and crossed the canal to take them in the rear. By 21 October Sharon's bridgehead was 25 miles deep and 20 miles wide, and the Arabs were joining the Russians in calling for a cease-fire. The Americans—alarmed at the Arab reaction if the defeat turned into a rout—supported them and the cease-fire began on 22 October. Sharon, however, claiming that the Egyptians had infringed it, resumed his advance on 23 October and by the following day had seized the town of Suez, had cut off the entire Egyptian Third Army, and was poised at Kilometre 101 on the road to Cairo. Under tremendous American pressure, the cease-fire was re-established, but Sharon held on to his gains and the Israelis were able to use their stranglehold over the Egyptian Third Army in the subsequent negotiations.

Fury in the Arab world knew no bounds. After being humiliated in 1949, 1956 and 1967 they had in mid-October seemed on the verge of a military triumph at last. Now it had all turned to ashes and only the concerted efforts of the superpowers were saving them from a fourth knock-out. Their bitterness was intensified by the feeling that the Israelis had cheated them by breaking the cease-fire on 23 October.

Oil as a diplomatic weapon

They vented their anger on the West. By late October, oil deliveries from Arab countries had already been reduced by 25 per cent (from 20 million to 16 million barrels per day). At a meeting in Kuwait on 4–5 November they resolved on a further decrease to between 14 and 15 million barrels a day—the main weight of the cuts falling on the USA and the Netherlands, who were regarded as particularly sympathetic to Israel.

On 18 November, however, Britain and the other EEC members (excepting the Netherlands) were exempted from these additional cuts 'in appreciation of the political stand taken by the Common Market countries in their communiqué concerning the Middle East crisis'. (This communiqué, issued on 6 November, had called for a return to the cease-fire positions occupied on 22 October, for Israel to end the occupation of the territories occupied since 1967, and it added that any settlement should take account of the 'legitimate rights of the Palestinians'.) Another factor was that Britain had withheld spare parts and ammunition for Centurion tanks supplied to the Israeli army—to the anger of the Israelis and at some cost to confidence in Britain as an arms supplier in the Third World. But this did please the Arabs.

The selective use of the oil weapon for applying diplomatic pressure was now firmly established. At a three-day summit meeting of Arab heads of state on 26–8 November, it was decided to draw up a list classifying states as friendly, neutral or 'supporting the enemy'. Though most EEC countries were by then receiving some 28·75 per cent less oil than in September, the cuts were thereafter steadily reduced. In January Britain's reduction had fallen to 17 per cent and was getting back to normal by February.

Arab oil and the British economy

By then, however, the decisive factor was no longer supply but price. The Heath Government, beset by a balance of payments crisis and falling coal stocks due to the miners' go-slow, had declared a State of Emergency and called a General Election. The explosive rise in the oil price was the last straw.

When OAPEC had raised the posted price of crude oil by 70 per cent to $5·11 on 16 October, this had added £400 to £500 million to Britain's annual oil bill. From 1 January 1974 it was estimated that the rise to $11·65 would add £1,800 million to the balance of payments deficit during the year. Put another way, *The Economist* estimated that the 70 per cent rise (to $5·11) was equivalent to a 4½ per cent wage rise and would add 2½ per cent to total industrial costs.[1] The rise to $11·65 was probably equivalent in its internal effect to a wage rise of 15–20 per cent.

It was at this moment that the British political system showed up at its worst. On 23 December, when the $11·65 oil price became known, it was clear that the crisis was a national one of really gargantuan dimensions. Nothing could save the British economy except a really drastic recutting of the coat according to the shrunken cloth. This could only have been done with a united lead from all parties, sinking their differences. They proved unable to do this, and unable even to join forces to explain the situation to the miners, at heart amongst the most deeply patriotic of communities in the land. But the opposition in Parliament could see no further than the chance to make the Government fail, and, despite the efforts of Joe Gormley, the leadership of the NUM allowed itself to be swayed by those whose aim was in any case to bring British industry to a halt, whatever the cost. The result was that the nation, already crippled, tore itself to shreds with a disastrous strike and settlement and with a divisive General Election, sentencing itself to another three years of agony even worse than that which had gone before.

8 The Strike that Brought Down a Government

The Coal Board's offer

On 10 October, two days after the announcement of Stage 3 of the Government's counter-inflation policy, the NCB had offered the miners a package which made full use of every loophole in the code. In all this amounted to the largest increase (with the possible exception of the Wilberforce award after the 1972 strike) which the miners had ever been offered. It was made up of the 7 per cent Stage 3 norm, another 1 per cent for holiday pay, 4·3 per cent for 'unsocial hours' on night shifts and 0·7 per cent for odds and ends, plus another 3·5 per cent if they accepted the NCB's productivity scheme—a total of 16½ per cent.

The Government had every confidence that an offer within Stage 3 would be accepted. Edward Heath, realizing that the miners' acceptance was crucial to success (as it had been in Stage 2) had had a meeting in July at No. 10 Downing Street with Joe Gormley, held in strict confidence on both sides, to try to discuss what kind of offer would be needed if the miners were to accept Stage 3.[1] According to the *Sunday Times*, both Heath and Gormley thought that they had reached an agreement.

This may well have been so, but the NCB made a fatal—and almost incomprehensible—tactical error. They offered the entire package at once with every conceivable loophole included: holiday, unsocial hours, productivity deals.[2] Whether he wanted to or not, Gormley could not conceivably have carried the moderate majority of the NUM National Executive to accept the first offer in the round of negotiations. If they had done so both he and they would have been irrevocably discredited. As one Conservative Minister later put it to the *Sunday Times*, 'If you're going to help the moderates they've got to be seen to be fighting like tigers.' Bert Ramelson, the Communist Party's Industrial Organizer, was jubilant: 'The Government failed because they gave the Right nothing to hold on to. It was a field day for us.'[3]

The Government were left with no room for manœuvre at all. If they authorized the NCB to offer an additional percentage under any pretext, they were sure that that pretext would be seized upon by other unions and would have the effect of adding that percentage to everyone else's claim. Maurice Macmillan, the Employment Secretary, lacked his father's common touch, and despite an evident sincerity which they respected, seemed unable to develop a relationship of confidence with any of the four groups in the industrial relations forum: the union leaders, the employers, the boards of the nationalized industries and his own colleagues in the Cabinet.[4] He recalled later that he thought at the time that the NCB's offer could not possibly be a final one. Whether this was due to ignorance, or lack of communication or lack of shrewdness (as in his handling of the compulsory ballot in the 1972 railway strike) he was clearly inadequate as the pivot in the most fundamental conflict facing the Government and society. Other Cabinet Ministers appear to have been unaware of the scope of the NCB's offer until after it was made, but some of them sensed its significance before Macmillan did. His predecessor Robert Carr, then Home Secretary, recalls his feelings after he learned of the offer: 'I thought about it, and quite suddenly I felt a dense of doom, as though a Greek tragedy was about to be acted out.'[5]

A State of Emergency

The NUM Executive rejected the offer on 8 November and launched an overtime ban on 12 November. This was aimed to reduce the large stocks of coal at power stations, which stood at a record 18½ million tons (compared with 15 million tons before the 1972 strike) in order to strengthen their hand for strike action later. The ban was effective because, although miners worked little overtime, their output depended heavily on weekend safety measures and other preparatory work.[6]

By this time, the Government were becoming concerned about the effects of the 25 per cent reduction in deliveries from the Arab oil states announced on 17 October, and the situation had been made worse by industrial action by the Electrical Power

Engineers Association (EPEA). The timing in relation to the Arab oil embargo was coincidental, though it undoubtedly strengthened the EPEA's hand. Their action was in support of a claim for implementation of an agreement on increased payments for stand-by duties, which had been on the point of being signed in late 1972 but had been blocked by the Government's pay freeze.[7] The EPEA announced on 24 October that its 31,000 members had voted overwhelmingly to ban out-of-hours work from 1 November. This meant that faults developing at night would not be dealt with until next day unless safety was involved, and that repairs normally carried out at weekends would have to be done during weekdays, thus putting power stations temporarily out of action when demand was high. Its main significance, however, lay in the restriction on flexibility. As the miners' overtime ban and the oil embargo threatened the fuel stocks at individual power stations, chaotic and unplanned cuts could only be avoided by the complex procedure of shedding the load from one station and switching to another on the National Grid. No one had the technical skill to do this other than the power engineers, so their non-co-operation could have disastrous effects.

Accordingly the Government declared a State of Emergency on 13 November. A licence was required to consume electricity for advertising and display, or for space heating in premises such as offices, schools and shops. (On 15 November the restriction on schools was relaxed). All Government departments and nationalized industries were instructed to reduce consumption of fuel and electricity by 10 per cent, and on 5 December further restrictions included a 63°F temperature limit in offices and the reduction of street lighting by up to 50 per cent. A road speed limit of 50 mph was imposed and petrol coupons were issued at Post Offices in readiness for petrol rationing, in case the situation became more serious.[8]

The Downing Street meeting

On 28 November, Heath invited the entire NUM National Executive to meet him, together with the Cabinet Ministers directly involved, at No. 10 Downing Street. There can be little doubt that, at this meeting, Joe Gormley had every intention of finding a way to honour his informal agreement with Heath to accept a generous maximum offer under Stage 3, but he could not do this unless he could convince his members that the miners had won some clear advantages over others by being treated as a 'special case'. He had originally hoped that the miners' 'unsocial hours' payments would give him this special case but this had now, unwisely, been included in print in the Stage 3 White Paper, so it would be available to all unions. Gormley had no desire to plunge the country and the miners into another winter of hardship, particularly as he knew that many members of the public would regard a miners' strike as a stab in the back when the country was already fighting for its life against the attack by the Arabs' oil weapon. He did, however, need to be seen to win enough for his men to carry them with him—in other words, to be 'fighting like a tiger'. It seemed to him inconceivable that Heath would not offer him enough at this meeting to carry his executive to a settlement.

The Communist Party and Labour Party Marxists in Gormley's team, however, had other ideas. They had since 1972 been reinforced by Arthur Scargill, now President of the Yorkshire Area NUM and a member of the National Executive. His declared political aim remained unchanged—to bring down the Government by bringing British industry to a halt,[9] and the oil crisis gave his faction an unprecedented opportunity to further this aim.

The Cabinet Ministers lined up on one side of the room and the NUM executive on the other. The proceedings illustrated the shortcomings both of summit meetings and of meetings of large delegations; the combination of the two was fatal. The faction which was determined to prevent an agreement being reached had no difficulty in outflanking the moderates and making it impossible for them to make concessions. The fact that neither side could play the delaying card—'I'll have to refer that to my Cabinet (or Committee)'—meant that manœuvre was restricted and both sides found themselves trapped by arguments expressed during the cut and thrust of discussion.

All that Heath could offer was that the Relativities Report, due out at the end of the year, might offer some scope for improvement. During the meeting the leader of the Marxist faction, Mick McGahey, said something to the effect that he was 'determined to break the Pay Code and get Heath out of office and that he would do anything to achieve it'.[10] Heath subsequently indicted him publicly on television for proposing to by-pass the constitution by using the industrial power of the miners to force political change. McGahey angrily denied this, but at least some of the union leaders who were at the Downing Street meeting appear to have been taken aback by his words, whatever they were.[11]

At the end of the meeting the NUM Executive held a meeting of their own in a room set aside for them in 10 Downing Street, to consider a proposal to call a pithead ballot on whether to continue the overtime ban.

They rejected the proposal by twenty votes to five (two abstaining). Only two men from Durham and three from the craftsmen's sections voted for a ballot. The remainder of the moderates voted with McGahey. Gormley, who was entitled only to a casting vote in the event of a tie, was powerless.

Whitelaw becomes Employment Secretary

Heath had long intended to replace Maurice Macmillan by transferring William Whitelaw from Northern Ireland, but Whitelaw was, throughout the summer, engaged in crucial negotiations to bring Protestant and Catholic politicians together to form a power-sharing executive. These negotiations reached their peak in the autumn, and there really did seem to be a prospect of peace in Northern Ireland at last. Whitelaw was the only British minister who had ever succeeded in winning the trust of a majority of moderate Protestant and Catholic politicians and Heath felt that he must not take him away. After the meeting with the NUM Executive, however, the change could be delayed no longer and Whitelaw became Employment Secretary on 2 December.

Whitelaw's reputation as a conciliator was such that there was a burgeoning of hope, all over the country, that he would somehow solve the dispute with the miners and get Stage 3 accepted as Stage 2 had been. Whitelaw, however, was in no state to wade into the incredibly complicated web of wages, bonuses, productivity, prices and union politics involved in industrial relations. 'I was', he said later, 'totally exhausted. I was emotionally affected by all that I had been involved with in Ireland. I was not mentally conditioned for home politics. I made several mistakes.'[12]

The same could be said of most of the Cabinet. They were under immense pressure from all sides. Anthony Barber, Chancellor of the Exchequer, was working a 100-hour week grappling with the financial crisis caused by the oil embargo and had to rush out a mini-budget on 17 December to cut public expenditure by £1,200 million. Other ministers were preparing plans for maintenance of essential services in the event of a major breakdown of public utilities and communications, and even for the implementation of the contingency plans for emergency regional government. (A framework for this is maintained in existence to cope with nuclear attack or massive natural disasters such as the crippling or isolation of part of the country by floods.) Heath himself had no rest even at weekends. On Sunday 9 December he chaired an all-night session of talks at Sunningdale, hammering out an agreement with Protestant, Catholic and Southern Irish political leaders to create the power-sharing Executive for Northern Ireland; his load was made even heavier by the transfer of Whitelaw. And he had to spend the next weekend in Copenhagen for a Common Market summit on the oil crisis, fraught with tension by the ruthless determination of President Pompidou (then a dying man) to preserve French interests at no matter what cost to others. Enoch Powell, who had no love for Heath, can hardly have been trying to help when, with much publicity, he expressed unctuous concern 'for the mental and emotional stability of the head of Government'.[13]

On 6 December the Central Electricity Generating Board (CEGB) gave warning of 'grave danger' to the nation's power supplies. Since the miners' overtime ban began, there had been a reduction of 35 per cent in coal deliveries to power stations and, although oil storage tanks and tankers at sea carried nearly three months' stocks, these would not last through the winter unless there were substantial cuts in consumption.

On 12 December the train drivers' union (ASLEF) decided to join the battle. ASLEF was blocking a wage settlement covering all the three railway unions which the others wished to accept. ASLEF refused to submit the dispute to arbitration, and called a work-to-rule and overtime ban. Like the NUM, ASLEF's executive contained a strong politically motivated element and their action was intended to exacerbate the energy crisis by restricting the movement of fuel. This was organized by an informal co-ordinating meeting between ASLEF and NUM on the following day.

Meanwhile, William Whitelaw was doing his best to settle the power engineers' and miners' disputes. He managed to make a reasonable settlement with the EPEA and then invited Gormley to an informal and unpublicized meeting in a London hotel room on a Sunday evening. Having only just taken over, Whitelaw intended this meeting to be exploratory, but Gormley had clearly interpreted his appointment as Employment Secretary as an indication that the Government was adopting a more conciliatory attitude in order to reach a settlement. He was therefore surprised and disappointed when Whitelaw had nothing specific to offer. The meeting achieved very little, but they did agree to examine the possibility of some additional money being found for the miners by paying them for 'washing and waiting time'—that is, for time spent waiting for transport to the coal face and in taking pithead baths after their shifts. In the event, after an exhaustive inquiry, it transpired that this would yield only five minutes more pay per day than they had already been offered.[14]

The other card which Whitelaw could have played at this stage was the 'Arab card': a special energy supplement, quite separate from Stage 3, to meet the unprecedented situation arising from the other squeeze on the nation's jugular vein, the Arab oil embargo. This would undoubtedly have given Gormley what he needed to rally the moderates on his executive and most, at least, of the other unions would probably have accepted it as a special case rather than endure the hardship of a three-day week. At least two members of the Government's 'think-tank' suggested this in December as a way out, but the Cabinet would not accept it.[15]

The three-day week

On 13 December (between his Sunningdale and Copenhagen weekend conferences) Heath announced that industry would be restricted to a three-day working week from 30 December. The TUC reacted angrily. At a meeting of the National Economic Development Council (NEDC) on 21 November they contended that there were adequate coal stocks for another nine or ten weeks,[16] and called for the three-day week to be postponed for a

further two weeks. Heath refused, stating that the power stations
were receiving only two-thirds of their normal supplies and that
the Government must ensure that they were able to maintain
essential power supplies until the spring. His assessment of the
gravity of the situation appeared to be confirmed by an article in
the *Sunday Times*, pointing out that if coal stocks at power
stations fell below 6 million tons there would be no flexibility on
the grid and massive random cuts would result in chaos. Unless
there were a 20 per cent reduction in demand this situation would
be reached in late January.[17]

The forecasts of the effect of the three-day week were alarming. NEDC at its January meeting predicted that in February
$1\frac{3}{4}$ million would be temporarily unemployed, with another $3\frac{1}{2}$
million on short time; that many firms would go bankrupt; that
even after normal working was resumed, British industry would
be held back for many months as the raw material pipelines were
refilled; and that export delivery dates would be missed and trade
gaps and inflation would soar.

In the event, however, the three-day week had far less effect
than predicted. Many firms offered their men the chance of
longer hours on their three working days, and most responded
to these offers, so that average take-home pay in January fell by
only £2 (to £35.71 from £37.69 in December) and remained
steady (at £35.53) through February.[18]

Unemployment also rose far less than expected—from 2.1 per
cent in December to 2.4 per cent in January and February, and
by the end of February only 680,000 workers were on short time.
Industrial production was maintained at 75 per cent of normal
even though working hours were cut by 40 per cent or more[19]—
a clear indication of the slack available to be taken up in industry.
On 13 February the CBI reported that output had actually been
rising during the past two weeks, and that a number of companies
were reporting normal production figures.

The miners' strike

Meanwhile, negotiation was continuing in the attempt to end the
miners' overtime ban and avert a strike. At the NEDC meeting on
9 January the TUC, at that time alarmed about the prospects of
unemployment and short-time working, formally offered an

undertaking that, if the Government would treat the miners as a special case, the other unions would not use this as an argument in negotiating their own settlements. The Chancellor, Anthony Barber, peremptorily rejected this offer (neither Heath nor Whitelaw were at the meeting). The TUC repeated it in writing to the Government next day but the Cabinet rejected it, Heath declaring in the House of Commons that it would be unfair on the millions of other workers who had already settled under Stage 3.[20]

Len Murray, in retrospect, was amazed at this rejection. He considered that the Government could not lose by accepting the TUC's undertaking. If the unions failed to honour it, this could be used against them in carrying public support for tougher policies. If the deal had enabled Stage 3 to succeed, the Government could have claimed it as a triumph.

Gormley, on the other hand, was more sceptical: 'Why shouldn't the other unions use the NUM as an argument for their own claim? That's what negotiation is all about.' And another moderate, Sid Vincent, at a Northwest Area Miners' conference on 26 January asked 'Would the miners, if they were in the same position, sell their souls for the benefit of others?'[21]

After another barren meeting on 21 January between Heath and TUC leaders, the NUM Executive met on 24 January to decide whether to call a pithead ballot for a strike. They voted by sixteen to ten for a ballot asking the miners to give the executive a free hand, with authority to call a strike if necessary.

On the same day (24 January) the Pay Board published their Relativities Report. This presented a clear opportunity for a fresh offer to the miners but, because the Pay Board had taken the view that the relativities mechanism should not be used during an industrial dispute, Whitelaw had not foreseen its implications. He later admitted that he threw away a chance: 'Barbara Castle said on the day it came out that she couldn't understand why on earth I hadn't used it to settle with the miners. She was quite right. I had never really thought of it. It was short-sighted of me to let it be published and then not to use it.'[22]

On 4 February the result of the pithead ballot was announced: an overwhelming vote (81 per cent) to give the executive the free hand it wanted.[23] On 7 February Heath announced the dissolution of Parliament and a General Election for 28 February.

Gormley, fearing that a strike would help the Conservatives, proposed suspending it until after the election, but was again unable to carry his executive with him. The strike began on 10 February.

Picketing in 1974

The fact that it took place during the General Election campaign had two effects on picketing during the strike. First, intense efforts were made by the NUM to discourage violence and mass picketing, since the public reaction to Saltley left them in no doubt that both these would be playing into the Conservatives' hands. Secondly, the election was seen as a trial of strength between Government and unions ('Who runs Britain?') and this caused a closing of union ranks, so that mass picketing was unnecessary. Other unions, including NUR and ASLEF (railways), TGWU (other transport) and GMWU (power station and gas workers), all called upon their members not to handle coal or alternative fuels.[24] Another factor was that, since Saltley, the laws on picketing had been clarified by certain court decisions, as a result of which a very large crowd of pickets could now be held to be intimidating.[25] The NUM therefore decided that pickets at mines, ports, power stations and steelworks should be limited to six men[26] and this proved sufficient as, in contrast to the 1972 strike, not many non-union transport drivers took part. Very few union members attempted to cross picket lines.

The Government had, nevertheless, taken precautions against any repetition of massed or violent picketing. A special operations office was formed at Scotland Yard to give early warning of flying or massed pickets and to co-ordinate the movement of police reinforcements to prevent violence, intimidation, obstruction and other breaches of the law.[27] In the event these precautions proved unnecessary.

Just as the General Election affected the strike, so the strike affected the election. It was the strike which brought it about. Indeed, as David Butler and Dennis Kavanagh commented: 'It was unprecedented for an outside challenge to Government policy to force a dissolution, but the issue was one on which ministers thought it impossible to change course without a new mandate.'[28]

9 The Shattering of a Dream

Heath's reluctance to call an election

Up till October 1973 the Conservative Government—which could, if it chose, remain in power until June 1975—had little thought of an early election. 1973 had thus far been a good year, and the Government and most of the press were confidently predicting the continuation of the growth on which the economy seemed to be set. By early November, the oil embargo and the miners' rejection of Stage 3 had suddenly and radically changed the picture. Conservative Party strategists, foreseeing an economic downturn, began to revise draft manifestos and to talk of an election as early as the spring of 1974.[1]

The Conservative Party employed an organization to run private opinion polls, and by early January these pointed insistently to a Conservative win if the election were held on 31 January or 7 February, but probable defeat if it were held any later than that.[2]

Heath was, and remained, strongly against an election, not on tactical but on national grounds. Defeat would destroy all he had aimed to do, while a Conservative victory would be a triumph for the Tory hardliners and would destroy the prospects of government by co-operation with the unions, which had always been his dream. He had been deeply impressed by the German success in co-operation between government, employers and trade unions which had enabled their workers to produce more and to live so much more prosperously than British workers. On one occasion, as Heath was taking his leave after a visit to Bonn, Chancellor Willy Brandt mentioned the people waiting for his next appointment: 'There are sixteen union leaders out there. They are the men I run Germany with.'[3]

There were three others in the Cabinet who felt the same as Heath. William Whitelaw was himself a dedicated conciliator.

Francis Pym, having taken over from Whitelaw in Northern Ireland, was concerned (rightly, it proved) about the effect that an election campaign would have on the prospects for survival of the power-sharing Executive, a delicate seedling which had just been planted in January 1974. Robert Carr was both an ex-trade unionist and an essentially moderate man. Others—notably Lord Carrington—were urging that the Party must catch the tide and so, almost unanimously, were the local Conservative constituency branches.

The NUM Executive decision on 24 January to call for a pit-head ballot probably made an election inevitable—even though the Labour Party were somewhat alarmed by the prospect. On 28 January, Mick McGahey captured the headlines with a statement that, should troops be called in, he would appeal to them to 'aid and assist the miners'. This was at once repudiated by Joe Gormley and by James Callaghan, then Chairman of the Labour Party, who said, 'We utterly repudiate any attempt by the Communists or anyone else to use the miners as a battering-ram to bring about a general strike or to call on troops to disobey orders.'[4]

Heath and Whitelaw continued to make desperate efforts to avert both the strike and the election. On 30 January Heath offered to reopen the miners' case to the Relativities Board if they would resume normal working, but it was too late. They were only prepared to delay the strike for 'money on the table' and this was understandable, since the surge towards a national strike by a large union cannot be halted too easily. Early in February, Whitelaw again invited the NUM Executive to meet him but they snubbed him, saying that they were too busy.[5] Heath reluctantly succumbed to the clamour of his advisers and announced the dissolution on 7 February. Once again he proved to be too late.

The election of February 1974

The election campaign itself was packed with errors and disasters for the Conservatives. Whitelaw, despite the NUM's snub, did refer their case to the Relativities Board on 8 February, *after* the announcement of the election, and thus appeared to undermine the reason for calling it. Worse was to follow, for on 21

February the Relativities Board released statistical evidence suggesting that the miners were entitled to at least 8 per cent more than the NCB offer. Harold Wilson regarded this as the turning-point of the campaign and made the most of it.[6] Heath received another unpleasant blow from Enoch Powell, who said that he would not stand for re-election as a Conservative, as he thought the calling of the election was 'fraudulent' and advised people to vote Labour. The final blow was a remark by the Director-General of the CBI (Campbell Adamson), two days before polling day, that the Industrial Relations Act had 'sullied every relationship at national level between unions and employers' and should be repealed.[7] This remark was made at a meeting which Adamson thought was private and he did not expect to be quoted. He at once offered to resign, but the offer was declined; most CBI members agreed with his statement, even if not with its timing.

Polling on 28 February produced one of the most inconclusive results ever, and demonstrated the worst shortcomings of the British electoral system. The seats and votes the parties gained were as follows:[4]

	Seats	Votes	% of total vote
Labour	301	11,646,391	37·1
Conservative	297	11,872,180	37·8
Liberal	14	6,058,744	19·3
Others	23	1,795,590	5·8

The twenty-three 'others' included eleven Ulster Unionists, who would in previous Parliaments have voted with the Conservatives but who were on this occasion flatly opposed to them because of the Sunningdale agreement and the installation of a power-sharing Executive. Some Conservatives later reflected ruefully that this was the penalty for their leaders acting as Government rather than party men.[9] As Whitelaw and Pym had feared, the election polarized Protestant opinion and spelt the doom of the power-sharing Executive.[10] The twelfth Northern Irish seat was won by the sole representative of the power-sharing Executive, Gerry Fitt, a Catholic who, as a member of the Social Democratic and Labour Party, could be expected to vote Labour.

There were seven Scottish Nationalists and two Welsh Nationalists. Their votes were unpredictable, and would presumably be tactical and conditional upon favours to their cause. There were two Independents, ex-Labour MPs who had successfully challenged left-wing constituency machines which had discarded them, but neither was to survive the next election in October 1974.

The Communist Party's forty-four candidates secured only 32,743 votes (0·1 per cent of those voting and only 1·8 per cent of the vote even in the seats they contested). The National Front, with fifty-four candidates, polled more than twice as many, with an average of 3·9 per cent in the seats contested. Both showings were poor enough, but the National Front had now established itself as the fourth party in England, and was on a rising curve, as will be seen later.

The glaring anomalies—sadly all too familiar in British elections—were that neither the Conservatives nor Labour had as much as 40 per cent of the vote; the Conservatives had more votes but fewer seats; and the Liberals, with nearly 20 per cent of the vote, had only just over 2 per cent of the seats.

The election was, as usual, on a Thursday. By Friday it was clear that neither Conservative nor Labour would be able to form a majority Government, though the final pattern of seats was not clear until Sunday. The weekend was spent in discussions between Heath and the Liberal leader Jeremy Thorpe about forming a coalition. Even if they had succeeded, however, the resulting Government would still have been in a minority. It was never really a starter. Liberal constituency workers, with the full momentum of an election campaign to unseat the Conservatives, were in no mood to join them. They might conceivably have done so for a guarantee of legislation to introduce proportional representation before the next election (Heath could offer no more than a Speaker's Conference on electoral reform). This would have had the effect of ensuring the Liberals more than a hundred seats at the next election, but few Conservative or Labour MPs were willing to see this. Certainly no minority Government could have hoped to force such legislation through even if they had wanted to. As for a 'Grand Coalition' between Conservatives and Labour, neither side was prepared to consider it, and it would have been impossible, in the prevailing situation, to have found enough common ground to do so.

So Harold Wilson took power on 4 March, with a brave and practical warning that he intended to govern Britain as he judged best, daring Parliament to plunge the country into another election if they preferred that. They did not.

Why Heath failed

Edward Heath's dream of a united industrial state, like Germany or Japan, run by the Government, the employers and the unions in co-operation, seemed to have a better than even chance of realization in September 1973. It was shattered primarily by a *diabolus ex machina*, the Arab–Israeli war, and the quadrupling of the price of oil, which torpedoed both his external and internal economic policies.

The miners' original challenge to the NCB pay offer was made quite independently of this. Later, however, it gave the miners' executive greatly added power, which its Marxist wing understandably exploited to the full. Without that power—and but for the Government's desperate economic plight arising from the oil situation—there is little doubt that a settlement would have been reached by taking account of the Relativities Report and that Stage 3 would have survived. But, since the oil price *was* quadrupled, this is a theoretical might-have-been.

Joe Gormley emerges as one of the more honourable characters in this drama. He clearly did his utmost to avoid both the short-term damage which the nation would suffer from the strike, and the longer-term damage of the inflation which was to follow it. His position, however, was fatally compromised by the naïve generosity of the Coal Board in putting everything in the shop window, leaving him nothing he could 'fight like a tiger' to win for his men. So he was outvoted.

Had Vic Feather still headed the TUC, with his experience, prestige and common sense, he might well have found a way of helping Heath and Gormley to avert this damage. He would certainly have wished to do so.[11] Whether Murray wished to do so or not, he had not yet built up the necessary power to influence the situation.

Enoch Powell certainly did not help Heath, as the leader of his party, in any way. He later reappeared as an MP wearing the colours of the Ulster Unionist Party.

The rest of the Conservative Party acted as political parties do. The constituency workers and most of the Cabinet were con-

cerned more with winning the election than with the agony of
Britain (so, no doubt were their opposite numbers in the Labour
Party). Under the prevailing electoral system this was inevitable
(see Chapter 20).

William Whitelaw's remarkable achievement in bringing
Protestants and Catholics together in Northern Ireland proved
fatal to the Conservative Party in that it alienated the Unionists,
who could have been earlier relied upon to keep it in power. And
the election proved equally fatal to Whitelaw's achievement of
power-sharing.

Whitelaw himself emerges as a figure little less tragic than
Heath. Recalled from Ireland just as his work was bearing fruit,
he was in no way briefed or fit to charge into the chaotic brawl of
a major industrial dispute combined with a disastrous blow to the
economy. He will—unfairly—suffer in his own mind from the
chances he threw away. But, like Heath, he emerges as an
honourable man, caring more for the country than for party
advantage—more for peace in Northern Ireland than for winning
the next election.

Heath himself made serious mistakes, all through his administration. Despite all the evidence of public opinion polls in
1969–70, he was wrong to try to give such a major role to the law
in industrial relations. It damaged both respect for the law and
the harmony between Government, employers and the unions—
the very harmony he was most urgently seeking. He was tough
and efficient as a manager, both in the Cabinet and in conference, but he was respected rather than liked. He lacked the
ability to communicate his sincerity and idealism, and to carry
people with him, either personally or on the television screen.

In the end, it was his determination to put what he judged to be
national interests before party interests—notably his refusal to
call an election at the moment of greatest political advantage—
which brought him down, first from leadership of the nation and,
a year later, from leadership of his party. And this, too, reflects
little credit on the British political system.

PART II
1974–77

10 Harold Wilson's Minority Government, 1974

Back to work

After his unsuccessful weekend attempt at a Conservative–Liberal Coalition, Mr Heath resigned and Mr Wilson became Prime Minister on 4 March as the head of a minority government for six months—the shortest parliament since 1681.[1]

His first priority was to get the miners back to work. He did this by settling for rises of between £6·71 and £11·21 per week—only slightly more than recommended in the Relativities Report, which was published on the same day.[2] For the majority of underground workers this was roughly double the NCB's offer of $16\frac{1}{2}$ per cent. Details of the settlement were:[3]

	Surface workers		Underground (unskilled)		Underground (skilled)	
	£	%	£	%	£	%
Old basic rate	25·29		27·29		37·69	
NUM Claim	35·00	38	40·00	47	45·00	22
Settlement	32·00	26	36·00	32	45·00	22

The settlement cost the country £103m (compared with £98m recommended by the Relativities Board and the original NCB offer of £44m). This meant an increase in coal prices to the consumer of 48 per cent.

The miners resumed work on 11 March, having lost $5\frac{1}{2}$ million working days. Emergency regulations and the three-day week were ended.

Wilson and his Cabinet gave a courageous impression of firm government, and rapidly restored confidence. Declining any kind of coalition or 'arrangement' with other parties, they chose to place themselves at the mercy of Parliament, so their legislative programme was restricted; but they could claim the right to govern, and they did. Wilson said that, if defeated on a vote of confidence, he would ask the Queen to dissolve Parliament and demand a fresh mandate—which he and the other parties knew he would get. Tactically, Heath had played into Wilson's hands by trying and failing to form a coalition, because he had thereby forfeited any claim to ask the Queen to defer the dissolution and invite *him* to try to form a government.[4] Knowing that no one was anxious to face another election, therefore, Wilson was on much firmer ground than his successor was to be in 1977, when Labour again had to govern as a minority in Parliament. By April, the public opinion polls showed a Labour lead of 16 per cent.[5]

On 20 March the new Chancellor of the Exchequer, Denis Healey, introduced his budget, raising income tax and corporation tax and extending value-added tax to sweets and petrol. He also authorized large increases in prices of electricity (30 per cent), steel (25 per cent) and rail freight (15 per cent) to cover the increased prices of oil and coal.

No peace for industry

The Government announced that they would introduce fresh legislation, and abolish the NIRC (though the Court continued to operate—and to impose fines on trade unions under the Act—until July). The Government also cancelled a number of expensive projects, including the third London Airport at Maplin and the Channel Tunnel.

On the other hand, they announced on taking office that they would *not* repeal Stage 3 of the Conservative Counter-Inflation Act, and this gave the Conservatives a reasonable excuse not to create an immediate constitutional crisis by voting against the Government's programme in the March Speech from the Throne. The TUC set out to prove that it intended to help the Labour Government to manage the economy and to enable it to govern; it advised unions to aim only to maintain their members' standard of living, not to try to raise it, and to settle within Stage 3. Most of them did.

Not all, however: there was a larger than usual number of strikes, as often happens when a Labour Government takes power, because unions think it will give way more easily. There were more strikes in the summer of 1974 than in the year before, and in the year as a whole 9 million days were lost (excluding the 5½ million lost in the miners' strike)—2 million more than in 1973.[6]

Inflation and a collapse of investment

During the six months of minority government, inflation gathered momentum. The Retail Price Index rose by 10 per cent and wages by 16 per cent.[7] These figures were, of course, equivalent to an annual rise of 20 per cent in the cost of living and an annual rate of wage escalation of 32 per cent (in the event wages rose 28 per cent on the year). The response to the TUC call to settle within Stage 3 was patchy. By any calculation, at least a quarter of the settlements were outside the guidelines—but almost half of the wage escalation (13 per cent out of the 28½ per cent) could be ascribed to Heath's provision for threshold payments, which Wilson described as a 'built-in twist to the wage-price spiral'.[8]

Industrial production started well, rising by 4 per cent between March and July, but fell back again so that the rise over the six months was only 2 per cent. This disparity with wage rises created a classic inflation situation and, as a result, investment confidence collapsed and the Financial Times Industrial Ordinary Share Index (FT Index) plunged from 313 in March to 197 in October, continuing its fall to 146 on 6 January 1975—a fall even greater than in the 1929–31 stock market collapse.[9] At the same time the balance of payments declined and the books were balanced only by massive borrowings from the oil states against the hope of future profits from North Sea oil.[10]

The Pay Board was abolished on 25 July, having settled over 8,000 claims for 18 million workers under Stage 2 and 8,000 claims covering 16 million workers under Stage 3.[11] The statutory incomes policy was abolished on the same day and replaced by the voluntary 'Social Contract' between Government and unions, which will be discussed in Chapter 14.

At the same time Michael Foot, the Employment Secretary, set in motion a Royal Commission on the Distribution of Incomes and Wealth, under Lord Diamond—a chartered accountant who had been a member of the Labour Cabinet in 1968–70. This was a positive attempt to make a start on ironing out the large differences between rich and poor. The Diamond Commission's Report, when it came out, in the event indicated that there were smaller differentials in income than in most countries, but more substantial differentials in wealth—that is, capital and possessions; but as it was not published until well into 1975, it will be more appropriate to examine it in Chapter 15.

The Advisory, Conciliation and Arbitration Service (ACAS)

Another innovation was the Advisory, Conciliation and Arbitration Service (ACAS), set up under the chairmanship of Jim Mortimer, an ex-trade union official who had been a member of the Prices and Incomes Board. Of its members, three were nominated by the TUC, three by the CBI and three by the Government in consultation with them (all the three government nominees were, in fact, academics). ACAS relieved the Department of Employment of its conciliation role, and initially took over the staff and offices of that section as a going concern. The aim was to try to free the conciliation service from official pressures—that is, from Ministers and civil servants in the Department who, wittingly or otherwise, could not avoid to some extent influencing decisions in accordance with Government policy and thinking. ACAS proved in the event to be a remarkably successful body, due not least to the patience, honesty and compassion of Jim Mortimer. As with most such bodies, only its failures hit the news, not its many thousands of successes. Its functioning will be examined more fully in discussing the Grunwick dispute in Chapter 16.

The Trade Union and Labour Relations Act, 1974

The Industrial Relations Act was formally supplanted on 31 July 1974 by the Trade Union and Labour Relations Act (TULRA), with further and subsequent legislation in the Employment Protection Act of 1975 (EPA). The working of both of these Acts, as of ACAS, will be examined more closely in Chapter 16, in the context of the Grunwick dispute.

It may, however, be useful at this stage to summarize some of the main points of TULRA. It abolished the NIRC and repealed the Industrial Relations Act, retaining only the provisions on unfair dismissal, the code of practice on industrial relations (though this was later to be repealed by the EPA), and the provision for industrial tribunals and for conciliation.

TULRA specified and extended some of the rights and immunities enjoyed by trade unions, including their immunity from being sued for any tort arising out of a trade dispute. These immunities, however, were confined to unions certified[12] as 'independent'—that is 'not liable to interference by an employer . . . (arising out of the provision of financial or material support or by any other means whatsoever) tending towards such control'.

Most of the immunities were continuations or minor extensions of those in the 1906, 1967 and 1971 Acts but there were some important new ones, in particular that a person, union official or Union acting in contemplation or furtherance of a trade dispute could not be sued for inducing some other person to break a contract of employment *or a commercial contract*. The significance of this was that it specifically permitted the blacking of goods. TULRA also permitted a threat of breaking a contract or of inducing some other person to do so, and (again only in a trade dispute) gave immunity from prosecution for the *tort* of intimidation in so doing (though not from *criminal* prosecution).

Regarding picketing, TULRA did no more than extend the provisions to a 'trade dispute' as being able to be applied more widely than the previous 'industrial dispute'. The Act (like the 1906 and 1971 Acts) gave pickets immunity from prosecution, in a trade dispute, for attending anywhere (except at or near a person's home) 'for the purpose only of peacefully obtaining or communicating information or peacefully persuading any person to work or abstain from working.' The Act did not give the pickets the *right* to stop any person or vehicle if those concerned did not wish to stop or to listen to their persuasion. (The Government attempted to insert the right to stop vehicles, but did not press this because of police objections through the Home Secretary.) The Act did not give any immunity from prosecution for other offences such as obstruction, insulting behaviour, intimidation or assault, and did not attempt to define what was 'reasonable' or 'peaceful'. There was no guidance on what was and was not permissible in the way of 'mass picketing' (as at Saltley in 1972 and as was to arise at Grunwick in 1977).

TULRA repealed all the provisions which limited closed shops. It was open to unions to negotiate an agreement with an employer—or an 'arrangement' which did not need to be in writing—that 100 per cent of employees would be members of one or more specified unions. The EPA later made provision for application through ACAS to a Central Arbitration Committee (CAC) which had the power to make an award requiring the employer to recognize such an agreement even if he did not wish to do so. Once such an agreement or arrangement, voluntary or compulsory, had been made, the employer was obliged to dismiss any worker who was not a member of the union concerned. Unless the worker could substantiate 'religious belief' as his reason for not joining the union, he could not claim that his dismissal was unfair. These provisions were to play a major role in the violent Grunwick dispute in 1977.

TULRA initially (like the Industrial Relations Act) gave every worker protection against expulsion from a trade union by way of arbitrary or unreasonable discrimination. This was later repealed, and all he could thereafter do, if such expulsion cost him his job in a closed-shop factory, was to appeal to a review committee set up by the TUC.

On the other hand, if an employer dismissed a worker because he *did* join or propose to join a union (this could clearly not apply to a closed shop) the dismissal would be classed as unfair. This too was to be one of the issues at Grunwick.

The Act caused considerable concern because it appeared to give extensive power to trade unions and in particular to open the door to any individual or union, claiming furtherance of a trade dispute, to picket any establishment whether it was involved in the dispute or not. The picketing of power stations and the Saltley Coke Depot by miners in 1972 and 1974 had been controversial. But was it legal? And would it be legal for, say, school teachers on strike to picket a power station on the grounds that merely picketing a school would not apply any effective pressure on the Government or the community, whereas picketing power stations would?

These anxieties were expressed by the Director General of the CBI, Campbell Adamson, in a letter to *The Times* on 11 June 1974, while TULRA was still a Bill under debate in Parliament. He drew attention to the 'great increase in the opportunity for trade unions to exert power', not only greater than their power under the 1971 Act, but greater than at any time before it. He went on:

If the Bill is passed as at present drafted, unions, their officials and their shop stewards will be free in law to strike or indulge in other industrial action or to 'black', blockade or boycott, or threaten to do so, whenever they like, officially or unofficially, constitutionally or in breach of procedure, in respect of a trade dispute anywhere in Great Britain or in the rest of the world. Secondly, it will be lawful to use the picket line for the purpose of establishing boycotts or blockades whether against an employer in dispute or against employers, companies, public corporations or bodies which have nothing to do with the dispute in question.

We have already experienced in the 1972 miners' strike the picketing of oil-fired power stations to bring pressure on the Government by stopping the supply of electricity. It would have been unlawful under the pre-1971 law (as well as under the 1971 Act). In future this will be entirely lawful and it will then be possible for powerful unions to blockade public utilities or hold up the nation's food supplies at the docks, whenever they are unable to get their own way in a wage dispute by more traditional means.

I believe that we should all be fully aware of the implications of this Bill as it stands at the moment.

In the event, the extension in the Bill of immunity for inducing another person to break a commercial contract (as opposed to a contract of employment) was defeated in Parliament in 1974, but was later reinserted in 1976 when Labour had an overall majority.

The backlash

To add fuel to the fire, Protestant extremists in Northern Ireland staged a two-week strike against the power-sharing executive, which they brought down on 28 May 1974. This strike will be described in the next chapter, but its significance in the present context is that the strikers—highly organized and using intimidation—brought Northern Ireland's electric power generation almost to a halt in furtherance of a purely political dispute, with no industrial aspects at all—indeed the strike was condemned by the TUC and the major unions concerned all appealed to their members to keep working. This strike was clearly unlawful (even if there had not been intimidation) in that it was in no way 'in contemplation or furtherance of a trade dispute'. But it succeeded in its political aim, and no action was taken against the instigators or participants. If they could do this for a supposedly 'fascist' purpose (as some felt the Chileans had done against President Allende in 1973), it could even more easily be done by any other totalitarian group seeking to make the mixed economy fail and to destroy parliamentary democracy.

For this reason, the public reaction against the implications of TULRA was broadly based, and by no means restricted to the middle class. On the one hand the National Front—which always predominantly attracted manual workers—began to gain ground. In another field, a retired army officer, General Sir Walter Walker, founded an organization of volunteers to maintain essential services in a crisis. He claimed that his organization was non-political, that it would act only if help from its volunteers was requested by the Government, and that it would meet such requests from either a Labour or a Conservative Government. His initial support was from middle-class people but it later widened enormously, and he claimed to have on his register the names of a large number of trained power station workers and other skilled, semi-skilled and unskilled men, who could operate a wide range of essential services.

His organization was, of course, never likely to be called upon by either a Labour or Conservative Government for a number of reasons. Even if it produced hundreds of thousands of volunteers, they would not be able to work without at least the tolerance of trade union members in associated industries. Trade unionists are generally tolerant of the use of soldiers, provided that their use is confined to essential services to save life or health, but they would certainly not have extended this tolerance to Walker's volunteers. Indeed, their use would undoubtedly have exacerbated any situation of industrial conflict, and have done great damage to social harmony as a whole.

There were other causes for anxiety about law and order on a much wider range of issues. The Protestant strike in Ulster has already been mentioned. The IRA, frustrated by lack of progress in Northern Ireland, switched their attacks to England, where they killed forty-four people during 1974 in terrorist attacks— many more than in the whole of the previous century. And in June 1974, in a march by a Trotskyist group against the National

Front in Red Lion Square, a young man was killed: Kevin
Gately, the first to die in England in a political demonstration
for over half a century. These incidents will be discussed in
succeeding chapters.

11 The Ulster Workers' Council Strike, 1974

The Protestants in Ulster

The Ulster Workers' Council (UWC) strike in 1974 had wide implications, not only for Northern Ireland but for Great Britain as well. It was launched in the teeth of opposition from the trade union movement, and was Fascist rather than Marxist in its politics; yet it totally succeeded in its aim of bringing down the power-sharing executive at Stormont. It succeeded partly because of an organized and effective system of intimidation, and partly because it was supported by a substantial number of key managers, some coerced but some willing; and it succeeded because the stopping of the power stations, in an isolated province with only its own small grid and no means of alternative supply, was professionally organized and produced a credible threat of a total breakdown of electricity supply and with it a collapse of urban life and livelihood.

The background against which industrial disputes (and politics) are conducted in Northern Ireland is radically different from that of Great Britain, in that the conflict between the Protestant and Catholic communities transcends every other political conflict, such as the normal conflicts between Conservatives and Socialists, or social classes, or management and workers. This communal conflict also transcends the battles for wages and working conditions. Whereas in Britain there is usually a mixed aim, industrial and political, in the case of the UWC strike the aim was wholly political: there was no wage demand, no conflict with management—just the simple and declared aim of bringing down the Assembly and the Executive, with the claim that the Assembly no longer represented the views of the majority who had elected it and that the policies of the Executive were now contrary to the majority's wishes. The UWC claimed that the voting figures for the twelve Northern Irish members for the

British Parliament in February 1974 indicated a change of mind amongst the voters—though this argument could equally have been applied to the interpretation of by-election results in the last year of the Labour Government in 1969–70, or again in 1977. Whether the UWC strike was morally justified or not, however, it was an avowed attempt to use industrial power to reverse the constitutional process. As such it has lessons for Britain which should not be disregarded.

Protestants in Ulster have always been more militant—and arguably more vicious—than Catholics. For over 300 years a Protestant minority wielded power in Ireland as a whole. Partition in 1922 placed them in a majority of two to one in the six Northern counties, but they remained well aware that reunification would put them back into a minority (of 27 per cent) in a thirty-two-county Republic of Ireland. This prospect has remained the cornerstone of Unionist politics, and the hierarchy has always managed to retain the loyalty of the majority of the Protestant working class by ensuring that they enjoyed advantages over their Catholic neighbours which would be lost if they were to be absorbed into the Republic. Against this background, the Stormont government used the powers devolved to it from Westminster to impose or condone discrimination between the two communities from 1922 to 1965.

Alexis de Tocqueville pointed out that the pressure which exploded into the French Revolution developed, not when oppression of the *ancien régime* was at its height, but when it began to be relaxed. The same applied in Northern Ireland. In 1965 the Stormont Prime Minister, Terence O'Neill, decided to tackle the problem of discrimination and to improve relations with Dublin. He exchanged visits with the Irish Prime Minister, Sean Lemass (and was denounced by the Reverend Ian Paisley for entertaining a 'Fenian Papist murderer') and made a start on eliminating the preferences for Protestants in such matters as housing allocation and the often flagrant gerrymandering over the fixing of ward boundaries for local government elections.[1]

As de Tocqueville would have predicted, the Catholics demanded that the action be speeded up, and in 1967 they formed a civil rights movement which began to march and demonstrate. Equally predictably, the more militant Protestants, led by Paisley, sensing the prospect of the erosion of their privileges and eventually of reunification, organized counter-demonstrations.

Clashes ensued, leading to the first fatal casualties in August 1969—and to the start of the violence which led to the killing of over 1,800 people during the next eight years.

Shortly before the first fatal casualties, the Unionist Party had overthrown its leader, Terence O'Neill, but militant Protestants were still dissatisfied with the firmness of his successor, James Chichester-Clark, in maintaining the Protestant ascendency. In September 1969 two trade unionists, Billy Hull and Hugh Petrie, formed a Workers' Committee for the Defence of the Constitution, initially amongst the predominantly Protestant work-force in the Harland and Wolff shipyards, but they later expanded it to attract Protestant factory workers from all over the country.[2]

In all, thirteen people were killed in Northern Ireland in 1969 and another twenty-five in 1970. Though these figures were horrifying at the time, they were small compared with subsequent casualties running into hundreds each year. In 1969 and 1970 the fighting had been communal—between rival crowds or gangs, usually with sticks and stones and petrol-bombs, though guns were increasingly used from June 1970 onwards. In 1971 the Provisional IRA—which had broken away from the more ideological but less violent Official IRA—introduced a new dimension with their urban guerrilla campaign. Their main tactic was indiscriminate bombing of public places, and by August 1971 another twenty-one people had been killed, bringing the total in the two years since August 1969 to fifty-nine.

Direct rule

By that time Brian Faulkner had replaced Chichester-Clark as Prime Minister at Stormont, and he became convinced that Protestant fury was on the verge of explosion. He persuaded the British Government to make their greatest blunder, the introduction of internment without trial. With IRA bombings growing each month—thirty-seven in April, forty-seven in May, fifty in June and ninety-one in July—Faulkner argued that, since no one dared give evidence to convict the bombers, known IRA men and supporters must be arrested and interned without trial under the 1922 Special Powers Act—otherwise, he said, the Protestants would take the law into their own hands and he could not be answerable for the consequences.

The British Government gave way, and 342 people were arrested on 9 August 1971. These came, in the main, from the traditional nationalist areas in the Catholic slums in Belfast, such as the Ardoyne and the Lower Falls. In these small, tightly knit communities there was scarcely a family which did not see a father, son or brother—or at least a cousin or a neighbour's son —arrested. The result was predictable. The IRA reacted with increased violence—and with a degree of support from the Catholic population never seen before or since. Compared with the fifty-nine killed in the previous two years, 231 were killed in the subsequent six months, before the British Government assumed direct rule in March 1972.

As the IRA violence exploded in the autumn of 1971, residents of hard-line Protestant areas in Belfast—such as Woodvale and the Shankill—began to form vigilante movements; and by the end of the year these were amalgamated into the paramilitary Ulster Defence Association (UDA). At the same time the Ulster Volunteer Force (UVF)—a militant Protestant organization which had been revived to carry out some bomb attacks in 1966, using the traditional title of Lord Carsons' volunteers in 1912— decided to fight the IRA by using their own terrorist methods against them. Billy Hull's Workers' Committee—now renamed the Loyalist Association of Workers (LAW)—was a leading force in the formation of the UDA, but at that time kept clear of the UVF.

Early in 1972, with rapidly escalating violence, the appearance of Protestant as well as Catholic terrorists, and of Protestant paramilitary bodies marching the streets, the British Government decided that they could not continue the element of dual control, whereby British soldiers, though ultimately responsible to London, carried out a security policy set out by the wholly Protestant Stormont Government. They therefore told Faulkner that the British Government would take sole responsibility for security. Faulkner, knowing that he could not carry the Unionist Party with him if he accepted this, resigned. The Stormont Parliament was prorogued and the British Government exercised direct rule from 24 March.

The announcement of direct rule from London marked the end of fifty years of political domination by the Protestants, and they knew it. They reacted on 27 March with a two-day strike led by one of the leading 'loyalist' politicians, William Craig.

(The title 'loyalist' was originally used to denote a desire to remain part of the UK but, from this time onwards, 'loyalists' consistently opposed and defied the policies of the British Government, so it became a misleading term. They were certainly no longer loyal to Britain. So, where possible, other terms will be substituted and 'loyalist', where used, will be in quotes.)

On the first day of Craig's strike, many thousands tried to go to work, but widespread intimidation induced 190,000 Protestant workers to stay at home on the second day. Under the guidance of Billy Kelly, a trade union convenor in the power stations (in which 75 per cent of the workers were Protestants), power cuts were imposed which shut down virtually every heavy industrial works in Belfast and the surrounding area. The strike—though avowedly short and sharp—clearly demonstrated the ability of the militant Protestants to bring the life of the Province to a halt if they chose to do so.

The year 1972 saw 468 people killed in Northern Ireland—almost twice as many as in any other year, before or since. The Protestant terrorist movements became increasingly active and from 1972 onwards, in every year, more Catholics were killed in sectarian murders by Protestants than Protestants by Catholics (not including those of either community who were victims of indiscriminate bombings).[3]

In 1971 and 1972 all the suspected terrorists interned without trial had been Catholics, but on 5 February 1973 the first two Protestants were interned. Craig called another general strike and at the same time Protestant groups—often teenagers calling themselves 'Tartan Gangs'—rampaged in Catholic areas, looting, burning and shooting. Also early in 1973, LAW planned a civil disobedience campaign. All of this proved too much for Billy Hull, who was one of the few 'loyalists' who really did feel some loyalty to the British Government and to British soldiers—he had been three times wounded in the Second World War—and was also a loyal trade unionist. He refused to go along with these ideas and the extremists, led by Petrie, walked out on him and LAW collapsed. From then on, the 'loyalists' were as much at war with Britain, and with the trade unions, as were their enemies in the IRA. Nevertheless, it was a three-cornered battle. They attacked civilians of the other community more often than they attacked the British Army, and the soldiers' main task was to prevent them from killing each other.

Power-sharing and the Protestant reaction

In March 1973, one year after the imposition of direct rule, the British Government published a White Paper whereby a new Stormont Parliament was to be elected by proportional representation. The British Government would retain responsibility for security and law and order and also for electoral matters, to eliminate any possibility of further gerrymandering, but the new Stormont Assembly would be empowered to elect an executive with full power of administration over the Province, *provided* that the executive contained a fair proportion of members of parties representing the Catholic community—including those who wished for a united Ireland—that is, a power-sharing executive.

The elections were held in June 1973 and resulted in a large overall majority (though not a majority of Protestants) in favour of power-sharing. Of the Protestant Unionist members elected, twenty-two (with Faulkner) supported the new constitution. These, with eight of the Alliance Party, one of the Northern Ireland Labour Party and nineteen of the Catholic Social Democratic and Labour Party (SDLP) made up fifty in favour of power-sharing, facing twenty-eight Protestant members (in three groups led by William Craig, Harry West and the Reverend Ian Paisley) opposed to it.

On 1 January 1974 the power-sharing executive took office, led by Faulkner. His cabinet of eleven included six Unionists, one Alliance man and four Catholic SDLP Ministers led by Gerry Fitt.

This was the high point of hope for reconciliation in Northern Ireland and, for its short life, the power-sharing executive worked efficiently and harmoniously. It was, however, doomed because, between the June elections and the taking of office in January, the Sunningdale meeting had taken place, in December 1973. This, as was described in Chapter 8, was at the height of the crises which was to bring down the Heath Government and just after William Whitelaw (whose patience and negotiating skill had brought about the power-sharing agreement and had given the electorate the confidence to support it) had left the Northern Ireland Office to try to resolve the threatened miners' strike.

Heath, who was under very great strain, did attend the Sunning-dale Conference and agreed with the Dublin Government to include an 'Irish Dimension' and a 'Council of Ireland' in the proposed constitution. This was all that Paisley and his supporters needed to alarm Protestant voters, with warnings that it would lead inexorably to their absorption into the Republic and the final destruction of their privileged position in the Province.

In the British General Election of 28 February 1974, only one Northern Ireland member who supported power-sharing was elected to Westminster, and he was the republican SDLP leader, Gerry Fitt. All the other eleven members were hard-line anti-constitution men who campaigned exclusively on an anti-Sunningdale ticket. Not a single Protestant supporter of Faulkner was elected. Although it is possible that the combined votes of the Catholics and of those who voted for the defeated Faulkner candidates may still have represented more than 50 per cent of the total votes, the result was disastrous for power-sharing in that its opponents in Northern Ireland had a plausible case that the majority of power-sharing supporters elected to Stormont in June 1973 had now been repudiated.

Preparing for the strike

On 10 December 1973, immediately after the Sunningdale meeting, the militant Protestants announced the formation of an Ulster Army Council (a mirror image of the Army Council of the IRA in Dublin) comprising the UDA, the UVF, the Ulster Special Constabulary Association (USCA) and the Red Hand Commando (RHC).[4] They completed plans for a strike in January, but Craig had shrewdly advised them to wait and see what happened in the miners' strike and the British General Election.

Meanwhile, Billy Kelly, the convenor in the Belfast East power station, had been busy for the previous six months preparing detailed plans for action, in conjunction with shop stewards in the coal and oil industries as well as in the power stations, and organizing the UWC, which now had a twenty-one-man executive. Their chief organizers were Petrie and Kelly, and Tom Beattie, who worked in the Ballylumford power station, which provided more than half of Northern Ireland's electric power.

Other predominant members were Harry Murray, a shipyard member who had been a long-standing member of the old LAW, and Glen Barr, a charismatic and energetic UDA officer in his thirties, an anti-power-sharing member of the Stormont Parliament, who was elected Chairman of the UWC and proved an able and articulate spokesman on television.

The UWC executive generally distrusted Stormont politicians and kept people like West, Craig and Paisley at arm's length. They also got on quietly and assiduously with preparing the strike —and especially for the stoppage of electric power—with no attempt to work up popular support, which they were confident they could get, if necessary by intimidation. This bothered the politicians, who were aware of the planning of the strike, but feared that it might fail for lack of response. Harold Wilson's newly elected minority Government in London—which had other problems on its mind—also misinterpreted the lack of popular involvement in the movement and did not take the threat of a power stoppage seriously. As a result, neither Wilson nor Faulkner made adequate preparation for maintaining essential services.

Distrust between the UWC and the politicians was exacerbated when Paisley deliberately sabotaged the UWC plan to call the strike on 8 May, by leaking it to the press. The UWC therefore decided to launch the strike a week later without bringing in the politicians. Paisley and some others turned up at a routine meeting of the UWC executive in an hotel on 13 May to find it already in session with plans nearing completion. The executive told them that the strike was to be declared the following evening, to coincide with the vote in the Stormont Assembly on the Sunningdale agreement. Paisley and Craig (who was not present but heard of the decision by telephone) both strongly opposed the timing, but they had become mere passengers and they eventually accepted the UWC decision. The Ulster Army Council issued a statement warning that 'If Westminster is not prepared to restore democracy, i.e., the will of the people made clear in an election, then the only other way it can be restored is by a *coup d'état*.'[5]

The strike begins

The strike was declared at 6 pm on Tuesday 14 May. Initial

response by Protestant workers on Wednesday morning was poor. At 9 am all roads into Belfast were still open and most firms reported that 90 per cent of the work-force had turned up. But Kelly's well-organized power station men cut power supplies to 60 per cent and big factories were finding it difficult to maintain production by the end of the morning.

Meanwhile, the UDA went round the shops and businesses in Belfast instructing them to close, with warnings of petrol-bombs if they did not comply. Most of them did. At the Harland and Wolff shipyard all the 8,000 workers were invited to hear UWC speakers during the lunch break and they were told that any cars left in the workers' car parks after 2 pm would be burned. Almost all of them left immediately and the yard closed down. By the end of the day commercial life in and around Belfast was coming to a standstill.

The power cuts gathered momentum. Kelly's task was made easier by the fact that the Northern Ireland grid was served only by the four power stations in the Province, because the single power line linking it to the grid in Southern Ireland (which crossed in the militantly republican area of South Armagh) had been blown up by the IRA and was closed throughout the strike.

During the afternoon, Ballylumford was producing only half its normal capacity of 1,080 megawatts and large areas of the Province were suffering four-hour power cuts. By the evening, 75 per cent of Londonderry area was without electricity and the strike began to affect food supplies in the city.

Faulkner and the British Government still did not appreciate the seriousness of the strike, which they assumed would only last for one day. Faulkner was convinced that the UWC and the uniformed groups of the UDA did not represent majority Protestant opinion and that the intimidation and suffering would lead to them being repudiated by the public. He also believed that the Protestant middle class—businessmen, managers, shopkeepers, farmers and professional men—would rally to the established authority, but he was wrong; many of them felt as strongly as the Protestant workers that Sunningdale would lead to reunification and the loss of their privileged position. This proved to be a fatal error of judgement by Faulkner, particularly over the power station managerial staff.

On Thursday 16 May intimidation and hijacking intensified. Many buses were withdrawn. The UDA erected thirty-seven roadblocks around Belfast, and the British Army—under orders not to provoke violence—did not try to remove them. Nor did the Royal Ulster Constabulary (RUC), some, at least, of whose members made little attempt to conceal their sympathy with the aims of the strike.

Meanwhile, the British Government's policy was to let the strike run out of steam and not provoke a clash between the army and the UDA unless the UDA started shooting.

The UWC's alternative administration

One of the most remarkable features of this strike was that the UWC set up its own *de facto* Provisional Government. It appreciated that a total breakdown of essential services had commonly proved to be the downfall of strikes, neither the public nor the strikers being willing to let that happen. The UWC therefore enlisted the help of technical experts from the power stations, from the aircraft factory, from the gas and oil industries and from the farms to manage the life of the community during the strike. They found suitable people to take charge of fuel and power, petrol supplies, animal feed and other essential services. Individuals or organizations with problems—hospitals, for example—were invited to approach the UWC rather than Government offices, and the UWC set out to demonstrate that it alone had the ability to provide what they needed—or to withhold it. This was a masterly ploy to destroy the credibility of Faulkner's executive and establish their own.

On Friday 17 May four large car-bombs were set off in the Republic—three in Dublin and one in the border town of Monaghan. Twenty-eight Southern Irish people were killed. Three of the cars were traced to Protestant areas of Belfast and Portadown and, although the UWC, UDA and UVF all disowned and condemned the bombings, many people interpreted them as a demonstration of what the Protestant paramilitaries could do if they chose, either in the North or—as a warning of what would be in store for Dublin in the event of reunification—in the South.[6] There was certainly little doubt that the bombings had been done by Protestants, not by the IRA, though they may well have been Protestant mavericks, not connected with the UWC strike. No one was ever arrested.

Meanwhile, the strikers attempted to achieve recognition as a negotiating authority at government level by offering to guarantee 60 per cent power supplies and maintain all essential services if the Secretary of State for Northern Ireland, Merlyn Rees, would agree to cut off commercial and industrial consumers from the grid. Rees refused to have any dealings with them, saying that this was a political, not an industrial strike. By Saturday 18 May all big industries faced closure, and farmers were becoming worried about suffocation of livestock through the lack of powered ventilation. Officials of the Northern Ireland Electricity Service warned that power supplies could only be maintained at 30 per cent, and that this would be reduced rather than increased if troops moved in, as junior managers and technicians would walk out.

This was confirmed on Sunday 19 May, when six military engineers in civilian clothes visited Ballylumford and concluded that the Army could not operate the power station without the participation of control room staff—which they knew they would not get, and so did the UWC.

By the morning of Monday there were 172 roadblocks and massive intimidation by large bodies of UDA men marching the streets and forcing shops and businesses to close and people not to go to work. The RUC were ordered not to interfere unless life was at risk and the Army took no action against the barricades. The impression gained ground amongst all sections of the public that the strikers would win and that the Government (in London and Stormont) lacked the will to act against them.[7]

On Tuesday, Len Murray, General Secretary of the TUC, led a 'back to work' march of workers to the shipyards—with more courage than success. Of the 10,000 shipyard workers, only 200 followed him. All over the Province power cuts of up to twelve hours were common. Farm livestock were dying, and the UWC themselves were getting worried.

On Wednesday, the Army deployed 15,000 troops to clear roadblocks in Belfast. The UDA did not resist—indeed they agreed to remove the barricades themselves. Thereafter the UDA confined themselves to human barricades and the UDA commander, Andy Tyrie, ordered his men to avoid confrontations with the Army. He probably realized that a large number of them were still loyalists in the true sense of the word and would baulk at opening fire on British soldiers. The significance of this

—and of the opportunity it offered—appears to have been lost on the British Government.

The collapse of the Government

Meanwhile, Faulkner's executive itself was beginning to break apart. There were disagreements over proposals to water down the 'Council of Ireland' plan in order to pacify the Protestant population, and the Catholic SDLP members were demanding more positive action by the British in using the Army to break the strike, and especially to maintain oil and petrol supplies, but the British Government remained adamant that the Army must not be used as strike-breakers.

The IRA lay low throughout. Apart from the twenty-eight killed by the bombings south of the border, only two people were killed during the strike. On Friday a gang of 30 UDA and UVF men decided to raid a number of Catholic pubs which had stayed open in the predominantly Protestant district of Bally-mena. One of them, Thomas McClure, murdered two Catholic brothers who owned one of the pubs and who resisted the raid. Most of the Protestants were drunk and all were later arrested, McClure being sentenced to life imprisonment. The incident alarmed UWC, UDA and UVF leaders who vehemently disowned and condemned it.

The British Government was meanwhile urgently considering a plan to arrest all known UWC leaders and move in the Army in force. The Ballymena killings would have provided them with an additional pretext and it is probable that if they had done so the strikers, after an initial explosion of resistance, would have given way rather than suffer the odium of causing the public suffering which would follow a collapse of essential services and provoking large-scale shooting on the streets between 'loyalists' and British soldiers. Whatever their leaders' views may have been, the majority of Protestants did feel some loyalty to Britain. Wilson, however, decided to take a middle course—to use the Army to maintain oil and petrol supplies, but not to break the strike as a whole and not to risk an explosion by arresting the leaders. On the evening of Saturday 25 May he made a broadcast. It began firmly enough:

What we are seeing in Northern Ireland is not just an industrial strike. It has nothing to do with wages. It has nothing to do with jobs—except to imperil jobs. It is a deliberate and calculated attempt to use every undemocratic and unparliamentary means for the purpose of bringing down the whole constitution of Northern Ireland so as to set up there a sectarian and undemocratic state, from which one-third of the people of Northern Ireland will be excluded.

After a reference to the Ballymena killings, he went on:

Those who are now challenging constitutional authority are denying the fundamental right of every man and woman—the right to work.

But then he included a highly controversial passage:

The people on this side of the water—British parents—have seen their sons vilified and spat on and murdered. British taxpayers have seen ... over £300 million a year this year, with the cost of the Army operation on top of that, going into Northern Ireland. They see property destroyed by evil violence and are asked to pick up the bill for rebuilding it. Yet people who benefit from all this now viciously defy Westminster, purporting to act as though they were an elected government; people who spend their lives sponging on Westminster and British democracy and then systematically assault democratic methods. Who do these people think they are?

This had the effect of rallying support for the UWC and of discrediting Faulkner, who was enjoying Wilson's support. Though the Protestant terrorists were more vicious than the IRA in sectarian murders, it was not this which Wilson attacked. Although it was not his intention, he was taken by the Protestants to imply that it was *they* who blew up buildings and that it was *they* who murdered British soldiers—in fact, of the 214 British soldiers killed up to that date, Protestants had killed two. But the ultimate insult was to label them as 'spongers'.

After that—despite a rather lame avowal by Wilson of support for the power-sharing executive—the end was swift. Next day (Sunday) the SDLP members warned that, unless the Army took over the distribution of petrol and oil, they would resign from the executive. The Army did take this over, including depots, tanker-lorries and petrol stations, next morning. The UWC replied by calling for a total stoppage (though in the event they postponed it by twenty-four hours), including the water and sewage works. Power output fell to 10 per cent. There was a danger of raw sewage flooding areas of Belfast.

At this stage the twenty-two Unionists in the Assembly who had supported power-sharing told Faulkner that they could no longer guarantee their support. He tried to persuade Rees to open talks with the UWC, but Rees refused. Faulkner resigned. The UWC called off the strike on Wednesday 29 May. The British Government resumed direct rule.

The power-sharing experiment had been destroyed. Though the circumstances and the political motivations were very different, it was the second time in 1974 that an elected administration had been brought down by an avowedly political strike.

The UWC strike succeeded for five main reasons. First, the isolation of the provincial grid, with one predominant power station (Ballylumford) and only three other minor ones, enabled the UWC to exercise a degree of control over supplies which would not have been possible in Britain itself; and they planned and executed this control well. Secondly, the intimidation—by large paramilitary bodies on the streets—was ruthless and effective, so that at the critical moment any other essential services could be totally disrupted and everyone knew it. Thirdly, the Security Forces made little or no effort in the first week to protect people from this intimidation, or to remove the large number of barricades on the roads; in the case of the police, a contributory factor was the sympathy which many RUC men felt for the aims of the strike; in the case of the soldiers, it was a policy decision because it was feared that forceful action could have provoked large-scale violence between the UDA or UVF and the Army, which—if the IRA had exploited the opportunity—could have plunged the Province into an anarchic collapse of order. (Though when the Army did remove the barricades there was no resistance, and it proved that the IRA were just as fearful of such a confrontation as the Government was.)

Fourthly, the Army could not have run the electric power system without the participation of junior and middle managers, and it was clear that if the Army came in they would join the strike. Fifthly, the British Government missed the best opportunity for firm action—immediately after the successful removal of the barricades on Wednesday 22 May.

Had the Army and the RUC, on that day, arrested the UWC, UDA and UVF leaders, protected people who wanted to work and operated such services as they could (including, probably, water, sewage, and transport) the strike would probably have collapsed. There would no doubt have been an initial and damaging stoppage of power, but the best tactics would have been to accept this, so that the community would have to endure the suffering. The power workers, faced with public revulsion and deprived of their organization and leadership, would in due course have given way.

All these things are easily commended with hindsight. Had they been done and the fears of anarchic violence proved correct, the others with hindsight would have said, with some justice, that surrender was the proper answer. Yet the lessons remain. Intimidation was seen to prevail. A political strike—in this case with not even a pretence of industrial aims—defied and defeated the parliamentary democratic process. This was a dangerous precedent for Britain and has provided both encouragement and vicarious experience for those who wish to use industrial action —whether their philosophy tends towards Marxism or Fascism— to defy or destroy parliamentary democracy in Britain.

Paisley's strike in 1977

Three years later—in May 1977—a group of militant Protestants tried to repeat the process, this time led, not by people involved in power generation or the shipyards but by two politicians, Ian Paisley and Ernest Baird (who had in 1974 been one of Craig's lieutenants).

The strike was a dismal failure and a humiliation for Paisley and Baird. Its aims were—by contrast with 1974—not sufficiently specific to appeal to popular opinion: that is, a vague demand for more offensive action against the IRA and for the return of power to a majority (i.e. Protestant) government at Stormont. Another factor was that the economy in May 1974 had not yet been hit by the effects of the oil price rise and by the wage explosion of 1974 and 1975, whereas in 1977 there was an acute awareness of economic depression and unemployment. Full use was made of this by Government information services before the strike. A public opinion poll (NOP) just before the strike showed 78 per cent disapproval; of the 53 per cent of Protestants who expected to be involved, only 18 per cent said they would be doing so voluntarily. Most of the 8,000 Harland and Wolff shipyard workers opposed the strike.

On the first day (Tuesday 3 May 1977) about 50 per cent stayed away from work, largely as a result of intimidation—but this time the RUC acted firmly and confidence was maintained. The Northern Ireland Secretary, Roy Mason, was firm from the start and on the third day (Thursday 5 May) had a long meeting with power station workers at Ballylumford, convincing them that they could and would be protected from violence. Kelly, the key figure in 1974, had promised Paisley that Ballylumford would support the strike but the majority of the work-force stayed at work. By the fourth day (Friday 6 May), despite intimidation both at work and at home, a large majority of the Ballylumford workers (268 to 171) voted to continue work. The second week showed support dwindling further and on Friday 13 May the strike was called off, having achieved none of its aims.

Paisley's 1977 strike failed for reasons which were in many ways the mirror-image of the reasons for success of the UWC strike in 1974. It was led by politicians and not by men close to the shop floor. The intimidation was just as vicious—more so in some ways—but it was firmly dealt with by the RUC. Power station workers were, if they so requested, protected at home as well as at work. Barricades were removed at once. Above all, the British Government was fully prepared, took the propaganda initiative and acted firmly. The people were left in no doubt about the suffering and the loss of jobs which would result if the strike succeeded.

It would be tempting to conclude that the Protestant extremists, especially Paisley and Baird, were fatally discredited by the strike. The history of Northern Ireland encourages no such complacency. Nevertheless, Paisley's strike did give the Government useful experience in the handling of political strikes which may have undone at least some of the damage caused by its failure in 1974. The most important lesson was the success of informing the public what was really behind the strike and what was at stake for them.

12 Bombs in England

England's most violent year

To add to Harold Wilson's troubles, more people were killed in political violence in England in 1974 than in all the previous seventy-three years of the twentieth century. Altogether, forty-five people were killed in England in 1974—forty-four by terrorist bombs, and one in a riot in Red Lion Square (see next chapter). The bombs were all placed by the Provisional IRA, with the declared aim of sickening the British Government and public of having anything more to do with Northern Ireland.

One of the results of the bombing campaign was the introduction of the Prevention of Terrorism (Emergency Provisions) Act of 1974, which banned the IRA and increased the powers of the Government and police regarding deportation, search at points of entry and the period for which suspects could be held for questioning.

All the IRA cells operating in Britain were made up either of people coming over from Ireland or from members of the 1½ million Irish immigrants in Britain (with the exception of one half-English girlfriend of an IRA man). They were, however, supported in their aims by the International Marxist Group (IMG), one of whose leaders, Tariq Ali, offered on BBC Television to give favourable consideration to requests for the IRA for shelter for operations in Britain. IMG also sponsored the Troops Out Movement and called regularly for support for the IRA in their journal.[1]

Anatomy of a bombing campaign

On 4 February 1974, just before Edward Heath called for the dissolution and the General Election, a coach blew up on the M62 motorway, killing twelve people. This was a civilian coach but it was known to be used regularly to carry soldiers stationed in Yorkshire to and from weekend visits to parents and friends in Lancashire. Nine of those killed were soldiers and the other three were a mother and two young children—a complete family. The bomb was found to have been placed in a suitcase in the baggage compartment of the coach, just under where the family was sitting. Later Judith Ward, the half-English girlfriend of an IRA man, was sentenced to thirty years' imprisonment for the murder of the twelve people.

During the spring and summer, three more people were killed, one of them by a bomb in the armoury of the Tower of London at the height of the tourist season in July. This room was a well-known attraction for mothers and children—most of the forty-one injured were children and the one killed was a woman. It was hard to find a motive for this other than indiscriminate hatred, and it had an adverse reception both in Ireland and in USA.

In October and November, bombs were placed in pubs in Guildford and Woolwich, close to Army barracks. Of the seven people killed, some were soldiers off duty and some civilians, one of them a girl. Once again, IRA members were convicted.

The heaviest casualties, however, were in Birmingham, where twenty-one people were killed and 162 injured by two bombs placed in crowded pubs on pay night, nowhere near any Army barracks. This was the climax (and the end) of a bombing campaign in the Midlands, which had begun in April 1974. In all, fourteen IRA members were convicted for these bombings and a fifteenth (James McDade) was killed by his own bomb. In the course of the police investigations leading to their arrests, much was learned about the organization and methods of IRA bomb cells (or 'Active Service Units') in England.

The cells varied in size between five and twelve and were centred on the homes of Irishmen, mainly in and around London and Birmingham, and in pubs frequented by the Irish community. There was seldom if ever more than one cell operating in any one city at a time and, whenever the police had enough information to make a series of half a dozen arrests, there was a complete cessation of bombing in that area—until a new cell had been set up.

The key figure was the cell leader. He was an IRA officer and was usually the only man in contact with the IRA Army Council in Dublin—and possibly the only one whom they knew by name.

In accordance with normal practice in underground organizations, the cell leader had strict instructions not to take part in
operations, because he was too valuable, because he might give
leads into the higher organization and, in the event of the cell
being broken up, he would be required to form a new one. These
instructions were not always obeyed.

The cell leader worked to a general brief from Dublin, for
example to bomb pubs near Army barracks or to disrupt commercial activity or shopping centres. He recruited and trained
the members of his cell and co-ordinated the work of its three
groups—sometimes separate and sometimes overlapping—a procurement group, a bomb factory and a bombing team.

The procurement organization in Britain operated mainly by
smuggling commercial explosives and detonators manufactured
and stolen by the IRA in Ireland, though sometimes thefts were
also arranged in England. The materials needed for making delay
fuse systems—watches, batteries, wires, etc.—were usually
bought in local shops by those working in the bomb factory.

The bomb factory—an imposing name for a bench in the back
room of an IRA man's house—usually included two or three
experts; one was the bomb designer, familiar with explosives;
next was an 'electrician', who made the delayed-action (or occasionally radio-controlled) firing system; and there was sometimes
also an expert in making up containers, such as suitcases or
shopping-bags, designed so as not to arouse suspicion.[2] Like the
cell leader, the bomb factory experts were usually regarded as
too valuable to be hazarded on operations.

The bombing team itself was headed by a bomb officer, and
his home was usually the 'safe house' from which the operation
was mounted (it also often housed the bomb factory). His task
was to brief the men or women[3] to place the bombs and put the
delay mechanism into operation; also to brief any others, such
as drivers, look-out men, or people to create a diversion. All of
these were 'expendable'. Their tasks were easily learned, though
they had generally been in the cell for long enough for the leader
to make sure of their reliability, and possibly to commit them
sufficiently to have a hold on them against their defection.

The cell leader or bomb officer might sometimes brief one of
the cell members to telephone a warning, often to a newspaper,
and usually about twenty minutes before a bomb was timed to go
off. This was regarded as so important, however, that one of the

two officers would often do it himself; and in order to ensure that the police did act quickly on it, the IRA (by telephone) at this time had agreed code-words with the police which were usually known only to the cell leader or his immediate deputy. The warning was regarded as important for two reasons: first because massive casualties were damaging to the IRA cause, particularly because they shocked the Irish-American community which provided most of their funds; and secondly because, if the timing of the warning went wrong, the rank-and-file bomb-layers might themselves be so shattered by the casualties they had caused that they would break down under interrogation. This was what happened in the Birmingham pub bombings in November 1974.

Between April and August 1974 there were a large number of bombs (and hoax calls) in Birmingham—though no one was killed. On 2 August the police simultaneously raided three suspected houses. They found two bomb factories and arrested five people, all of whom were later convicted.

At least one man got away, however, who may or may not have been the cell leader—Mick Murray. He was a senior IRA officer—and a determined one. Within three months, around the Irish pubs, he had recruited a fresh cell, of which he certainly was the leader.[4]

The new cell launched its first operation on 5 November 1974 and one of the bomb-layers, identified from fingerprints, was James McDade. On 14 November McDade laid another bomb—but this one had a defective timing mechanism, which fired as soon as McDade pulled the pin to set it in motion. He was killed.

This mistake in the bomb factory—several other bombs disarmed in this period were found to have the same fault, a screw which was too long and made a short circuit—was probably a symptom of the haste with which Murray had tried to get his new cell into operation. This haste may also have accounted for an error in the timing of the warning call for the pub bombs on 21 November; it came only seven minutes before the first bomb went off—and caused carnage which lost support for the IRA all over the world.

The bomb officer (John Walker) and four of the layers all caught the boat train for Belfast from Birmingham New Street station, which pulled out twenty minutes before the bombs went off. By a blend of good background intelligence and efficient police work, all five were arrested as they tried to board the boat in Heysham four hours later. Under interrogation next morning one of them, when he heard the results of the bombing, broke down and made a full confession, implicating the others. Most of them then made statements too and four other members of the cell—this time including Murray—were traced and arrested in Birmingham. All were convicted—Murray both for this and for one of the August bombs, in which his fingerprints were found on the clock mechanism, which he had either handled or assembled.

Public reaction and the law

After the November bombs, one of the Government's main problems was to control the fury of the public. In Birmingham, particularly (where there were over 100,000 Irish immigrants), men with Irish accents were attacked by their fellow workers, some Irish shops were smashed and some Irishmen's homes were set on fire. One (who had unwisely painted on his wall the Long Kesh emblem indicating that he had been held as an IRA suspect in Belfast) had his house set on fire three times.

Television had brought the horror of the carnage into people's homes, in colour. One man, at least, thought that it should have been brought home more vividly still. He was a fireman—and one of the first into one of the pubs after the bombs went off. In the beam of his torch he saw a torso, with no arms or legs, and a spongy mess where its head had been. The torso was not only wriggling; it was also, through the spongy mess, screaming. The fireman asked the police to let the television cameras record it live and let the public see what bombing really meant. It is probably as well that the police refused, or many more Irishmen would have been attacked.

The bombing, not surprisingly, increased the public demand for the death penalty. Even a year later (during which nine more people were killed by the IRA in England) 88 per cent of those questioned in a public opinion poll still favoured capital punishment.[5] Many police and prison officers supported this view, but most senior police officers opposed it, on the grounds that it would reduce rather than increase the prospects of detection and conviction of terrorists, because people would be less likely to come forward with evidence and juries more reluctant to convict;

also, since a death sentence would clearly require a unanimous verdict, it would open the way for defence lawyers to object to jurors until they could be sure that at least one would vote for acquittal—they had objected to thirty-seven in turn in the Angry Brigade bombing trial in 1972. Perhaps the most convincing reason of all was that the death penalty would encourage the IRA to employ young teenagers to do even more of the killing than they already did, confident that no one under 18 could be hanged.

The Prevention of Terrorism (Temporary Provisions) Act was rushed through Parliament within a week of the Birmingham bombs, and was renewed in 1975, 1976 and 1977. This made it a criminal offence to belong to the IRA, or to solicit or provide funds for it, or to give it propaganda support. It increased the Government's power to deport or exclude people born outside Britain who were suspected of supporting terrorism. It also empowered the police to demand proof of identity from people entering the country from Northern or Southern Ireland, and (subject to the Home Secretary's approval) to extend the time of holding suspects for questioning from two to seven days. The Act did not, however, change the rules for investigation of evidence, nor introduce capital punishment, nor identity cards, as many were advocating. The restriction of the liberty of the ordinary citizen was, in practice, nil.

The mildness of the legislation was an endorsement of the stability of British society. There was, not surprisingly, a clamour for tougher measures but, on the whole, they were about right. On the one hand, anything less would have caused the risk of a still angry public taking the law into their own hands, as had happened with the Protestant vigilantes in Northern Ireland in 1972. On the other hand, overreaction would have created a more brittle society and would in the end have played into the hands of those who wished to undermine it.

Though there was still some IRA terrorism in England in subsequent years—nine people were killed by it in 1975 and one more in 1976—the new legislation did have, or at least contribute to, the desired effect.

In the broader context of Britain's agony, the burst of terrorism in 1974 drew the people together. All parties in Parliament rallied to the support of the Government in dealing with it and perhaps, in its way, it increased the revulsion against violence, both in industrial and political affairs.

13 Red Lion Square and Windsor Park

Political demonstrations in London

Kevin Gately was killed in Red Lion Square on 15 June 1974 when a group of demonstrators attempted to break through a police cordon. He was the first man to be killed in any political demonstration in England, Scotland or Wales since 1919.

Compared with the mighty confrontation at Saltley, which had great political, social and economic significance, the events that day in Red Lion Square were little more than a sordid scuffle. About nine hundred members of the National Front (NF) were marching to a meeting in Conway Hall. About two hundred students, mainly members of the International Marxist Group (IMG) broke away from a counter-demonstration in order to try to block the entrance of the hall, and charged the police cordon positioned to keep the two demonstrations apart. Writing in *The Times* three days later, Bernard Levin expressed what was probably the view of the majority of the public:

> Saturday's repulsive spectacle of rival gangs of totalitarians flexing their weedy muscles in the centre of London has been given a genuinely tragic dimension by the death of a young man in the mêlée, though that is being gleefully turned to political advantage by the Left-Wing gang, who are already claiming him for their own mythological purposes as a martyr to fascism and police brutality.[1]

Because Kevin Gately's death was the first in a riot for half a century, the incident became the subject of much public debate and the Government ordered a public inquiry by Lord Justice Scarman. The public debate and the inquiry have thrown a valuable light on the conduct of demonstrations in Britain.

The Red Lion Square demonstration was one of 1,321 political demonstrations in London in the years 1972–4. Only fifty-four of them involved disorder. In these, 623 arrests were made and 373 people were injured, 297 of them being police officers.[2] The great majority of the injuries were light, including those in Red Lion Square, where forty-six policemen and eight demonstrators were injured.[3]

In the fifty-four demonstrations in which disorder occurred, students or recent graduates of universities predominated both in the leadership and in the rank and file. Sir Robert Mark, then Commissioner of the Metropolitan Police, commented on the contrast between these demonstrations and the great majority, which are peaceful:

> Although support of the public at large for police aims and methods is a major factor in keeping down the temperature at demonstrations and minimizing casualties, the lack of fatal and serious casualties has allowed unjustified complacency in the public attitude to political demonstrations. These are occasionally both violent and frightening and there have emerged a small minority of extremist causes whose adherents leave no doubt of their belief in the use of force and lack of scruples to further political aims.[4]

The philosophies and the malign influence of some of these same groups have sometimes also been apparent when an industrial dispute is used as an occasion for a political demonstration, or simply for attacks on the police by demonstrators unconnected with the dispute (e.g. at Grunwick in 1977; see Chapter 16).

Planning the marches to Red Lion Square

The build-up to the Red Lion Square incident began on 13 April 1974, when the National Front booked the largest assembly room in Conway Hall, which is on the corner of the square (see map) to hold a meeting on 15 June to protest against Government immigration policy.[5] The NF had held meetings in this hall for the previous four years and one of these had been picketed by left-wing demonstrators in October 1973, when there were scuffles with the police and a number of people were injured and arrested.

On 7 May Martin Webster, NF National Activities Organizer,

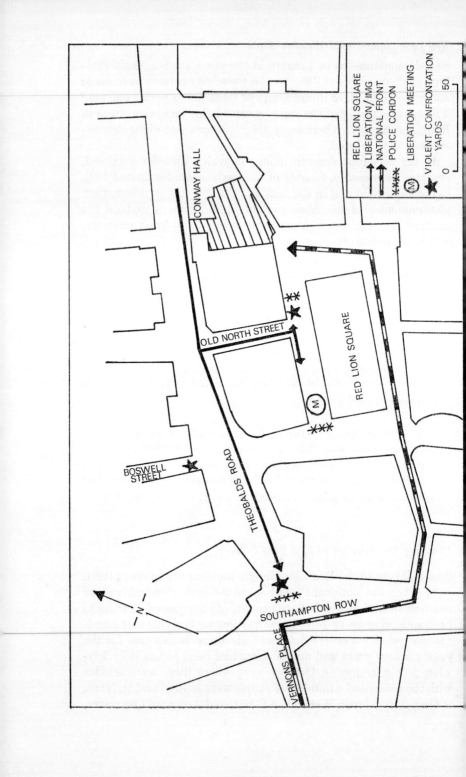

CONWAY HALL

OLD NORTH STREET

RED LION SQUARE

THEOBALDS ROAD

BOSWELL STREET

SOUTHAMPTON ROW

VERNONS PLACE

N

RED LION SQUARE
LIBERATION/IMG
NATIONAL FRONT
POLICE CORDON
LIBERATION MEETING
VIOLENT CONFRONTATION
YARDS
0   50

sent a long and detailed letter to Cannon Row Police Station, setting out plans for the march and subsequent meeting. Copies of this letter were sent to Holborn Police Station, in whose area the march would end, and to Special Branch. Webster forecast that approximately 1,500 would take part in the march, would move off from Westminster Hall at 2.30, stopping to deliver a letter at No. 10 Downing Street, and march through the West End to Conway Hall. He drew attention to the counter-demonstration which had occurred in October 1973. These plans were agreed by the Public Order department at Scotland Yard.

On 4 June a newspaper contact informed Miss Kay Beauchamp, secretary of the London Area Council of Liberation, of the impending march. Liberation was a movement based on the 'broad left'—mainly the Communist Party of Great Britain and the left wing of the Labour Party; it had previously been known as the Movement for Colonial Freedom. The President was a Labour peer, Lord Brockway, a veteran campaigner against racial discrimination, and on matters of immigration it was diametrically opposed to the NF.

Kay Beauchamp consulted Liberation's general secretary, Steven Hart, and they booked a small room for a meeting in Conway Hall for the same day, 15 June. This room had a separate entrance from Theobald's Road, not from Red Lion Square (see map).

On 6 June Liberation called a meeting of organizations which might take part in a counter-demonstration. These included representatives of the CPGB, IMG and the International Socialists (IS)—the movement which later became the Socialist Workers' Party (SWP). They were invited by Steven Hart (son of Labour MP Judith Hart, and aged twenty-two at the time) and this caused apprehension amongst some of the more experienced members of Liberation. So did the booking of the simultaneous meeting in the same hall as the NF, which Lord Justice Scarman described as a 'mischievous ploy' which 'carried public order implications which Liberation ought to have foreseen'.[6] Scarman noted that, on the Council of Liberation, only Lord Brockway seemed to be apprehensive. The National Union of Students also clearly appreciated the dangers and were well aware of the damage which violent confrontations could do to the public image of students; they, like Lord Brockway, urged Liberation to cancel the meeting, but to no avail.

Next day, 7 June, Liberation issued 8,000 leaflets advertising their demonstration. One of these was shown by the police to Peter Cadogan, General Secretary of the South Place Ethical Society, the lessees of Conway Hall. Cadogan sought and obtained assurances from Liberation and the NF that neither meeting would interfere with the other, and that they would use the separate entrances on Theobald's Road and in Red Lion Square. He also sent a registered letter to IMG when he heard that Liberation had invited them to take part, warning them that any interference with the other meeting would lead to loss of access to the hall.[7]

On 11 June Kay Beauchamp and Steven Hart discussed the route for their march with the police at Scotland Yard. Hart had requested the same route as the NF but the police asked him to use Theobald's Road, drop off the 100 ticket holders for their meeting to enter through the back entrance, and for the main body to move on for their open-air meeting in Red Lion Square via New North Road, thus entering the Square from the north side. The NF would be entering the Square—and Conway Hall —from the opposite side, so that the two demonstrations should not meet. There was subsequently some argument as to whether this last point was made clear; some, at least, of the demonstrators certainly expected to be able to turn left on entering Red Lion Square and to establish 'pickets' outside the door through which the NF would be entering. It is equally certain that the police had no intention of allowing this to happen.[8]

Sequence of events, 15 June 1974

The Liberation demonstration, 1,000 strong, moved off from the Embankment near Charing Cross at 2.48 pm and reached the Theobald's Road entrance to Conway Hall at 3.30. Only thirty broke off to enter the hall—indicating that the main aim was the street demonstration, not the meeting. The remainder continued and turned into Old North Street, reaching the north entrance to Red Lion Square at 3.36. The leading group carried a CPGB banner, and was followed down the column by other groups with the banners of IMG, IS and the CPEML.[9]

At this time the NF demonstration, 900 strong, was still some some distance away. Neither of the two bodies of marchers had any offensive weapons as such, though both carried poles which could be used as weapons. The contingents of the Liberation march had their banner poles, and the NF carried a large number of Union Jacks on stout wooden flagpoles topped by ornamental metal spikes. The NF also deployed two 'defence parties' at different points in the column, each consisting of about 100 men who appeared to have been chosen largely for size. Scouts were sent forward to identify side-streets from which counter-demonstrators might emerge to attack the column, and members of the defence parties were ready to move forward to man the exits from these side-streets.

When the Liberation march entered Red Lion Square at 3.36 from the north, the NF were approaching it from the other side. They reached the Vernon Place junction with Southampton Row at 3.53, where they were stopped by the police.

Meanwhile, the leaders of the Liberation march were directed by the police to turn right along the north side of Red Lion Square, that is away from the entrance to Conway Hall. This they did and the leading contingent of about 200 behind the CPGB banner moved to the north-west corner of the Square where they began a meeting addressed by Sydney Bidwell, MP.

Observing this, the leaders of the IMG contingent, headed by a banner extending the full width of the road, marked time in Old North Street, allowing the tail of the marchers in front of them to get clear of the entrance to Red Lion Square. To the left of this entrance there was a police cordon across the road, barring the way to the entrance to Conway Hall. The leading ranks of the IMG contingent linked arms, and charged this cordon. This charge took the police by surprise and the cordon almost gave way. Behind it was a detachment of mounted police, and the police officer in charge of the operation (Mr J. H. Gerrard) called by radio for two detachments of the Special Patrol Group (approximately forty men) who were in reserve in vans nearby. These men formed a wedge and, with the mounted police, passed through the original cordon and began to push the demonstrators back. As the demonstrators withdrew, a number of people were left lying on the ground, one of whom was Kevin Gately. He was picked up by the police and taken to a St John Ambulance detachment waiting nearby, but he died some hours later from haemorrhage of the brain, caused by a blow on the head. The possible causes of his death are discussed on page 163.

By 3.50 pm (that is, approximately twelve minutes after the IMG contingent had charged the cordon) Red Lion Square had been cleared and remained free of disorder for the rest of the afternoon.

Having been driven out of the Square, the IMG detachment moved down Theobald's Road towards the junction with South-ampton Row, which they reached just before the head of the NF demonstration was halted by the police at the exit from Vernon Place on the other side of Southampton Row. Here the left-wing demonstrators[10] halted of their own accord, presumably hoping to block the advance of the NF march. The two groups of demon-strators shouted insults across the road, and individuals from both sides came forward into Southampton Row. Some from the left-wing side threw clods of earth, pebbles, metal and wooden objects, and there were between three and four hundred demon-strators on the left-wing side. A cordon of forty to fifty police formed a cordon on the NF side and another eighty or ninety stood in the centre of Southampton Row.

Just before 4 pm twelve mounted policemen arrived, and the police officer in charge in Southampton Row (Chief Super-intendent Cracknell) fearing that another left-wing assault in Southampton Row would bring them into direct contact with the NF marchers, began to drive them back down Theobald's Road. More violence ensued, and there are photographs showing demonstrators seizing the reins of police horses and of one wield-ing a banner pole as he charged a police horse. A number of policemen drew their batons to protect themselves and their horses, and newspaper reporters were more critical of the way the police behaved here than in the earlier incident in Red Lion Square itself. In particular, there was a second body of policemen behind the demonstrators in Theobald's Road, having come down from the original confrontation in Old North Street, and it was difficult for the demonstrators withdrawing before the mounted police to get away. Subsequently, another group of about seventy formed up again under one of the IMG leaders, Mr Heron, in Boswell Street (a side street off Theobald's Road), where there was more violence and the police made further arrests. The number of injuries, both in Theobald's Road and Boswell Street, was small, and none were serious.

By this time (about 4.20 pm) the NF marchers were entering Conway Hall, having been allowed by the police to turn into

Southampton Row when the left-wing demonstrators had been cleared at 4 pm, and to move round the other side of Red Lion Square. There was no trouble between them and the main body of the Liberation demonstration, which continued its meeting peacefully at the north-west corner of the square until 4.50 pm.

Altogether, 923 police had been deployed to keep 900 NF marchers and 1,000 Liberation marchers apart. Fifty-one demonstrators (all from the left-wing contingents which broke away from the Liberation march) were arrested. Of the fifty-four injuries reported, forty-six were to police officers.

Public comment and public inquiry

That evening, all the broadcast news bulletins commented fully on the incident and so did all the papers on Sunday and Monday. Argument continued in the correspondence columns and on television and radio. Two weeks later the Home Secretary (Roy Jenkins) appointed Lord Justice Scarman to 'review the events and actions which led to disorder in Red Lion Square on 15 June and to consider whether any lessons may be learned for the better maintenance of public order when demonstrations take place'.

Of the large number of press reporters who were eye-witnesses almost all (with the exception of those writing in the extreme left-wing press) seemed to agree that the initial confrontation in Red Lion Square was a deliberate attack by the IMG contingent, though some were critical of the subsequent police action in driving the left-wing demonstrators out of Theobald's Road. Amongst the most critical of the latter incident were Peter Chippendale and Martin Walker of the *Guardian*, so it is worth quoting their account of the original confrontation which resulted in the death of Kevin Gately, under the headline:

'LEFT GUILTY OF FIRST CHARGE—POLICE OF SECOND'

The two reporters first described how they were standing in front of the police cordon at the junction of Old North Street and Red Lion Square watching the main Liberation march filing past and turning to the right as directed. They said that there were about 120 police in all, a foot cordon three deep in front and about a dozen mounted police behind. They continue:

At this point a slight gap opened up in the march as a row of demonstrators beneath the banner started to mark time. Their arms were linked, and pressure built up behind them from the other marchers who had entered the narrow street.

Within ten seconds the marchers in front, unaware of what was happening, had moved forward, leaving a clear space between the demonstrators with the banner and the police cordon. (While all this was taking place the NF march was a considerable distance away.)

We are in no doubt at all that at this point the marchers around the banner deliberately charged the police cordon. We did not see or hear a pre-arranged signal, but the move had the appearance of being planned. Although we were standing just in front of the police we had to run away from the demonstrators as they charged towards us.

The banners and placards being carried were in many cases fastened to thick battens, some of which had been sharpened to a pointed stick. Some of them were lowered to make what were in effect lances to charge the police.

In the immediate rear of the front rank of the charging demonstrators were two banners, one of the International Socialists and one of the International Marxist Group.

The initial police reaction was comparatively slow. Their cordon bent badly as fighting broke out. The mounted police came in almost immediately, gently using their horses to stop the policemen on foot from being pushed further back and overwhelmed.

Serious fighting started, and spread along the Square as the first half of the march realized what was happening. The majority of the marchers bringing up the rear hung back, and the serious fighting was confined to a group of about 200.[11]

During the next few days, there were a large number of letters to the press, most of them critical of the demonstrators and sympathetic to the police. One, however, is worthy of particular note. It was in *The Times* of 19 June 1974, and purported to come from Mr J. W. Thomson, of 17 Onslow Gardens, Kensington, SW7. He claimed to be politically neutral, and gave an account, in what seemed to be 'middle-class, middle-aged' language, of the events in Red Lion Square, describing how the peaceful demonstration was assembling outside Conway Hall

1. Saltley. Pickets push forward into the path of a lorry (*Press Association*)

2. Arthur Scargill at Saltley. The gates are closed. Compare age of miners at Saltley with that of the demonstrators at Grunwick [Plates 5 and 6] (*Press Association*)

3. Red Lion Square
   15 June 1974
   (*The Daily Telegraph*)

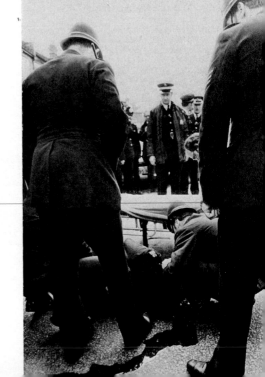

4. PC Wilson. The pool
   of blood that checked
   the violence at
   Grunwick
   (*Press Association*)

when 'a body of mounted police rode into the demonstrators, a manœuvre which amounted to a deliberate act of terrorism.' He went on to accuse the BBC and the press of deliberately falsifying their reports. He added:

> The extent of the aggression of the police at this demonstration is difficult to imagine for those accustomed to think of their country as being democratic and as inheriting a recent tradition of non-violent political activity. . . . I apologize for the length of this letter but I appeal to you to publish it in the hope that some readers will realize that the broadcast versions of political events, for all their influence and apparent verisimilitude, do not necessarily offer accurate or representative interpretation.

The police, as a matter of routine when there is a published complaint against them, went to call on 'Mr J. W. Thompson' at 17 Onslow Gardens, Kensington, SW7, to find that the address was 'unoccupied premises'. In a letter drawing attention to this an officer from Scotland Yard commented: 'The substance of the letter must lose its credibility unless its authenticity can be established.'[12]

Lord Justice Scarman, having heard all the evidence, was in no doubt that the IMG assault was

> . . . a deliberate, determined and sustained attack . . . it was unexpected, unprovoked and viciously violent. It was the beginning of the afternoon's violence in the course of which one young man sustained a fatal injury and an unknown number of demonstrators and 46 policemen were injured. A heavy responsibility rests on those who instigated and led that assault.[13]

One of the IMG leaders, Mr D. J. Bailey, was in the Square at the top of Old North Street when the leaders of the Liberation march were told that they had to turn right, and Mr Bailey heard that instruction. At the Inquiry, he commented, 'The police had broken the agreements that we made, and from then on everything was very much up for grabs, I would say.'[14] Bailey went back down Old North Street and spoke to Brian Heron, who was in charge of the IMG contingent. Scarman comments:

F

At this moment or a few seconds afterwards Mr Heron must have realized that the march was now turning right and not left into the Square. If, as he says, he was unable to hear what Mr Bailey was saying he had the evidence of his eyes as to what was happening a few yards ahead. The truth is that the IMG were determined, by force if necessary, to turn left and to 'picket' (i.e. to obstruct) if they could, the main entrance to Conway Hall.[15]

Commenting on the assault on the police cordon, and on the legality of a 'mass picket' in such circumstances, Scarman adds:

> The assault was inexcusable. .... The explanation which I accept is that the IMG, believing (because Mr Hart had told them so) that they would be turning left, had planned a 'mass picket' outside the entrance in the square to Conway Hall. This unlawful tactic is not to be confused with the lawful process of peaceful picketing in the course of a trade dispute. In this case the IMG's purpose was by the obstacle of their presence in mass to deny the National Front, when they arrived, access to the hall—unless the police were prepared to use force to disperse the 'picket', in which event it would not be difficult to set up the cry of police 'brutality'. The turn to the right at the foot of Old North Street deprived them of this opportunity.[16]

The effects of the demonstration

Of the groups which organized the Red Lion Square demonstration, the only one which advanced its cause was the NF, however little they deserved to do so. They set out to give a display of order and dignity to contrast with the disorder and violence of the left. They meticulously observed police instructions and maintained strict discipline. Television films showed the NF marchers, standing stock-still with closed ranks on one side of Southampton Row while 'dirty, hairy lefties' swarmed about in a chaotic battle with the police on the other. The implied menace of the 'defence sections' and of the metal spikes on top of the forest of Union Jack flagpoles made less impact on the public than the pictures of students hitting out at policemen and charging them with banner poles. The result was precisely what the NF would have wished—publicity for the purpose of *their* demonstration, discrediting of their detractors, increasing applications for membership and a substantially increased vote both at the next General Election and at subsequent by-elections.

By contrast, all the aims of IMG seem to have been set back by the incident, and even the death of Kevin Gately (who was not a member of IMG) rebounded against them. The public blamed them for it.

IMG's behaviour also damaged the reputation of the Liberation movement and hampered the efforts of others who genuinely wished to liberalize immigration policy.

Police tactics

A few days after the riot in Red Lion Square, the International Socialists published a poster headed 'Murdered by the Police' above a photograph of the unconscious Kevin Gately being carried away. Next day at a Press Conference Tony Gilbert, the organizer of the Liberation march, made the same accusation. At the Scarman inquiry, however, he unreservedly withdrew it.

The evidence is overwhelming that Kevin Gately fell whilst in the middle of the crowd of demonstrators, of which he was never near the front rank. He was a very tall man—all photographs show him standing head and shoulders above the others around him. If any policeman had at any time been close to him, still more so if any policeman had struck him, there would unquestionably have been a number of demonstrators who would have seen it and accused the police. There were none, so the inference is clear. Kevin Gately fell to the ground in the middle of the crowd, either overcome by the crush, or struck a glancing blow by a banner pole. Whether the head injury which killed him was from such a blow, or from being trampled upon by the crowd, will never be known. What is quite certain is that he was not trampled upon by the police, as all eye-witnesses report that his body came into view lying on the ground as the crowd withdrew.

Nevertheless, the police did make some errors in the handling of the Red Lion Square demonstration. First, it was a mistake to permit the NF and Liberation marches to get so close to each other. This error probably arose from the fact that police took Liberation at its face value—that is, a movement which had no record of violence in demonstrations, and which certainly did not intend violence on this occasion. It is hard to believe, however, that the police were not aware (as Peter Cadogan of Conway Hall became aware) that Liberation's General Secretary had invited the participation of IMG, who had a very different record, extending back to Grosvenor Square in 1968. If the police were aware of that they should have been aware of the risk they were taking in approving routes which took the two demonstrations within 50 yards of each other in Red Lion Square.

They also made two tactical errors in the handling of the demonstration itself. First, when the IMG contingent had revealed their violent intent on entering Red Lion Square, the police should have positioned a cordon in Theobald's Road to prevent them from taking that as an alternative route to confront the National Front march. There were police reserves in the vicinity who could have easily done this but, in criticizing the police officer in charge for failing to foresee this eventuality, it is only fair to note that the time between the IMG assault on the Red Lion Square cordon and when they moved back down Theobald's Road was less than 15 minutes, and hectic minutes at that.

Ironically, the other tactical error was of precisely the reverse nature. When the police advanced to clear the demonstrators confronting the National Front march across Southampton Row, there was another police cordon by then behind them impeding their retreat down Theobald's Road. The officer ordering the clearance, who was on foot, could not see this, but the mounted police should have seen it and do not appear to have drawn the officer's attention to it.

This is one of the particular advantages of using mounted police. Another advantage is that demonstrators are more frightened of an animal than of a man; while they know that policemen will be taken to account if they use excessive force, this restraint cannot be applied to a police horse, which they fear is much more likely to 'lash out' at them than a human policeman.

Horses are, however, particularly vulnerable. They can be frightened by demonstrators charging them or hitting them with sticks, or by throwing fireworks at them, or (as in Grosvenor Square in 1968 but not in Red Lion Square) by demonstrators spreading ball bearings under their hooves. The photographs of mounted policemen in Red Lion Square with raised truncheons were all of stationary horses hemmed in by demonstrators who, it must be assumed, were seizing the reins or attacking the horse in other ways. One close-up photograph[17] specifically shows this happening. The rider has no other way of protecting his horse.

A number of policemen on foot also drew their truncheons. One demonstrator (Mr Mullen) was injured by a blow on the head from a truncheon, but not seriously. Six others reported being injured in the demonstration but none of these were by truncheons, so, if any police officers did use their truncheons unnecessarily, this cannot have been to any great extent.

Demonstrations and the law

The Scarman inquiry on Red Lion Square was specifically asked to 'consider whether any lessons may be learned for the better maintenance of public order when demonstrations take place'. A number of suggestions were made, both by the Commissioner of the Metropolitan Police and others, and were fully examined in the Scarman Report.[18] Some are discussed in Chapter 19.

There is, however, good reason to criticize the way in which the Courts deal with cases of violence, intimidation and damage on political demonstrations.

The 623 persons arrested during demonstrations in London in 1972–74 were charged with a total of 758 offences, including threatening or insulting words or behaviour, assault, obstruction, possession of offensive weapons and criminal damage. The total number of convictions was 575. Of these, 91 were given absolute or conditional discharges or bound over; 431 were fined; 35 received suspended sentences; and only 18 were imprisoned. Of the 18 prison sentences, 12 were for one month, 2 for two months (both for assaults on the police) and 4 for three months (3 of them for assault on police). Of the fines, 246 were £10 and under, 92 between £10 and £20, 32 between £20 and £30 and only 20 over £30. The average fine for assualt on the police was £24, and the average fine for possession of an offensive weapon was £20. Considering that 297 police officers were injured, these sentences seem very light.

The same applies to the convictions and sentences for the Red

Lion Square demonstration. The 51 people arrested were charged
with 82 offences. Of the 53 convictions, 12 were given absolute
or conditional discharge or bound over, 36 were fined, and 3
given suspended sentences. No one served a sentence of imprisonment. The average fine for assault on the police was £32, and the
average fine for possession of an offensive weapon was £10.[19]

And Lord Justice Scarman had this to say:

> On such evidence as I have seen there may well be good reason
> to wonder whether magistrates do always appreciate the
> gravity of an offence against public order. Abuse of liberty
> endangers liberty itself: it is a serious offence to depreciate the
> currency of freedom by resorting to violence and public dis-
> order—thereby encouraging a move to introduce into the law
> greater restriction upon the rights of all of us.[20]

The Windsor Park Free Festival, 1974

In August 1974, within a few weeks of the incident in Red Lion
Square, there was another violent confrontation between police
and demonstrators at the Windsor Park Free Festival. The Free
Festival was the third of its kind and not to be confused with Pop
Festivals, which are devoted primarily to music and are not generally either political or violent. The advertised purposes of the
Free Festivals were 'social and political protest, drugs and mass
sexual activities'.[21] During the 1973 Festival, there had been 272
arrests, 202 of them for drug offences.[22]

The 1974 Free Festival was attended by about 8,000 people,
mainly students, and the organizers had declared that their aim
was to 'change society' and to force changes in the laws by mass
breaking of those laws—especially of the laws relating to drugs.
The Festivals (similar to the Saltley Coke Depot incident in this
respect only) exemplified the dilemma of the police in dealing
with an organized mass breach of the law when the lawbreakers
are ready to use violence.

In the event the violence, coupled with the filth of the camping
conditions, were such that the majority of those who took part
were disgusted. An attempt to hold a fourth Free Festival at
Watchfield in 1975 drew many fewer people and thereafter the
idea petered out.

The 1974 Festival was by far the most violent of the four. The use of Windsor Great Park was itself a breach of the law, as were many of the activities inside the camp. There was considerable resistance to the police when they went in to arrest drug sellers and others. After five days, 364 people had been arrested, 296 of them for drug offences. The camp was becoming a health hazard and the number of violent incidents between campers and inhabitants in Windsor was increasing. A Citizen's Action Committee had been formed, and the police came to the conclusion that there would be a serious risk of disorder if the camp remained for a second weekend, as the organizers clearly intended.

On Thursday 29 August the police broadcast instructions to the campers to leave, which most of them did, but a hard core of about 500 remained, armed with sticks and bottles and other missiles and prepared for siege. The police moved in at 11 am, and met with organized resistance directed by the camp public-address system. Some individual policemen found themselves isolated and surrounded by several hundred violent and abusive 'hippies' and some of the younger constables, who had not been involved in demonstrations before, undoubtedly overreacted. Hatred was intense on both sides, the constables having been disgusted by the filth of the campers for the past five days. Some drew their truncheons to rescue captured comrades, and in thirteen cases were successfully sued by the victims.

The Festival organizers had got wind of the operation and had positioned two buses beside the stage which they had selected for their 'last stand', inviting the BBC camera team to film it from the top of one bus and ITV from the other. This was a brilliant piece of media-handling by the organizers, since the cameras were seldom beamed onto the violence at the first blow, and swung round to film it when the police reacted and made their arrests, some pretty roughly. Nevertheless, the publicity rebounded and the overwhelming majority of the public sympathized with the police. A further 220 arrests were made and 116 people were injured, 70 of them policemen.[23]

Harold Wilson and his Home Secretary, Roy Jenkins, had many problems to cope with in 1974, their year of minority government, and they had more than their fair share of political violence.

14 The Social Contract

The General Election of October 1974

Harold Wilson called a General Election on 10 October 1974 in order to convert a minority into a majority Government in Parliament. He had perhaps been hoping for a continued rise in popularity, as had happened in 1966, when he had converted his 1964 overall majority of four into one of ninety-six. During the late summer of 1974, however, the Labour lead of 16 per cent in June had begun to decline sharply. He only caught it just in time and, though he gained eighteen seats from the Conservatives, he had only an overall majority of three (or five if he assumed that Gerry Fitt, of the Northern Ireland SDLP, would always vote with him). The narrowness of the majority was to give him and his successor constant trouble.

The full figures were:[1]

	Seats	Votes	%
Labour	319	11,457,079	39·2
Conservative	277	10,464,817	35·8
Liberal	13	5,346,754	18·3
Welsh Nationalists	3 }	1,005,938	3·5
Scottish Nationalists	11 }		
Northern Ireland	12	702,094	2·4
National Front	—	113,579	0·4
CPGB Com. S.	—	17,426	0·1 (—)
Others	—	81,491	0·3
Total	635	29,189,178	100

The Liberal vote declined, but not disastrously. The Communist Party (presumably because of lack of funds for two sets of lost deposits within a year) fielded fewer candidates and so got fewer votes—only 17,426. By contrast, the ninety National

Front candidates polled 113,579, drawing support from all parties, but particularly from Labour in some working-class constituencies with high immigrant populations in London and the Midlands.

The most significant gains were those of the Scottish Nationalists, whose share of the vote in Scotland rose from 22 to 30 per cent, promoting some uneasiness about the long-term reliability of North Sea Oil revenues for the British Government. And the prospects of power-sharing in Northern Ireland were set back by a further swing of the Protestant vote to hard line 'loyalists'.

Inflation and lack of confidence

The decline in the British economy which had begun in February 1974 gathered momentum after Labour's re-election in October on almost all fronts—rising inflation, falling production, falling industrial investment and rising unemployment.

Inflation (measured as an increase in the Retail Price Index from its value one year previously) was running at 12 per cent in February 1974; it reached 17 per cent in July 1974, 20 per cent in February 1975 and peaked at 27 per cent in August 1975. The index of industrial production (1970 = 100) was 110·1 in the second quarter of 1974 and bottomed at 99·7 by the third quarter of 1975. Fixed investment by manufacturing industry, having been high through 1973, began to decline in 1974 and to plunge disastrously in 1975. Unemployment rose from 577,000 when Wilson came to power in February 1974, and had doubled to 1,132,100 by the end of 1975.[2]

Amongst this almost unrelieved gloom there were a few glimmers of hope for the future. The balance of payments deficit, having risen from £835 million in 1973 to £3,668 million in 1974, fell in 1975 to £1,687 million. Though a major reason for the fall was the rather melancholy one that the slump in production and consumption reduced the import bill, an encouraging feature was that the deficit in 1975 was accounted for almost entirely by oil imports.[3]

On a more constructive note, the Government on 31 January 1975 introduced a bill to set up the National Enterprise Board (NEB) with initial capital of £1,000 million, as a means of infusing more public capital into industry. In some cases the NEB

assumed 100 per cent ownership (e.g. of Rolls-Royce) or 95%
(of British Leyland). In other cases it took 50 per cent (e.g. of
Ferranti) or a minority holding (e.g. 24 per cent of International
Computer (Holdings) Ltd).

This method of public investment marked a new line of action
by the Labour Party, and was really an extension of the highly
successful joint investment in BP, in which the British Government had owned just under 50% since the 1930s. While the
Government had always had a nominee on the BP Board, it had
not in practice interfered with the commercial decisions and the
public had thus shared in the large profits made by the company—a very much more successful undertaking than any of the
nationalized industries. The appointment of a successful indus-
trialist, Sir Don (later Lord) Ryder as first chairman of the NEB
suggested that the Government intended to leave the Board
free to operate under commercial rather than political considerations.

In January, too, the stock exchange began a sudden and rapid
revival after the FT Index had bottomed at 146. It doubled (to
292) by March 1975 and topped 400 in January 1976. This was
mistaken by some people as an indication of revival of confidence
in investment but this (as indicated above) was not so. The stock
exchange merely reflected a realization in the City of London
(particularly amongst the big investing institutions such as
merchant banks and insurance companies) that the Government did not intend to exert excessive political control over industry; nor to indulge in the extensive nationalization programmes
which the left-wing-dominated Labour Party National Executive
Committee had been demanding, but rather to encourage and
participate in new investment and allow industry to recover its
profitability and so regenerate its own investment. Less than
5 per cent new industrial investment is by new share issues;
10 per cent is from bank and other loans; over 80 per cent is
from reinvestment of retained profits.[4] So the stock market rose
because the big institutions had curtailed their *selling* of industrial
shares to other buyers. It was to be two more years before they
began any substantial increase in new investment in British
industry, but at least they stopped pulling out of it.

This revival of confidence was also a reflection of the belief
that the Government's Social Contract with the trade unions was
going to succeed and that, if it did, inflation would at least not

reach the galloping levels of the Weimar Republic or Latin America.

The origins of the Social Contract

The concept of the Social Contract (or rather this particular application of Rousseau's eighteenth-century concept of the relationship between government and people) was developed by the Labour Party in opposition during the Heath administration of 1970–4. The first record of its use in this context was by Anthony Wedgwood Benn in *The New Politics: A Socialist Renaissance*, a 1970 Fabian Society tract in which he wrote:

> It is arguable that what has really happened has amounted to such a breakdown in the social contract, upon which parliamentary democracy by universal suffrage was based, that that contract now needs to be renegotiated on a basis that shares power more widely, before it can win general assent again.[5]

The phrase was used again by James Callaghan at the Labour Party Conference in 1973 in the context of the agreement for co-operation worked out between the Labour Party and the TUC, of which Jack Jones, of the TGWU, was one of the principal authors. It thereafter became the cornerstone of the Labour Party manifestos for the two 1974 General Elections.

In the October 1974 manifesto the contract was spelled out. In return for price control, food subsidies and a freeze on rent increases, coupled with the inclusion of certain items in the proposed legislation on industrial relations, the trade unions had promised to moderate their wage claims. On 24 June 1974, the TUC unanimously agreed that negotiators should seek wage rises only to the extent needed to keep up with the cost of living, after tax and taking account of threshold payments. They also agreed that collective bargaining should be based on the following guidelines:

(1) Twelve-month intervals between major increases.

(2) Priority for agreements having beneficial effects on unit cost and efficiency, for reforming pay structures and for improving job security.

(3) Low pay target of £25 a week minimum basic rate.

(4) Elimination of discrimination (notably against women) and improvement of certain non-wage benefits such as sick pay, pension schemes and progress towards a four-week paid annual holiday.

(5) Full use of ACAS in solving disputes.

At the TUC's Annual Congress in September 1974 the Amalgamated Union of Engineering Workers put down a resolution rejecting the contract. The resolution was moved by Ken Gill, a Communist member of the union executive, and the CPGB thereafter referred to it as 'The Social Con-Trick'[6]—a phrase also taken up by the Labour Party Marxists such as Arthur Scargill. In the subsequent debate Len Murray described it as 'the only way forward which stands any chance at all in the country at the present time'. The AUEW eventually withdrew their resolution without a vote 'without retracting' and 'in the interests of unity and the return of a Labour government'.[7]

In the same month Michael Foot said:

> The Labour Party and the trade unions, united as never before in the way they believe they can serve the nation, offer a combination of cures for the immense problems which certainly face us. They are designed to produce a new industrial climate, a much wider sense of social justice, a new confidence that the Government will keep faith with the people and that the people as a whole will therefore respond to the national need.[8]

The Social Contract was a brave attempt to stem the flood. In both Stages 1 and 2 (i.e. until late 1977) it induced the great majority of workers to accept a degree of restraint which amounted to a steady fall in their real standard of living, in a period of massive and rising unemployment—a remarkable achievement in political leadership, whether right or wrong, by any standards.

Stage 1

Stage 1 was launched in a pamphlet delivered through the letter box of every household, *Attack on Inflation: A Policy for Survival*,[9] being a summary of the Government's White Paper which had been published on 11 July. Setting the target of reducing inflation to single figures by the end of 1976, the Government and the TUC agreed to limit wage and salary rises to £6 a week between 1 August 1975 and 1 August 1976. Anyone earning £8,500 or more would get no increase at all. As with previous incomes policies, there was to be a twelve-month interval between major pay rises.

The choice of the £6 figure (as opposed to a percentage) was avowedly aimed to give the greatest benefit to the lowest paid—reflecting the influence of Jack Jones, whose TGWU contained a high proportion of unskilled workers. It was recognized, however, that this would not keep up with inflation and that even the lowest paid would suffer a fall in their standard of living. A £6 rise for a man earning £24 a week would be a 25 per cent rise. If he had children he would pay little or no income tax, but this rise would still not match the current inflation rate of 27 per cent unless he also increased his earnings from overtime. For a man on the average manual worker's earnings (then about £50 a week) £6 was only 12 per cent; and income tax would in most cases reduce this to about 10 per cent, leaving him with the prospect of a very harsh fall in living standards. Yet the overwhelming majority of workers accepted the Government and TUC lead and public opinion polls showed widespread support for it.

At its Annual Congress the TUC endorsed the incomes policy, including the £6 limit, by a large majority (6,945,000 for and 3,375,000 against). As so often before, the tone had been set by the miners, who had voted for it by 60·5 per cent to 39·5 per cent in August 1975.

Unemployment, however, continued to rise. Reaching the million mark in August 1975, it passed 1¼ million and rose to nearly 1½ million (6·1 per cent of the work force) by January 1976. The Stage 1 White Paper made it clear that this would be inevitable so long as inflation continued, since rising costs were causing a high rate of bankruptcies and redundancies. As Harold Wilson put it in bold type on the back of his pamphlet to every household: 'One man's pay rise is not only another man's price rise: it might also cost him his own job—or his neighbour's job.' All the same, lower spending power also lowered consumer demand and thus itself contributed to bankruptcies and redundancies.

Though it failed to stem unemployment, the incomes policy did have its effect on inflation. The Government estimated that the £6 rise would add 10 or 11 per cent to the national wages bill (including overtime) but in the event it added 14 per cent. Labour costs only accounted for just over 50 per cent of total price increases in 1975 (import costs accounting for 21 per cent)[10] but the wage restraint in Stage 1 did contribute to a halving of the inflation rate from 27 per cent in August 1975 to 13·8 per cent in August 1976.

The Employment Protection Act, 1975

An important element in securing the co-operation of the trade unions was the Employment Protection Act (EPA) which added to the powers already given to them under the 1974 Trade Union and Labour Relations Act (TULRA—see Chapter 10). The EPA was introduced as a Bill in Parliament in August 1975 (concurrently with the Stage 1 White Paper) and came into force bit by bit during 1976. The EPA will be examined in operation in Chapter 16 in the context of the prolonged 1976–7 Grunwick dispute, but a brief look at some of its provisions will be appropriate at this stage.

As was mentioned in Chapter 10, the EPA greatly strengthened the ability of unions to obtain recognition from an employer as the official negotiating body for his workers, and to negotiate an agreement or informal arrangement with the employers for a closed shop. Should the employer decline to reach such an agreement, the union could apply through ACAS and the CAC for an 'award' of recognition. Under the Act the employer 'shall observe' this award, but it did not specify how he could be compelled to do so.

The EPA obliged employers to disclose information required for collective bargaining to representatives of recognized unions. The Act did, however, leave the employer with certain safeguards. He did not have to disclose information which would be against the interests of national security, or would contravene another law, or cause substantial injury to the employer's undertaking for reasons other than its effect on collective bargaining; nor information relating specially to an individual (unless the individual were agreeable) nor information which had been communicated to the employer in confidence, or obtained by him for the purpose of legal proceedings.

Most of the EPA concerned the rights of employees. They were protected from dismissal for joining a trade union (though they could be sacked—and in practice would have to be sacked—for not joining a union in a closed shop). It included other regulations about unfair dismissal, re-employment or compensation and about minimum notice. It required an employer to make guarantee payments for not more than five days in any three months for loss of work due to short time or lay-offs (though not if this were caused by a trade dispute involving any employee of the same firm or of an associated firm). And it specified time off, including time off without loss of pay in working hours for union meetings and activities (though this did not, of course, cover strikes as time off with pay). The Act also enabled people losing work as a result of a strike to receive unemployment benefit unless they themselves were participating in or directly interested in the dispute.

The EPA required employers to consult with representatives of trade unions concerned before making any members of those unions redundant. Such consultations had to begin at least 90 days before the first dismissal where 100 or more workers were to be dismissed in a 90-day period, or at least 60 days before the first dismissal where 10 or more workers were to be dismissed in a period of 30 days or less. The Act confirmed the scales of redundancy payments laid down in the Redundancy Payments Act of 1965, and extended and updated it to include a maximum redundancy payment of £2,400 free of tax for a man between 41 and 65 with not less than 20 years' service. It also gave a statutory basis for a temporary employment subsidy for employers willing to defer redundancies.

Concurrently, the Labour Party used its overall majority to introduce some of the provisions of TULRA (see Chapter 10) which had been excluded by Parliament—notably the extension of immunity from damages for inducing another person to break a commercial contract. In a guide to TULRA and the EPA, the Labour Research Department (which is run by members of the Labour Party's Tribune Group) commented: 'This crucial protection for union officials is a very valuable improvement of the original S3 of the 1906 Act because it now covers commercial contracts as well as contracts of employment, and thus protects action such as the blacking of goods.'[11]

The anxieties of employers and others about the extent to which this power might be exercised were discussed on pages 126 and 127, and an example of its use in the Grunwick dispute is described in Chapter 16.

15 The End of an Incomes Policy

James Callaghan takes over

In March 1976 Harold Wilson celebrated his sixtieth birthday, and he judged this to be an appropriate moment to retire to the back benches and invite the Labour Party to elect a new leader. Unemployment, after reaching 1,430,369 (6·1 per cent) in January, had fallen to 1,284,915 (5·5 per cent) in March. The rate of inflation was falling fast (from 27 per cent in August 1975 to 12·6 per cent in April 1976). Industrial production, having fallen below the 1970 level in the third quarter of 1975, had begun to climb again.[1]

The Labour Party's method of electing a new leader was a series of eliminating ballots by the Parliamentary Labour Party (that is, by the Labour MPs elected at the previous election). The final ballot was to be between the two most popular survivors from the previous one, to ensure that the winner enjoyed the support of an unequivocal majority of Labour Party MPs.

The process highlighted the division of the party into right and left—though none of the thirty or so members who publicly advocated a Marxist society in fact stood for election, as none would have attracted more than a humiliatingly small vote.

The left was represented in the first ballot by Michael Foot and Anthony Wedgwood Benn. Benn's views were equivocal, and he could best be described as a 'populist' who welcomed the participation of Marxists in the Labour Party without wishing to end Parliamentary democracy. Foot was above all things a parliamentarian, with radical but certainly not Marxist views. The centre candidates were James Callaghan (Foreign Secretary), Denis Healey (Chancellor of the Exchequer) and Anthony Crosland. The right of the party was represented by Roy Jenkins. The left were delighted when Michael Foot led on the first ballot: he gained $43\frac{1}{2}$ per cent of the vote on the final ballot to James Callaghan's $57\frac{1}{2}$ per cent. Full results were:

	1st ballot (25 March)	2nd ballot (29 March)	3rd ballot (5 April)
James Callaghan	84	141	176
Michael Foot	90	133	137
Roy Jenkins	56	—	—
Denis Healey	37	38	—
Anthony Wedgwood Benn	30	—	—
Anthony Crosland	17	—	—

The other leading figure on the right of the party, Mrs Shirley Williams, declined to stand. She later ran (in October) for election as deputy leader but was defeated by Michael Foot by 166 votes to 128, reflecting the continuous desire of the PLP to keep the left wing within the party rather than precipitate a split.

Stage 2

Callaghan at once set about introducing Stage 2 of the anti-inflation policy. Healey, who continued as Chancellor, introduced his Budget on 6 April. Declaring a target of reducing inflation to single figures during 1977, he proposed to make income tax concessions conditional on acceptance of Stage 2 pay limits. These were agreed between the Government and the TUC on 5 May. During the year 1 August 1976–31 July 1977 (Stage 2), it was agreed that there would be an upper limit for wage rises of £4 a week with a lower limit of £2·50; that the guideline should be an increase of 5 per cent in total earnings; that the twelve-month interval between major increases should continue to apply; and that the proposed tax concessions would be backdated to 1 April.

Controls on prices and profits were to continue, 'but the price control regime must be so modified as to encourage investment and jobs in our economy'. The Government realized that British industry was fast falling behind its competitors because of failure to replace outdated plant, and that this could be put right only by profits providing funds for reinvestment. The raising of public funds on the scale needed for investment through the NEB was incompatible with a policy of reducing taxation and cutting public expenditure, so they had little option.

The Government estimated that the guidelines would be exceeded and that total earnings would rise by 6½–7 per cent. *The Economist*, however, estimated that earnings would rise by 9–10 per cent and prices by 10–14 per cent, so that industrial workers' standards of living would continue to fall. (In the event, during the first nine months of Stage 2, earnings were to rise by 7½ per cent and prices by 14½ per cent,[3] so pay restraint worked better than price restraint, and the fall in the standard of living proved even greater than had been feared.)

On 16 June 1976 a Special Congress of the TUC gave a massive vote of approval to Stage 2—by 9,202,000 votes to 531,000. This vote of 95 per cent—compared with 67 per cent a year previously for Stage 1—was immensely encouraging for the new cabinet.

The collapse of the pound

Nevertheless, like the Conservatives during the earlier days of hope in 1973, the Government were sitting on two time-bombs: one was that their tiny majority in Parliament was threatened by a voting swing to the Conservatives revealed in by-elections (Labour had a fright at Rotherham in June with a 13·3 per cent swing against them and far worse was to follow): and the second was that international confidence in the pound was declining, so that foreign investors were withdrawing their money.

The run on the pound was caused partly by the realization that British industry was becoming less competitive owing to low productivity, poor industrial relations and lack of investment, with the result that foreign investors were investing their money elsewhere; and partly by the knowledge that Britain had been living on borrowed money since the quadrupling of the oil price in 1974—at a rate of roughly 5 per cent of her GNP. The Government were reluctant to curtail this borrowing as that would mean further cuts in public expenditure, an increase in unemployment in the public sector and more social and industrial unrest.

The pound, kept at around $2·40 until it was floated in 1971, had been drifting downwards at a steady but manageable rate, but on 5 March 1976 it fell below $2 for the first time. On 22 July the Government announced cuts in public expenditure of £1,012 million, but any good this might have done was soon nullified by the publication on 10 September of plans by the National Executive Committee (NEC) of the Labour Party to nationalize banks and insurance companies. This caused no surprise in Britain, where it was generally appreciated that the left wing dominated the NEC and that its decisions had little influence on the Cabinet or the Parliamentary Labour Party. The Cabinet firmly repudiated the plans, but the relationship between the Cabinet, the Parliamentary Labour Party and the NEC was not so well understood overseas as in Britain. By 27 October the pound had fallen to a record low level of $1·5710.

The Government had announced on 29 September that it was applying to the International Monetary Fund (IMF) for a loan of £2,300 million, which would not be subject to the unpredictable withdrawals of capital by Arab and other foreign investors. An IMF team came to Britain to set terms for this loan and agreement was announced on 15 December. To meet the IMF conditions, public expenditure was cut by a further £2,500 million. The Government sold £500 million of its share in BP and increased taxes on alcohol and tobacco. The pound gradually recovered over the next six months to $1·72.

Minority Government and the Lib–Lab pact

Late 1976 and early 1977 saw a series of disastrous by-elections for Labour. In November 1976 they contested three 'safe' seats on the same day and lost two of them. At Walsall North there was a record swing of 27·3 per cent from Labour to Conservative but this was partly explained by the fact that the previous Labour member, John Stonehouse, had just been convicted of some rather sordid financial dealings. The swing at Workington was 14·8 per cent and at Newcastle North, the only seat they retained, 10·6 per cent. Their overall majority in Parliament had vanished.

The crisis in Parliament came in March 1977. The Scottish and Welsh Nationalists, disgruntled with lack of progress on devolution, indicated that they would vote against the Government in a confidence motion. Since a General Election would clearly have resulted in a massive Conservative victory, Callaghan took the only possible course for survival and approached the Liberals. The Liberals declined to join a coalition, but made a pact not to vote against the Government on certain conditions

—notably that further large-scale nationalization would be suspended and that the Government would resist union pressure to abandon its pay policy.

This was a marriage of convenience between two desperate parties. Neither could afford to face a General Election. By-election swings indicated that the Liberals' 5·3 million votes would be drastically cut, while Labour would lose at least a hundred seats. This was confirmed in another by-election at Stechford on 31 March, just after the pact was announced, which Labour lost in a swing of 20·7 per cent to the Conservatives and the Liberals fell back into fourth place behind the National Front.

Tribune group members, already furious at the conditions imposed for the IMF loan, were bitterly resentful at being forced to abandon many cherished socialist ambitions for the duration of the pact, but a large proportion of them held marginal seats which would be lost in an election. After some angry confrontations at Parliamentary Labour Party meetings they accepted the political realities of their plight.

Wealth

Between July 1975 and October 1976 the Royal Commission on the Distribution of Incomes and Wealth (the 'Diamond Commission') published four reports.[4] These were packed with detail (they ran into over 1,000 pages in all with large numbers of tables and charts) and provided by far the best source of data ever produced on this very complex subject. Inevitably, any digest of conclusions must contain approximations, but certain facts do stand out very clearly. The unequal distribution of wealth and income between the small number of very rich and the great majority of wage-earners is a constant source of political and industrial strife. But in practice an even greater source of strife (and of governments' inability to control inflation and unemployment) are the differentials between groups of workers. As was described in Chapters 3 to 5, the real fury at Saltley and Shrewsbury was between regular workers, usually union members on a weekly wage with bonuses and overtime, and independent workers whose earnings could not be controlled either by legislation or union agreements. And the most intractable problems faced by the Callaghan Government in their attempt to maintain

an incomes policy in 1977 lay in the bitterness and frustration
of technicians and skilled workers at the erosion of the differentials to which they felt that their skill and training should
entitle them.

The first essential in understanding these problems is to recognize that wealth (possessions) and income (earned and unearned)
are very different things.

As defined in the Diamond Report, wealth generally consists of
marketable assets—houses, land, cars, jewellery, stocks, shares
etc. but does *not* include rights which cannot be sold, such as
pension rights. Diamond did attempt to produce data for five
different series of classifications[5], two of which (series D and E)
did include occupational and state pension rights, but figures
were not easy to interpret and Diamond found that they did not
make very much difference to the overall distribution of wealth.
Most of his figures were therefore based upon two series, both
covering the adult population (over 18). Series A was based on
Inland Revenue estate duty statistics, covering 18·8 million, just
under half the adult population. Series B covered the entire adult
population, 39·2 million, on the assumption that only 18·8 million have any marketable assets and that the remaining 20·4
million have no wealth at all.[6] Though this is obviously inaccurate,
the inaccuracy may be less significant than it seems in that people
with possessions do also have unquantifiable assets (such as the
prospect of growth in value of property), so the percentages reflected in Series B do probably give the fairest practicable reflection of the *proportional* distribution of wealth. The figures quoted
below are therefore Series B figures covering the 39·2 million
adults in Great Britain.

Ownership of personal wealth, 1960 and 1974

The richest	1960	1974
(a) Wealthiest 1%	38·2%	25·3%
(b) Next wealthiest 4% (2–5)	26·1%	24·6%
(c) Next wealthiest 5% (6–10)	12·4%	16·1%
Total		
(d) Wealthiest 10% ((a)+(b)+(c))	76·7%	66·0%
(e) Next wealthiest 10%	13·1%	19·5%
(f) Poorest 80%	10·2%	14·5%
	100%	100%

The first main conclusion is that the distribution of *wealth* is much less equitable than the distribution of *income* (which is discussed separately below). The second is that wealth has been redistributed fairly fast, but rather from the very rich to those already fairly prosperous than from the prosperous to the poor.[7]

Diamond estimates the total marketable personal wealth in Great Britain to be £157,062 million.[8] Distributed as above for 1974 this works out as follows:[9]

Distribution of wealth

1974 The richest	Number of people	Total wealth £ million	Average per head £	Change since 1960 (1974 value) £	
(a) Wealthiest 1%	392,000	39,736	101,360	Loss	51,690
(b) Next 4% (2–5)	1,568,000	38,637	24,640	Loss	1,500
(c) Next 5% (6–10)	1,960,000	25,287	12,900	Gain	2,964
Total					
(d) Wealthiest 10%	3,920,000	103,661	26,444	Loss	4,287
(e) Next 10% (11–20)	3,920,000	30,627	7,813	Gain	2,564
(f) Poorest 80%	31,360,000	22,774	726	Gain	215
Grand total	39,200,000	157,062	4,007		

From this it is possible to assess some theoretical figures as to how much there is to go round if we were to attempt total equalization of these assets. The poorest 80 per cent have average assets of only £726[10] but if everyone's wealth were pooled they would each have, in theory, the overall average of £4,007 worth of marketable assets—that is, an increase of £3,281.

It is only possible to make a rough guess at the difference this would make to incomes. If all these assets were invested in such a way as to earn 10 per cent return the incomes of the poorest 80 per cent would be increased by an unearned income of £328 per year or £6 a week. This is, of course, even more theoretical since the state would still, presumably, have to extract the revenue in some way which it now obtains by taxing the rich. Thus the actual gain to the poor (even if it were practicable to do such a redistribution) would be even smaller. The only function of figures such as these is to indicate the relatively small effect of even the most drastic redistribution. This, however, does not alter the fact that the inequities are excessive, have an abrasive effect on society, and are a major stumbling-block in negotiating any kind of incomes policy (see pages 185 to 189).

Incomes

The breakdown of incomes, both in the Diamond Report and in other Government statistics, deals with a different number of people—in this case 20·8 million instead of 39·2 million, because income data is only available from income tax assessments and most families are taxed as a single tax unit. Thus, the number of tax units is 20·8 million.

Diamond shows the lower limit for each range (e.g. of the richest 1 per cent) but figures have been interpolated to give an estimate of the average for each range. Diamond's figures are also based on the tax year 1973–4 but for the present context (with particular relevance to the discussion of differentials below) an attempt has been made to adjust these for inflation of incomes during 1974–6. An explanation of the method of adjustment is given in the notes on page 305.[11]

Estimated income distribution, 1976
For all individuals or families

Percentage of tax units* in 1976 (estimated from Diamond Report)	Average £ per year Before tax	After tax	Average £ per week Before tax	After tax	Number of incomes (tax units)
The richest					
Richest 0·1%	27,500	10,500	529	202	20,800
Richest 1%	9,900	6,300	190	121	208,000
Next 4% (2–5)	6,600	5,000	127	96	832,000
Next 5%	5,200	3,750	100	72	1·04 million
All tax units					
Richest 10%	6,250	4,550	120	88	2·08 million
Second ,, (11–20)	4,500	3,500	87	67	,, ,,
Third ,, (21–30)	3,800	3,050	73	57	,, ,,
Fourth ,, (31–40)	3,200	2,600	62	50	,, ,,
Fifth ,, (41–50)	2,850	2,350	55	45	,, ,,
Sixth ,, (51–60)	2,500	2,100	48	40	,, ,,
Seventh ,, (61–70)	2,100	1,800	40	35	,, ,,
Eighth ,, (71–80)	1,750	1,500	34	29	,, ,,
Ninth ,, (81–90)	1,400	1,200	27	23	,, ,,
Poorest 10% (91–100)	1,000	1,000	19	19	,, ,,
Average overall	3,000	2,400	58	46	20·8 million

* A tax unit is any individual paying income tax or a family which pays tax as a unit

As a rough check on these figures—and to carry them forward into 1977—the following may act as a guide.[12]

Earnings per week—average	*July 1976*	*April 1977*
All married men with two children		
Gross earnings (including overtime)	£74·08	£79·63
Nett after tax	£58·62	£62·47

These are for both manual and non-manual workers. Male manual workers (with two children) in July 1976 averaged £7 less: about £67 gross, £53 after tax. The overall average of £58 gross, £46 after tax includes younger (unmarried) people, women workers, pensioners etc.

Diamond also examined the effects of the 'social wage'—i.e. the direct and indirect benefits in cash and in kind, such as social security, health service, state education, school meals, council house subsidies, rent rebates and food subsidies. These made a very large difference to the family incomes of the poorest 10 per cent, slightly reduced the net share of the richest third but had, predictably, little effect on the middle incomes.[13]

As with wealth, the scope for equalization is limited. If, for example, it were possible to impose further taxes on all the richest 10 per cent so that no one in the country received more, earned or unearned, than £3,500 (£67 a week) after tax, all that this would yield to spread around the remaining 90 per cent would be £2·50 a week per family. As a wage increase on the overall average of £58 this would work out at little more than 4 per cent—an offer which most wage negotiators would describe as 'derisory'. Yet—without higher productivity—this is all there would be to go round.

Nevertheless, as with redistribution of wealth, the psychological factor is more important than the material one. With wage and pension increases in 1976–7 falling well behind inflation, the average family suffered a fall in standard of living equivalent to £4 a week.[14] So long as there are even 20,000 people, one in a thousand, with incomes of the order of £27,500, it is not unreasonable for the other 999 to say: 'OK—let them tighten their belts first. Then I'll tighten mine. I don't see why my wife and kids should suffer so long as they're getting ten times more than we are.'

Differentials

In reality, however, the main pressure is not for equalization but for differentials. When, in the summer of 1977, the miners called for a wage of £135, they were asking to be included in the richest 5 per cent, at more than double the average man's earnings. They felt that the skills and hardships of their job justified it.

The differentials in the engineering industry in June 1976 were recorded by the Labour Research Department as follows:[15]

	per year		per week	
Average earnings	*Gross*	*After tax*	*Gross*	*After tax*
Managing director	15,041	7,972	289	153
General manager	11,189	6,769	215	130
Company director	7,043	5,001	135	96
Chief engineer	5,769	4,269	111	82
Production controller	5,281	4,014	102	77
Skilled worker	3,432	2,756	66	53
Unskilled worker	2,704	2,236	52	43

Looking first at the differentials between managerial and shop-floor earnings: the average-sized firm in England employs about 800 people—roughly the same size as a section of a bigger firm controlled by the general manager in the table above. His salary in 1976 (£11,189) was about 3¼ times that of one of his skilled workers (£3,432) or 4¼ times that of the unskilled worker (£2,704), that is about 3½ times the average of all his shop-floor workers—before tax. After tax the ratio was about 2¾ to 1.

This differential was low by European standards. It was even low compared with the People's Republic of China, where the manager got a higher gross differential (4 to 1) over the average shop-floor earnings—and, since there is no income tax in China, his take-home differential was also 4 to 1. Between shop-floor workers themselves, too, the differential in China was higher than in Britain—but were based on political attitude and experience rather than skill. Under their 'eight-grade system' an experienced worker in China got three times as much as a newly joined young one.[16]

British executives pay was, in fact, not only low in terms of its differential, but also in terms of purchasing power, compared with equivalent grades in other countries. In June 1977 the *Daily Telegraph* published figures for comparison with other countries under the headline 'BRITISH EXECUTIVES BOTTOM OF WORLD PAY LEAGUE'.

Comparative pay of higher executives

	Gross pay	After tax	What that buys	Gross pay	After tax	What that buys	Gross pay	After tax	What that buys
U.K.	8,200	6,068	6,068	10,900	7,497	7,497	14,500	8,929	8,929
France	18,384	15,610	10,006	26,984	21,714	13,919	39,613	30,164	19,335
Germany	23,731	16,182	9,463	34,421	21,551	12,603	45,017	26,600	15,555
Holland	21,302	13,002	8,026	30,175	15,886	9,806	42,742	19,574	12,083
Sweden	19,000	8,467	4,784	25,760	9,627	5,439	34,667	11,067	6,253
USA	21,540	14,651	11,536	28,488	17,500	13,780	35,465	19,942	15,702

Of the countries listed, only Sweden showed lower purchasing power but the article suggested that differences in what was and was not included probably made Sweden and the UK roughly on a par.[17]

The salaries of working managers have not, however, generally been a cause of much contention in Britain. There is greater resentment over fringe benefits. Diamond recorded that in 1975 managers with a gross salary of £15,000 received fringe benefits worth nearly £4,000 (26 per cent).[18] By contrast the *Department of Employment Gazette* reported that manual workers received superannuation and other fringe benefits worth only about £220 (4·7 per cent).[19]

Another source of contention is unearned income because, once again, most of it seems to go to those who are already the most highly paid. The richest 1 per cent, whose incomes in 1976 averaged £10,000, got 30 per cent of it from investments, and of the £6,600 incomes of the top 10 per cent, 13 per cent was unearned.[20] The man who gets it claims that it is not 'unearned' as he has saved his capital from his earnings, but the man on the shop floor will say that the fact that the managers or the shareholders had enough surplus income to save was due to *his* efforts, rather than theirs. There is some weight in both these arguments.

The greatest bitterness, however, is over differentials between different groups on the shop floor and between supervisors and workers. The bitterness arose directly from the pay restrictions imposed in 1975 and 1976 (particularly the flat rate £6 increase in Stage 1) which were designed specifically to benefit low-paid workers. As a result, junior managers often found the men they supervised taking home more (by way of overtime and bonuses) than they were themselves, and skilled men who had been through several years of training or poorly paid apprenticeship often earned little more than unskilled process workers with only a few weeks' experience.

Thus, in June 1971, the average weekly earnings of a skilled engineering worker were 38·1 per cent above those of an unskilled worker but by June 1976 this differential had fallen to 26·9 per cent. Civil engineers, accountants, purchasing officers, and draughtsmen also saw their differentials over manual workers eroded.[21]

These resentments boiled over in 1977 with an expensive stoppage of work at British Leyland caused by a strike of skilled toolmakers and a major disruption of Easter holiday traffic by a strike of British Airways maintenance engineers (the latter costing the country £31 million).

It became clear during 1977 that the Social Contract was going to founder not because of resentment against differentials but because of frustration at the lack of them. The skilled man and the specialists knew that, despite their small numbers, they could bring the work of many thousands of process workers to a halt, and were determined to use their bargaining power. It was they who led the demand for a return to free collective bargaining.

The end of the Social Contract

During the trade union conference season in the summer of 1977, one union after another repudiated any extension of agreed wage limits negotiated between the TUC and the Government and for a return to free collective bargaining. In July, with the NUM and then the TGWU taking the decision, the Government had no option but to abandon the attempt. On 15 July, after a final and abortive round of talks with the TUC, Denis Healey announced a fresh Budget, reducing income tax at the bottom level from 35 to 34 per cent (instead of 33 per cent he had promised if the TUC had agreed to a maximum figure for wage settlements) and he also increased the tax-free allowance to benefit the lowest paid. A married man would not now pay any tax on the first £1,295 of his income. In exchange, the Chancellor called for voluntary restraint in order to keep the total increase in the nation's *earnings* bill down to 10 per cent in the hope of reducing the inflation rate from 17·7 per cent to under 10 per cent by July 1978. Since earnings would include an element of 'wage drift' from bonuses, overtime, redesignation of jobs, etc., this could not be achieved unless the rises in basic wages were a good deal less than 10 per cent.

The nation accepted the end of the Social Contract with equanimity. For different reasons, it was acclaimed in Parliament by both the right wing of the Conservative Party (as a move towards *laissez-faire*) and by the left wing of the Labour Party (more scope for trade union power). The moderate trade union leadership also welcomed it, since they had been severely restricted by having committed themselves to fixed wage limits for a year ahead, in their ability to retain the leadership of their rank and file, leaving themselves no way of being seen to be 'fighting like tigers' (see page 103).

Though the nation accepted the idea of the end of the Social Contract, and public opinion polls supported the 10 per cent voluntary target as 'about right', few accepted it as applying to themselves. Miners' leaders, both moderate and militant, regarded it as out of the question, and so did other groups as disparate as doctors and railwaymen.

The Government declared its intention of withholding funds from nationalized industries if their boards concealed higher wage settlements, but had little to say about how they would handle the subsequent threats of major stoppages of public utilities. It was also suggested that the Minister of Consumer Affairs would use his power to withhold approval for price rises from private firms which made wage settlements above the norm.

The end of the Social Contract was cautiously welcomed by the CBI, which saw advantages in being able to reward key men by higher differentials, while rising unemployment could be expected to impose some restraint on a wages explosion amongst semi-skilled and unskilled workers. Most employers, however, were sceptical about keeping the rise in their overall earnings bill down to 10 per cent. Most had already allowed in their budgets for rises of 15 to 20 per cent. The investing institutions —as reflected in stock exchange prices—also seemed content.

The Government's strategy was to control inflation by controlling the money supply. After seven years of almost continuous wage restraint by the Heath, Wilson and Callaghan Governments, sometimes statutory, sometimes by voluntary agreement in advance, everyone seemed to have had enough. There had been but one period of eighteen months (1974–5) in which re-

straint had, in effect, been lifted, and the memory of the con-
sequent 27 per cent rate of inflation was fresh in people's minds.
It was on this memory that the Prime Minister pinned his hopes.
There was also, as in 1969, an element of political desperation; it
would be some time before wage rises were fully reflected in price
rises and this might present the only hope of the Government
finding a 'window' of relative popularity in which to hold an
election.[22]

During that summer, however, many people in Britain had
become more concerned about another industrial problem—a re-
surgence of violence on the picket lines. After five years of relatively peaceful picketing since Saltley and Shrewsbury, a violent
confrontation involving as many as 18,000 demonstrators and
3,500 police built up outside the Grunwick film-processing
laboratory in North London.

16 Grunwick

The teacup and the storm

Between August 1976 and the autumn of 1977, the conflict around the small mail-order film processing firm of Grunwick in North London regularly hit the headlines. The conflict reached its peak between 13 and 24 June. During these two weeks of massed and violent picketing, 297 people were arrested, including a number of public figures, such as left-wing Labour MP Mrs Audrey Wise and the Yorkshire miners' leader Arthur Scargill. During the same period, ninety-seven police were injured, one seriously. Violence continued for a further two weeks, culminating in a mass picket and demonstration on 11 July, in which 18,000 people took part and 3,500 police were on duty; there were more arrests and injuries. Altogether, there were more mass pickets, more police on duty, more arrests and more injuries at Grunwick than in either of the most violent picketing incidents in 1972 at Saltley and Shrewsbury. The 1972 strikes involved the whole coal industry (250,000 men) and the building industry (2 million). Yet the Grunwick conflict was centred around one small firm with a maximum staff, much of it temporary and seasonal, of a little over 400—and only 270 at the time of the peak of violence in June 1977.

The explanation, of course, was that Grunwick raised an immense number of issues of principle, and, in particular, provided a test of the Labour Government's industrial relations legislation of 1974/6 in action—the Trade Union and Labour Relations Act (TULRA) and the Employment Protection Act (EPA).

It raised the issues of the right to join a union, the right not to join a union and the right to work; the procedures for trade unions to establish recognition by an employer as a negotiating authority for his workers; and the procedures provided in the

EPA for resolution of recognition disputes by the Advisory Conciliation and Arbitration Service (ACAS).

Grunwick also demonstrated the shortcomings of the picketing laws and of their relationship with other laws covering obstruction, intimidation, violence, threatening and insulting behaviour and the right of assembly; and the lack of definition of what constituted peaceful persuasion, of what was a reasonable number of pickets to exercise it, and at what point or in what circumstances either of these amounted in themselves to intimidation. Grunwick revived the controversy over the right of pickets to stop individuals or vehicles entering a factory, and whether or not the individuals or drivers should be obliged to listen to their persuasion.

It again raised the question (see page 127) of whether workers in industries not a party to the dispute should be protected by the law if they intervened: either by preventing people from going to work in the premises involved; or by picketing premises which were not in dispute (as at Saltley); or by blacking goods going into or produced by the firm in dispute. In particular it raised the issue of whether this should apply to the blacking of mail by post office workers.

The powers and performance of the police also came into the limelight. Was the law enforceable as it stood? Did it make unreasonable demands on the police? Was the discretion it allowed them too much or too little? And did they overreact?

The influence of the media on violence and on industrial disputes was again demonstrated. How far did all sides use or develop the dispute to gain publicity for their cause? Did the media increase the violence, or did they shock or alarm those concerned into reducing it?

And were the Asian immigrants who made up 75 per cent of Grunwick's 270 workers and ninety-one strikers being used as pawns in a political power game? By the right in the form of the National Association for Freedom (NAFF) and Conservative MPs like John Gorst; by the left in the form of the Communist Party of Great Britain (CPGB), Labour Party Marxists, such as Audrey Wise and Arthur Scargill, and Trotskyists like the Socialist Workers' Party (SWP)? By pressure groups such as the National Council for Civil Liberties (NCCL)? By the rival factions, moderate and militant, in the trade unions, competing for membership, leadership and prestige? And by individuals of all persuasions seeking personal publicity and power?

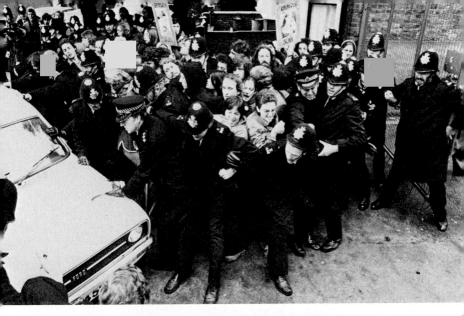

Intimidation at Grunwick. Pickets at rear holding placards with photographs of those still going to work (*Press Association*)

Grunwick salute: Fascist or Communist? Pickets or demonstrators? Compare with Plate 2 (*Associated Newspapers*)

7. Lewisham. Some of the weapons that were used (*Associated Newspapers*)

Early in the dispute, NAFF threw themselves behind Grunwick's founder and proprietor, George Ward, and he became a member of their Council. The Chairman of the NCCL, Jack Dromey, championed the strikers. After this many others came in on both sides. Writing about the peak week of violence, on 26 June 1977, the *Sunday Times* 'Insight' team commented: 'The whole panoply of the left, from International Marxists to Gay Liberationists, parades daily: "This is the Ascot of the left," one said. "It is essential to be seen here, best of all to get arrested." ' This intervention was of considerable embarrassment to Roy Grantham, the General Secretary of the principal union involved, the Association of Professional, Executive and Computer Staff (APEX).

How the dispute developed

George Ward was an Anglo-Indian born in New Delhi. He migrated to Britain in 1948, became a chartered accountant, worked for three years in Brazil and returned to Britain to found Grunwick, a small film-processing laboratory. Starting in a shed, in twelve years he built up a mail-order business which, in June 1977, was named by the consumer magazine *Which* as the fastest firm in the film-processing business, beating the giants like Kodak both in speed and prices.

In so doing, Ward had become a rich man and, at the time of the dispute, owned five racehorses. He had achieved this in the way in which small businessmen have traditionally risen from 'rags to riches' in both the nineteenth and twentieth centuries. He worked hard himself and employed dynamic and at times ruthless managers and supervisors; and he employed cheap labour, in this case mainly Asian immigrants, who would probably work hard for long hours to hold on to their jobs.

He was uncompromising in his methods to ensure fast and high output, especially during the rush season for 'holiday snaps'. All employees accepted that they would have to do compulsory overtime during the season, paid at time-and-a-quarter for the first six hours in any week and at time-and-a-half thereafter. They were told that they could not take holidays in July, August and September. Discipline was strict and Ward was determined not to allow trade unions to interfere with his high-pressure business in the competitive market.

G

In 1972, five of his workers joined the TGWU and tried to recruit others. Three weeks later these five were sacked though not, the firm claimed, for joining a union. They brought an action for unfair dismissal and lost. A few others walked out in sympathy, but the rest of the staff ignored their pickets and their protest petered out within a month.

Pay was low, though not at the bottom end of the income scale (see page 184). Compared with Kodak (£49·35) and Ilford (£38·88), basic weekly pay at Grunwick in August 1976 was £28·00.[1] With overtime, and after tax and national insurance, Mrs Jayaben Desai, the central figure of the 1976–7 dispute, was taking home £36·00 for a 50-hour week at that time.[2]

Strikers later claimed that since the dispute began, Ward had raised wages by 25 per cent in breach of the social contract. Basic pay in June 1977 was reputedly between £37 and £69 a week.[3] Most of Grunwick's Asian workers, however, were glad enough to have a job of any kind while there were 1½ million unemployed, and did not cavil at the wage. It was not wages which provided the spark for the dispute, but rather the strict discipline, the irritations of working long hours at high pressure in a hot summer and—above all—the lack of any effective means of airing grievances.

On Friday 20 August 1976 a nineteen-year-old worker, Devshi Boudia, was sacked after an angry scene with one of the directors, Malcolm Alden, who had censured him for not completing a batch of mail to catch the post, on which he had been deliberately 'going slow'. According to the Scarman Inquiry, Boudia admitted that he had provoked the incident, having first taken the precaution of obtaining the promise of a job elsewhere. After his dismissal he walked out with three or four sympathizers and they waited at the gate. Here they were joined later by Mrs Jayaben Desai and her son Sunil. She too had had an altercation with Mr Alden, who wanted her to do some extra overtime to get some outgoing mail into the post before the weekend. She refused, asked for her cards and walked out. This is noteworthy in view of the part played by Mrs Desai on the picket lines during the following year.

On Monday morning, 23 August, Mrs Desai, her son, Boudia and a few others were back outside the factory gates with placards, asking those going to work to sign a document supporting a union. Some of them signed, and a walk-out was arranged for

3 pm. About fifty walked out and, after an altercation with the management outside the gates of the factory in Chapter Road, they marched to a neighbouring Grunwick works in Cobbold Road where a number of them tried to break in and broke some windows. The police were called and they dispersed.

During 23 August, Mrs Desai took advice from the Citizens' Advice Bureau about forming a union. She approached the Brent Trades Council whose secretary was Jack Dromey, a twenty-eight-year-old ex-law student and 1976 Chairman of the NCCL. He advised her to apply to APEX, whose area organizer, Len Gristey, joined Dromey and Mrs Desai in forming a strike committee.[4]

By the end of August there were 137 on strike—ninety-one full-time workers and forty-six students on vacation work—and the ninety-one all joined APEX. There had not until then been any APEX members in Grunwick, nor, in fact, in any other film processing firm, and those who joined APEX did so after leaving the factory.[5]

APEX requested recognition by Grunwick and, having no success, applied to ACAS for conciliation. ACAS approached Grunwick to offer assistance on 31 August and again on 2, 10 and 30 September, but Grunwick declined their assistance.[6]

On 1 September APEX made the strike 'official' and on 2 September Grunwick sacked all the 137 strikers for breach of their contract of employment. When no further progress was made, APEX, on 15 October referred the dispute to ACAS for examination under EPA Sections 11 and 12 as a 'recognition issue'.[7] During the next two months ACAS had five meetings with Grunwick, to no avail.[8]

The National Association for Freedom intervenes

On 1 November, two new and powerful bodies entered the field from outside. The Union of Postal Workers (UPW) blacked all Grunwick's mail which, for a mail-order business, could quickly lead to its bankruptcy. This came to the notice of John Gouriet, a director of NAFF, who suggested that Ward should use NAFF solicitors to call on the High Court to order the Post Office to resume deliveries under the Post Office Act of 1969. The UPW realized that, under the law as it stood, Grunwick would probably get the High Court Order and, knowing that the idea of blacking mail was not popular with the public, backed down and called off their boycott on 5 November.[9]

The incident, however, had further impeded the conciliation efforts. At a meeting with the firm on 3 November, ACAS proposed a ballot of workers on the recognition issue under the provision of EPA Section 14. Grunwick agreed to provide names and addresses of their workers for this ballot provided that the UPW lifted their ban (which on that date was still in force).

At subsequent meetings on 10 and 17 November, however, Grunwick challenged the validity of including the sacked workers in the ACAS ballot, on the grounds that they no longer worked for the firm. They also said that they must seek advice from their lawyers on the provision of names and addresses of those who were still at work. On 18 November, Grunwick telephoned ACAS to say that their lawyers had advised them not to provide the names and addresses without further safeguards. There was also some argument over the wording of the ACAS questionnaire for the ballot. ACAS, who had originally set 20 November as the date for the ballot, temporarily postponed it.

After a further telephone call there was another meeting on 10 December, at which Grunwick agreed to the ballot on condition that their objections to two of the questions were resolved, on which they were consulting their solicitors. On 15 December they said that their lawyers could not fit in a consultation until 21 December, so ACAS asked for a meeting on the day after. Grunwick then said that they could not meet ACAS until after the Christmas break (4 January). ACAS informed Grunwick on 17 December that they had already postponed the ballot once and could not further delay it into the New Year; they would have to proceed with the ballot, with or without Grunwick s cooperation. After twelve more days, ACAS still had no names and addresses from the firm, so they despatched questionnaires on 29 December to those whose addresses had been given to them by APEX, all of whom were on strike. There were ninety-three of these, the ones who had been regular workers with the firm before they were sacked. They were asked whether they wanted a trade union to negotiate their pay and conditions and, if so, whether that union should be APEX. Ninety-one said yes, one said no and one was uncertain.

ACAS published its report on 10 March 1977, recommending

under EPA Section 12 that Grunwick should recognize APEX as a negotiating body for employees who were members of the union.

Meanwhile, at the end of February, Grunwick had commissioned an independent firm, Market and Opinion Research International (MORI), to take a ballot of those still at work. 86·4 per cent voted against joining a union but, although the ballot papers were not numbered, two workers who later joined the strike said that the ballot was conducted by departments in the canteen and that since the departments were small, those who were thinking of voting in favour of joining a union were afraid that they might be identified and sacked; also that no union officials were allowed to communicate with the workers before the ballot.[10]

On 23 March an industrial tribunal rejected an application from fifty-nine workers, sacked in September, that their dismissal should be declared unfair. The grounds for rejection were that it was lawful for an employer to sack *all* those involved in a strike and was unfair only if he discriminated by sacking some of them.[11]

On 19 April, Ward applied to the High Court for a declaration that the ACAS report recommending recognition of APEX for the purpose of collective bargaining was null and void and not binding on him on the grounds that it had not been properly conducted. He claimed that the questionnaire was biased toward APEX and had not been adequately translated into Gujerati: that none of those working for the firm at the time had been asked for their opinion (he claimed that their names and addresses were available from 21 December); and that the ninety-three whose opinions had been sought were no longer employed by the firm, having been fairly dismissed for breach of contract.

The failure of moderation

By this time the pickets had been manning the gates for forty weeks, right through the winter, a forlorn group, mainly of tiny Asian women (Mrs Desai was under five feet tall). They were having no impact on those still going to work, and still less on George Ward and his supporters in NAFF. They were losing heart. In the last week in May, Roy Grantham made a positive effort to encourage them and bring their case to the notice of the public and visited the picket line accompanied by four Labour MPs sponsored by APEX, three of them Ministers—Mrs Shirley Williams, Fred Mulley and Denis Howell.[12] Roy Grantham himself was a moderate man on the right of the party—he had lost his seat on the TUC General Council when he fell out with the left[13]—and so were the three Ministers. Up to this point, APEX and the pickets had acted on unimpeachably constitutional lines,[14] through ACAS, against an employer supported by a powerful pressure-group determined to keep the unions out of his firm. As Ward himself put it: 'We are not an anti-union company, merely non-union.'[15] Constitutional industrial action seemed to be no match for the tactics of NAFF.

Mass picketing

At the end of May, there was a marked change in the character and conduct of the dispute. Moderate trade unionism had failed, so extremism took over. The battle became one between the politically motivated right and the politically motivated left. And, as so often before, this led to violence.

Jack Dromey had thus far loyally followed the constitutional line in his capacity (one of many) of Secretary of the TUC Southern Region. But his personal philosophy was of the left— he was a member of the Labour Party's Tribune Group—and he came to the conclusion that more militant tactics were needed. Shirley Williams and the others were subsequently criticized for lending their names to what later proved to be very violent picketing, but it is probable that, by their visit, they were making a last-minute attempt to help moderation to succeed in the hope of heading this off.

In any event at the end of May, Dromey announced that there would be a massed picket on Monday 13 June. This was taken up by the Trotskyist SWP who, from 28 May onwards, published calls to its members to be there. Later, the CPGB (*Morning Star*) and the Communist Party of Britain, Marxist-Leninist (*Worker*), also came out in support. At this stage Jack Dromey and Mrs Desai do not appear to have been worried though Roy Grantham, who had accepted the need for a mass picket as the only remaining means of attracting public attention, began to have some anxiety about the allies who were joining him.

As the day approached the SWP mobilized its resources; though it had only a small membership (about 5,000—mainly students, graduates and white-collar workers) it ran a large printing works and had considerable financial backing. During the first ten days of June SWP issued 22,000 leaflets and put up 2,000 wall posters in London, calling out mass pickets for 13 June. They said that if the numbers were big enough, the police would not dare to provoke a confrontation, and that 'aggressive picketing can close the factory'.[17]

On Monday 13 June there were initially 200 pickets—later increasing to 700—crowding into the narrow streets outside the gates of the Grunwick factory by Dollis Hill underground station, and they endeavoured to form a physical block across the gates. The police, who had been formally notified of the mass picket by APEX, warned them that this amounted to an obstruction, as they were on a public highway. When they refused to move, the police formed a cordon to open access for those who were waiting to go to work. Violence broke out almost at once and during the day eighty-four people were arrested.

The police were accused of 'unnecessary brutality' and 'aggressive and provocative tactics', and during the day left-wing Labour MPs raised the issue in Parliament. They later suggested that overreaction by the police on the first day was responsible for much of the subsequent trouble. The Home Secretary ordered an inquiry but he and other Ministers, and the majority in both sides of the House, blamed the demonstrators and expressed sympathy for the police. Superintendent Hickman-Smith, who was in charge outside Grunwick on 13 June, was questioned by reporters on the site and commented:

> Everyone who wanted to go into work was being called a 'scab' and shouted at. There were about 200 people massing outside the gates and we had to put a cordon on to allow free access to the premises. I do not think there was any overreaction at all. We were quite impartial. We are put in situations like this and we have a duty to keep the highway clear and allow peaceful picketing.[18]

In contrast to the fighting with those who had come from outside, relations between the police and Roy Grantham and the official APEX pickets were good. During the day it was agreed

that an official picket of six APEX strikers could stand in front
of the police cordon to try to persuade people not to go to work,[19]
while other demonstrators would have to remain behind the
cordon or be charged with obstruction.

Next day, 14 June, the pattern was repeated. Some of the 270
people still at work—most of them, like the official pickets, being
Asian women—went in at the back entrance in a bus driven by a
Grunwick manager, and six official pickets, again separated from
the demonstrators, were established there too. Intimidation
increased. Threats were shouted at the people in the buses—'We
know where you live', etc., and banners carried enlarged photographs of some of those known to be still working. Another
thirteen people were arrested during the day.[20]

During 15 June the violence continued and five policemen
were injured. On 16 June, the fourth day of the mass picketing,
Roy Grantham was invited to speak to the workers inside the
factory and he crossed the picket lines to do so. Once inside he
received a hostile reception from a mass meeting of the staff,
chaired by John Gouriet. After Grantham had tried to speak,
Gouriet called for a show of hands and they voted overwhelmingly against joining a union. They also shouted that if any of the
sacked workers demonstrating outside were reinstated they would
walk out.[21] Roy Grantham was very angry, and said that the
occasion had been 'set up' by George Ward and NAFF as a trap.[22]

Meanwhile, postal workers at the Cricklewood sorting office,
which handled all mail for London's NW2 district, decided not
to handle any Grunwick mail, and in particular they held back
sixty-five sacks of mail which had arrived on 15 June.[23] They
took this action in defiance of the UPW, but next day the
Attorney General refused a request from Grunwick's lawyers for
legal action against the postal workers concerned, though he
said that there was nothing to stop anyone who was personally
affected from initiating a private prosecution.[24]

Meanwhile the numbers of pickets and police were building
up. Police estimates of the maximum numbers each day were
later given by the Home Secretary as follows:[25]

	Pickets	Police
Monday 13 June	700	308
Tuesday 14 June	700	503
Wednesday 15 June	700	356

	Pickets	Police
Thursday 16 June	700	521
Friday 17 June	1,500	688
Monday 20 June	1,200	556
Tuesday 21 June	1,000	765
Wednesday 22 June	800	631
Thursday 23 June	2,000	793
Friday 24 June	2,200	1,521

This increase took place in spite of appeals by Roy Grantham to keep the maximum down to 500. On 18 June *Socialist Worker* called for 'another Saltley' and later condemned Roy Grantham's call to restrict pickets:

> Grantham's move was not just a 'mistake'. He is a man of decidedly right-wing views—responsible, for instance, for a rule that prevents members of the Socialist Workers' Party holding any office in his union.[26]

Other far-left movements echoed the call. The Workers' Socialist League (which had broken away from SWP) said that 'Mass action can defeat any court order. Police and courts, the weapons of the capitalist class, must be challenged.'[27] The Communist Party of Britain (Marxist-Leninist) said: 'The mass picket is but one battle, the war must go on, but in more than one firm. The guerrilla approach is needed'.[28] And SWP on 2 July claimed that the police had proved that there was no parliamentary road to socialism, and said that the police, the judges, the employers' association and the Army were all on the same side. To defeat them would mean

> ... establishing secret contingents of socialist rank-and-file police and soldiers, prepared to change sides at crucial moments. It would also mean ensuring that the workers had enough force of their own to protect these rank-and-file soldiers and police against the vengeance of their superiors. There would have to be a workers' militia, prepared to fight the forces of the state until it had a monopoly of armed force in its own hands.[29]

With the ending of university terms, increasing numbers of

SWP and other students joined the mass pickets.[30] All of this was of increasing embarrassment to Roy Grantham and to Jack Dromey, who twice had to ask the SWP to refrain from handing out strike bulletins.[31]

By the end of the first week, 17 June, there had been 168 arrests and thirty-three injured—twenty-eight policemen and five demonstrators.[32]

The second week saw the intervention of a number of left-wing public figures. On Tuesday 21 June, eight Labour MPs joined the pickets—Denis Canavan, Martin Flannery, Joan Maynard, Ian Mikardo, Ronald Thomas, Stanley Thorn, Josephine Richardson and Mrs Audrey Wise. They were as far removed politically as would be possible within the Labour Party from Mrs Shirley Williams and the others who had attended a month earlier, and this underlined the change in the nature of the dispute. During the day Audrey Wise was arrested on a charge of obstructing the police in the execution of their duty. She was alleged to have seized the arm of a policeman who was in the act of arresting someone else, upon which the policeman, who clearly did not realize who she was, swung round and arrested her with words which have become immortal in Westminster: 'Never mind, love, you'll do instead.'[33]

On 23 June Mick McGahey appeared outside Grunwick with twelve Scottish miners, having earlier expressed his intention of 'doing a Saltley',[34] and Arthur Scargill also arrived with 150 Yorkshire miners.[35] Later, Scargill was arrested and charged with obstruction and Maurice Jones, the editor of the *Yorkshire Miner*, was also arrested; he was charged with insulting behaviour.

There was a strange sequel to this arrest. Jones, a member of the Communist Party, was released on bail but failed to appear. He was found to have fled to East Germany, where he asked for asylum. Later, in July, Arthur Scargill flew over to East Germany and persuaded him to return and answer the charge. On arrival at Heathrow he was rearrested, tried to break away and six policemen were needed to overpower him.[36]

The arrest of Scargill and Jones, however, was not the most significant event on 23 June. During this day of extreme violence, a policeman, PC Trevor Wilson, was struck on the head by a milk-bottle and severely injured. Newspaper photographs and television news showed him on the ground with a pool of blood spreading over the pavement from his head. Later, a twenty-one-year-old computer operator, Richard Maull (who was not a striker, or an APEX member) was charged in connection with this incident.

Like the famous picture of a policeman being held by one demonstrator and kicked in the face by another in Grosvenor Square in March 1968, the picture of PC Wilson had a dramatic effect and marked another turning-point in the dispute. The official pickets were horrified and some of them later visited him in hospital to express their sympathy and their disgust at what had been done in their name.

David Wheeler, writing in the *Listener*, was quick to capture the significance of the event:

'No genuine trade unionist would have thrown a bottle,' said one of the Grunwick strike organizers on ITN, a remark that will have divided the television audience as decisively as the strike itself has divided the nation. The bottle, as all the world knows, struck a young police constable in the head and will now, though shattered, live for years in British political history or (much the same thing) mythology. The incident marked the high point of a bad week for trade unions . . . However good a case the Grunwick strikers may have against the management, television has ensured that what will stick in people's minds is the blood running from the constable's head as he lay unconscious on the pavement.[37]

The violence subsides

Television is often accused of encouraging and exacerbating violence. On this occasion it undoubtedly acted to restrain it. All of those directly involved in the dispute itself (including APEX and the Grunwick strikers) realized that mass picketing led inevitably to violence, and that violence was the worst thing for their case. Though mass picketing and violence continued on Friday 24 June (fifty-four more were arrested and seventeen policemen injured) it was clear that those who were bringing violence to the scene were not welcomed by the strike committee. Roy Grantham agreed with the police to limit the number of pickets to 500.[38] The numbers fell from 2,200 on Friday 24 June to 900 the following Monday and thereafter (apart from the mass

demonstration on 11 July described below) there was a steady
decline throughout July both in the number of pickets and in the
violence.

Nevertheless, SWP continued each week to call on its members
to be at the Grunwick gates at 7.00 am every morning and to
step up the mass picket.[39] *Militant*, 'The Marxist paper for
Labour and Youth', run by the Trotskyist Young Socialist
faction of the Labour Party, also called for continued mass action
and condemned Roy Grantham s 'disastrous call' to limit the
pickets to 500.[40] Arthur Scargill took the same line, and both
papers joined him in calling for a mass picket of 20,000 on
Monday 11 July.

In the event 18,000 turned out, and 3,500 police were on duty
—one-sixth of the Metropolitan Police. The crowd initially
blocked the factory entrances, as at Saltley, and—for the first
time since the dispute began—the workers' buses did not enter
the factory on time at 8.00 am. Later in the morning, however,
the demonstrators moved off, led by the unlikely combination of
Roy Grantham and Arthur Scargill, on a peaceful march around
the area and the bus drivers took this opportunity to get the
workers in. Considering the size of the crowds (larger than at the
peak day at Saltley) the violence might well have been worse.
Seventy more arrests were made and thirty more injured, eighteen
of whom were police.[41] This brought the total number of arrests
since 13 June up to 377 and the total number of police injured
to 243.[42] When the Home Secretary announced these figures in
Parliament he drew attention to the fact that it was a misnomer
to call anyone at Grunwick a picket. 'There are people there who
are not picketing but are given the name. They are just there to
cause trouble.'[43]

After 11 July however, the temperature—and the numbers—
fell steadily. By Friday 22 July, pickets had dwindled to 100—
less now than the number of workers trying to go to work.[44]
At this point a split developed between Jack Dromey and Roy
Grantham. Dromey, fearful of a return to apathy and frustration,
called for a resumption of mass picketing, and especially for
another day of mass demonstration on 8 August. Grantham, on
the other hand, said that there would be no more mass pickets,
on that or any other day, that no one could be classed as a picket
without his authority and that he would not give that authority.
He succeeded in getting the strike committee to vote against

having a mass picket. *Socialist Worker*, however, urged its members to defy this decision and about 2,800 demonstrators turned out, mainly students, but were told by strike committee members that nobody had the right to take over the dispute from the people who had been involved in the dispute for fifty weeks. Some were noisy but, after urgent appeals from Jack Dromey to keep it peaceful, there was no violence.[45]

The postmen and the Courts

The main conflict had by now shifted to the postal sorting offices and the Courts.

On 28 June, Tom Jackson, General Secretary of the UPW, advised postal workers to cease their ban on Grunwick mail, on the grounds that it might prejudice the case for the granting of the formal right to strike which, as with power station workers, was restricted by law. The postal workers continued the ban and were warned by the Post Office management that they would be suspended without pay if they had not begun to sort the backlog of Grunwick mail by noon on 4 July. They refused. The Cricklewood sorting office, and all postboxes in the area, were closed, so that no one was able to post or receive any mail in the London NW2 district.

NAFF thereupon organized a 'pony express' on Saturday 9 July. Collecting all the mail from the Grunwick factory awaiting despatch, they distributed it to volunteers for posting all over the country. Postal workers in some sorting offices (e.g. at Luton and Nottingham) spotted the Grunwick brand-names and temporarily blacked individual packages, but these were soon released.[46]

Meanwhile, however, the closure of the Cricklewood sorting offices was having serious effects on other businesses in NW2. One managing director, Harold Shaw, applied to the High Court for an order to the Post Office to release his mail. The High Court refused and their decision was upheld by the Court of Appeal on 17 July. The Master of the Rolls (Lord Denning), while expressing sympathy for Shaw and for other firms suffering from the dispute in which they had no concern, said that the Post Office and the union had done their duty by warning the postal workers that they would be committing a criminal offence if they blacked the mail, but that they could not be held to blame if they were not obeyed. The Post Office was protected under Section 9 of the Post Office Act of 1969 from proceedings in tort for failure to deliver mail. (This protection is essential, as otherwise the Post Office would face suits for damages by firms or individuals which claimed to have suffered losses every time a letter was delayed or mislaid.) Lord Denning also felt that it would probably do more harm than good for the Courts to intervene in what was a very delicate industrial dispute.[47]

On Saturday 23 July, by arrangement with the Post Office, Grunwick were permitted to collect the sixty-five bags of mail which had been held in Cricklewood since mid-June. The sorters were then told that their suspension would be ended, but only if they were willing to handle all mail without discrimination. They refused. Ironically the UPW, despite disowning their action, was paying them £42·00 a week strike pay for fear that, if they did not, other postal workers would come out in sympathy. So London NW2 remained without postal services for another week. The Cricklewood sorters, however, received no further support from other sorting offices and eventually called off the boycott and returned to work on 31 July.

Meanwhile, on 4 July, the High Court began its hearing of the Grunwick case against the validity of the ACAS ballot and the Lord Chief Justice, Lord Widgery, gave judgement in favour of ACAS on 12 July. He ruled that the dismissed workers *did* have a right to take part in the ballot and that the fact that those still working for the firm had not done so was the fault of Grunwick for refusing to supply a list of their names and addresses. He said that George Ward might have done himself great harm by refusing to provide this list, since it was possible that the result would have favoured him, perhaps heavily.[48]

Grunwick appealed, and on 29 July the Appeal Court, under Lord Denning, reversed the High Court ruling, saying that ACAS had made a fatal error in balloting only the strikers and none of those still working at the time. ACAS then appealed to the House of Lords, who finally, on 14 December, ruled in favour of Grunwick, leaving ACAS free to call a fresh ballot of both strikers and workers.

While this case was still under appeal, the Government appointed a Court of Inquiry under Lord Justice Scarman to 'inquire into the cause and circumstances of, and relevant to, the dispute, *other than any matter before the High Court*'. This latter provision debarred Scarman from considering the question of recognition of APEX or the validity of the ACAS ballot, and thus presumably also barred him from recommending holding the ballot again with both those on strike and those now working with the firm. Scarman did, however, go fully into conditions in the factory and how the dispute began. He found that the 'sweatshop' conditions described by some strikers had no foundation in fact, but that some blame attached to both sides for the long and sometimes violent dispute: Grunwick for their lack of a proper industrial relations machinery, refusing ACAS offers of conciliation and refusing to seek a negotiated settlement; and APEX for calling on post office workers to act in a way which led to breaches of the criminal law, and for failing to foresee that their calling for a mass picket would lead to civil disorder. He added that Grunwick had acted within the letter but outside the spirit of the law and had thereby acted unreasonably, without the willingness to co-operate and compromise on which good industrial relations depend. He recommended (but had no power to order) that they either reinstate those strikers who were full-time employees, or make ex gratia payments (as advised by a mediator) to those for whom no vacancies existed.[49]

George Ward refused to do this, saying that those still working for the firm would not be willing to work with the strikers; that he saw no reason for ex gratia payments to people who had by their own actions terminated their employment; and that 're-instatement would be a surrender to the rampant illegality of brute force'.

He added that if a blockade involving the illegal cutting off of gas, electricity and water made it impossible to operate, Grunwick would 'generously recompense its loyal work-force and go into liquidation'.[50]

There is little doubt that, at this stage, Grunwick could have reached a compromise with APEX which would have ended the dispute and safeguarded their employees' jobs. Ward could have argued that, unless small firms like Grunwick survived, this would give greater power to the giant multinationals, like Kodak, which would not be in the interests either of the unions or of consumers; that he could only compete if his small staff accepted intensive work (with overtime pay) in the season, and that he could only take staff willing to do this; that his present staff certainly were willing; and that if he went into liquidation they would have little chance of other employment—nor even, in the case of the many working wives, of drawing the dole; that the bitterness was such that it was clearly impossible for the strikers to work alongside workers who had been subjected to their abuse and intimidation; that he could make no individual ex gratia payments but that he would subscribe to a fund organized by the union to pay to its members at their discretion. The chances are that Grantham, whom the Scarman Report had put into a conciliatory mood, would have accepted some compromise on these lines, bearing in mind that Grunwick had already declared their willingness to allow a union to negotiate on behalf of any members of staff who so desired.

Ward, however, preferred to fight the battle on the major political issue rather than on the needs for survival of a small firm providing work to people who wanted it. He was presumably still being advised by NAFF. His stance was clear from an article in *The Times* under his name on 1 September 1977. In this he condemned the Scarman Inquiry as a political con-trick, established because 'Grunwick had become an exceptional nuisance to those who see Britain's future as that of a collectivist, corporate state'.

This seemed to condemn not only the orthodox socialist state, but also the philosophy of the Heath Government in its attempt in 1972–3 to run the country as a joint venture by the government, the city, industry and the unions, as in Germany and Japan.[51] Sir Keith Joseph also condemned the Scarman Report next day,[52] and only one Conservative front bench spokesman who had previously spoken out in favour of APEX—James Prior —seemed to dissent. The continual confrontation with a particularly moderate trade union could hardly be in the interest of the Conservative Party as a potential government, but their leadership showed no sign of encouraging Ward to compromise.

The polarization of the Trade Union movement by this confrontation was underlined a few days later at the Annual Congress of the TUC, which voted unanimously to co-operate in cutting off supplies and services to Grunwick—with a rare closing of ranks from right to left. Frank Chapple, a leading right-winger and general secretary of the Electricians' Union, said that even if neighbouring inhabitants had to suffer by being cut off, this would be preferable to confrontations between mass pickets and police.[53] Services were not cut off, however, partly because Grunwick had arranged alternative supplies (including a generator) and partly because the factory was in any case at low pressure until the holiday season.

Conclusions

The mass picketing and violence at Grunwick took place in the shadow of Saltley, which was in the minds—whether with anxiety or with exhilaration—of all who took part. Yet—as pointed out at the start of the chapter—it was very different. The disrupting of Grunwick had no effect on the national economy, but principles were at stake. Partly because of this, and partly because of the exploitation of the dispute by both the political right and the political left, the violence was worse than at Saltley. Another factor was that, at Saltley, the violence was between miners and police without real hatred, whereas most of the violence at Grunwick was by people who had no direct connection with the dispute or with the union involved. Britain did, however, just retain its record of avoiding fatal casualties on picket lines, though the milk-bottle which hit PC Wilson was not far from killing him.

The dispute was a setback for moderation and patience in that they were tried and defeated. The inevitable result was extremism and violence. NAFF must take a great deal of responsibility for this (see pages 197 to 198).

The intervention of politicians was fit for a key by-election. Three Ministers in May, eight left-wing backbenchers in June. On the other side, John Gorst was in and out of the factory every day. Other guest stars—McGahey, Scargill, Sue Slipman (President of the National Union of Students and National Executive member of the Communist Party)—came in droves.

The two official leaders could hardly have been more different: Roy Grantham, moderation personified, who must have deeply regretted that his exasperation had ever led him to call for a mass picket; and Jack Dromey, who showed remarkable patience for nine months before he allowed his personal political views to lead him to accept allies who gravely damaged his case. Yet he, like Roy Grantham, was unquestionably opposed to violence throughout.

The people who earned most sympathy were the pawns in the

big power game—the Asian women on both sides: the pickets sticking patiently to their posts through autumn, winter and spring, and through a summer of violence in which they took no part; and those who continued working, enduring daily intimidation and abuse, the anxious awareness of 'spies' watching where the bus picked them up, and sometimes more than a mere implication that they and their families would be molested at home, as some of them were.[54]

The media, so much criticized by all sides in such disputes, showed up well. The newspapers admirably fulfilled their contemporary role of comment in depth. Television, while inevitably attracting political activists of both sides to posture before it, on balance probably reduced the violence by bringing it to the public notice, which led to the strike leaders taking action to control it.

The extreme movements of right and left emerged as both nasty and stupid. Neither did their cause much good. They, and their aims, are more broadly discussed on pages 234 to 242.

But the major lessons of Grunwick concerned the law: about picketing, the right to strike and the right to work; the right to join a union or not to join a union; recognition of trade unions; conciliation and arbitration; the right to intervene by those not a party to the dispute; the right to apply pressure by action against industries or services other than those in dispute; the right of public service workers to intervene over general or political issues by denying the use of their services; and the question of whether some, such as postal workers, should be restricted more than others in the scope of their industrial action.

The House of Lords' ruling on 14 December aroused demands from all sides to change the law. NAFF and George Ward demanded the repeal of the EPA. Roy Grantham, whose union had already spent £250,000 on the strike—which would continue —said that the EPA must be amended to compel employers to co-operate with ACAS. Jack Dromey said that the dispute would only be won by trade union muscle and condemned the TUC for failing to cut off essential services.

Joe Rogaly in *Grunwick* (an excellent Penguin Special published in October 1977) has put the case for the law playing a bigger part in industrial disputes, despite union objections. These, and other issues of the law, are discussed in Chapter 19.

17 The Growth of Violence on the Streets

The Right to Work March

Grunwick saw the most prolonged violence between police and demonstrators in 1976–7 but there was also, during these years, a disturbing escalation of political violence on the streets. This escalation began with the incident in West Hendon during the Right to Work March on 19 March 1976 and continued with a number of very violent battles between demonstrators and police, as in Lewisham on 13 August 1977, when the SWP attempted to break up a National Front march, and in the following week during a by-election campaign in Ladywood, Birmingham.

None of these incidents was concerned with industrial picketing, but arose from political demonstrations and marches and, as at Grunwick, the SWP played a major part.

The Right to Work Campaign was sponsored by the SWP (then International Socialists, IS) in 1976, to protest against unemployment, which stood at over 1¼ million. Thus far, IS had been a predominantly student movement only 3,000 strong; and so this gave them an opportunity to extend their membership more into the field of manual workers, where they had hitherto had only limited success.[1] Many working men were bitterly resentful of the failure of the Labour Government and of their trade union leadership (CPGB included) to provide them with work, and were ready to respond to a militant lead to express that resentment on the lines of the 1936 Jarrow march.

IS provided that lead. They organized a Right to Work March, starting in Manchester on 27 February 1976 and ending in a rally in London on 20 March.[2]

They mobilized about ninety unemployed workers, students and graduates for the three-week march, for which they raised substantial funds.[3] On the way, they entered a number of factory and construction sites to try to persuade workers to come out on strike, but they were disappointed by the lack of coverage in the media. They put this down (and it is a sad reflection that they were probably right) to the lack of any punch-ups with the police,[4] who had nowhere blocked their way nor given them any occasion for a confrontation.[5]

On 19 March they reached the outskirts of London in West Hendon, where a flyover was under construction at the crossing of their route (Edgware Road) over the North Circular Road at Staples Corner. The flyover was incomplete, so traffic was using what was later to become the slip road. The ninety marchers were at that time escorted by eight policemen, including a Chief Inspector and a Sergeant. They refused police direction to use the slip road and went on to the top of the flyover to try to talk to the construction workers, many of whom were on piecework and resented their interruption, so they did not get a good reception. This seemed to annoy the marchers and, as there was still a gap in the flyover bridge, they had to march back to do a U-turn into the slip road. The Chief Inspector was in front of them and, seeing the traffic lights further back had just released a flow of traffic, he raised his arms to hold up the marchers until the traffic was clear. He was suddenly set upon by the leading marchers and knocked to the ground, kicked and punched. Only one other policeman, the Sergeant, was within range to help him, the other six constables being further back along the column. Both the Chief Inspector and the Sergeant were badly beaten up, the Chief Inspector being kicked in the crutch and in the face and the Sergeant requiring fourteen stitches in his head.

West Hendon police station was only 200 yards along the slip road and, hearing the noise, the policemen in the station at the time ran out to help the Chief Inspector, the Sergeant and the six PCs, who were being overwhelmed. They were still hopelessly outnumbered, however; and when they attempted to make arrests, they too were attacked and a general riot ensued. Witnesses working in offices overlooking the spot described the violence as terrifying, and for a time anarchy reigned. When the police did manage to get some of those arrested into the police station, marchers invaded it and recaptured them.

Later, when reinforcements from three neighbouring police stations began to arrive, most of them were rearrested. In all, forty-one policemen were injured, three of them seriously. One was hit on the head by a large block of concrete thrown from the flyover above. Another, who had been kicked in the face, was off duty for four and a half months. None of the marchers was seriously hurt.

It was later suggested that a confrontation may have been staged in the Hendon area in order to get the publicity the marchers had hitherto lacked—particularly in order to avoid the next day's rally at the Albert Hall being a flop. Shortly before the attack on the Chief Inspector, they had appeared to passers-by to be deliberately blocking the road—which carries heavy traffic—but the police had not reacted. The Editor of *Socialist Worker* was present with several photographers, and their presses were all prepared to rush out a full-sized emergency edition on the incident overnight, ready for the rally. The incident also received considerable coverage in the national press on the morning of the rally so, if this was its purpose, it succeeded.

Of the forty-three marchers arrested, twenty-five were convicted, mainly for assault. Only one went to prison (for three months). All the others received suspended sentences or fines.

An analysis of the forty-three marchers charged reveals that twelve were students or graduates; thirty-five were in their twenties or their teens, eight in their thirties and none over forty. A number of those convicted had previous criminal records including convictions for assault and one, aged twenty-one, had fourteen previous convictions.

Six months later, 500 Right to Work marchers demonstrated at the TUC Congress in Brighton on 7–9 September 1976. Some had gone ahead on 5 September and shouted down the Employment Secretary, Albert Booth, at a Tribune Group meeting. TUC delegates had to run the gauntlet to get into the Congress meeting. Inside the hall they interrupted the meeting from the visitors' gallery, drawing a much-quoted rebuke from the General Secretary, Len Murray, as 'Trotskyist political boot-boys who represent no one but themselves'.[6]

Lewisham, 13 August 1977

In the summer of 1977, SWP continued their drive for new and more broadly based recruits and extended their campaign to attract more coloured immigrants, amongst whom unemployment was particularly high. They had launched this campaign earlier with the issue of two new papers, *Flame*, designed for blacks and *Chingari* ('the spark') for Bengali, Punjabi and Gujerati readers. Though only one of those charged at Hendon had been black, 1977 saw a big rise in immigrant membership of SWP and in coloured people turning out for their demonstrations. The activities of the National Front in high-immigrant areas of London and Birmingham presented SWP with the opportunity to harness the reaction to it. In the ensuing clashes, both NF and SWP brought each other much publicity.

The issue picked by the National Front was an extract from a routine police report which mentioned that, in South London in 1974, 80 per cent of mugging offences were by blacks and 85 per cent of the victims were white.[7] Then in May the police raided the homes of suspected muggers and twenty-four young West Indians were arrested,[8] twenty-one of whom were subsequently charged. The SWP at once formed a defence committee for the young blacks.[9]

NF decided to hold a march and rally in Deptford and Lewisham on Saturday 13 August to protest against mugging, and in particular mugging by blacks. They said that they wanted to demonstrate to the white population 'that they were not forgotten'.

In practice, of course, their aim was the political one of building up their membership and electoral support. In these respects, the Deptford and Lewisham constituency was a particularly promising one. The coloured population was about 14 per cent, one of the highest in Britain.[10] Unemployment was also running at 14 per cent. And in the 1976 local elections, the National Front and National Party had, between them, secured a record 44 per cent of the poll in Deptford.

As soon as the NF march was announced, the SWP also saw in this an opportunity for recruiting and publicity—since they knew that the great majority of the British population disliked the NF as much as they did the far left. They organized a counter-demonstration, and the next four issues of *Socialist Worker* called on its readers to turn out in force on 13 August to drive 'the Nazis off the streets' and to 'stop the Nazis marching, whatever the authorities do'. The front page of *Socialist Worker* on the morning of the march showed a picture of three young blacks, one carrying a baton, with the caption 'No Nazis in Lewisham'. The background of the picture was made up of anti-police *Flame* posters: 'The Police are the Real Muggers'; the implications were self-evident.

During the weeks before the march the Lewisham Council had called on the Commissioner of the Metropolitan Police to use his powers under the 1936 Public Order Act to advise the Home Secretary to ban the march, and tried unsuccessfully to get a High Court order for him to do so. When this failed, the Mayor, along with the Bishop of Southwark, Dr Mervyn Stockwood, called for a counter-demonstration in the morning on a different route from the NF march (which was to be in the afternoon).

This counter-march was organized by the All-Lewisham Campaign Against Racialism and Fascism (ALCARAF)—a broadly based body set up in January 1977, whose committee included representatives of churches, trade unions and political parties—amongst them a delegate from the SWP. This march went off peacefully—but SWP had encouraged their supporters to attend it, and this had the effect of concentrating them in the area in readiness for the NF march in the afternoon.

Since this would quite obviously be the result (virtually every newspaper predicted it) it is not easy to judge whether the Bishop was playing politics or being naïve. His subsequent letter to *The Times* suggests that he may merely have been piqued that the Commissioner of the Metropolitan Police declined to accept his advice and that of the Mayor. The ALCARAF march certainly helped to give publicity to the NF march and to mobilize the forces for the subsequent violence—two things which could do only harm to race relations.

The NF marchers, about 800 strong, assembled in Clifton Rise, opposite Deptford Town Hall, at 2.30 pm carrying Union Jacks and banners bearing provocative slogans, such as 'Stop the Muggers: 80 per cent of the Muggers are Black; 85 per cent of the Victims are White'. The police deployed about 3,500 men (as many as at Grunwick) and kept the SWP demonstrators away from them, but a number of these had occupied derelict buildings overlooking the route, from which they threw down bottles, dustbins, timber and chunks of masonry on the marchers and the police. Meanwhile, 200 Millwall football supporters, gathering for a match on their ground nearby, came and jeered at the SWP demonstrators, shouting: 'Up the National Front—kill the blacks.'

For a brief period, the NF march was split by SWP supporters who broke through the police, and it looked like disintegrating into individual fights; but the police broke them up and kept the column moving. It took them fifteen minutes to get the first 200 yards down New Cross Road, and the police then succeeded in separating the march from its attackers. This infuriated the SWP demonstrators, who switched their attacks to the police, while the NF march was directed on to a brief rally and then to Lewisham Station to disperse in special trains.

This clash differed from that in Red Lion Square in that there was only one march, not two (since the ALCARAF march was over before the NF one began). It was thus an attack by demonstrators who had gathered in the vicinity in which the NF march was forming up (Clifton Rise). The fighting between NF and SWP and its supporters took place within 200 yards of this point. Thereafter, the SWP supporters were attacking only the police. The police for the first time carried 'Perspex' riot shields, which they certainly needed to protect them from the missiles, and they confiscated a horrifying armoury of offensive weapons, including carving knives and a large iron pipe studded with bolts for use as a club. Some of the demonstrators also carried ammonia with which they attacked the policemen's eyes.

Two policemen were stabbed, one near Lewisham Police Station, some time after the NF march had dispersed. A brick was thrown through the windscreen of his van, which was then surrounded by demonstrators shouting 'Kill! Kill! Kill!' While he and his companion were temporarily blinded by broken glass, someone broke in and stabbed him in the back.

Of 134 requiring hospital treatment fifty-six were policemen of whom forty-one had head injuries, and most had other injuries as well, including forty in the legs, thirty-nine in the face and thirteen in the eyes. Six of the policemen had serious injuries, including those with stab wounds and two with eye damage from broken glass and ammonia. Of the 214 arrested, only forty-seven came from Lewisham.[12]

The Commissioner of Police was much criticized for failing to redirect or ban the march, but redirection would have achieved nothing, for wherever the NF march had formed up, the SWP demonstrators would have concentrated to try to stop it. As they were not marching, the SWP could not be 'redirected'. The only option open to the Commissioner would have been to ban *all*

marches and demonstrations for three months. Bearing in mind
that the great majority of demonstrations have nothing to do with
the NF or SWP and are wholly peaceful,[13] he felt that this would
be an unjustifiable interference with other people's freedom. All
the supporters of the NF and SWP combined were unlikely to be
as much as 1 per cent of the population, and it would have been
creating an undesirable precedent if, by threatening violence,
either of these fringe groups could cause such a ban to be imposed. It was, nevertheless, recognized that it might become
necessary if the street fighting were to reach the scale of the 1920s
and early 1930s in Germany, which resulted in the rise of Hitler
to power.

The NF, as after Red Lion Square, basked in a rather sickening halo of self-righteousness. They enjoyed another opportunity
to pose as a disciplined, law-abiding force. They carried no
weapons, attacked no one and claimed to have injured no one.
Nevertheless, their purpose was provocative, and they knew that
their cause could only be advanced by attacks from 'red terrorists
and muggers'. They did nothing to deserve the diversion of 3,500
police from other duties, of whom so many were injured in
protecting them.

The SWP themselves made no attempt to deny the use of
violence. In their report on the incident, they described their
reaction to the police clearing the path for the march:

> . . . the crowd of anti-fascists exploded. Sticks, smoke-bombs,
> rocks, bottles were thrown over the police heads at the
> Nazis . . .

and they later described their battle with the police after the NF
march had dispersed:

> Rocks were lobbed over the police shields, running fights de-
> veloped all along the road. People soon learned to deal with the
> SPG (Special Patrol Group) vans that screamed down the
> road. Bricks poured through their windows and put at least
> one out of action. A group of demonstrators besieged the
> police station and broke its windows. A match was put to what
> was thought to be a police motor cycle.[14]

The motor cycle, in fact, belonged to a *Sunday Times* reporter,
and one of the reporters from *The Times* was amongst those

seriously injured—by a brick in the eye. The SWP's National Organizer, Steve Jefferys, left *The Times* in no doubt about SWP's attitude to violence and to the police:

> The Socialist Workers' Party said that the stone- and bottle-throwing tactics of demonstrators at Lewisham had been justifiable and necessary . . . Mr Stephen Jefferys, a member of the Central Committee of the Socialist Workers' Party said: 'We want to make it absolutely clear to the police that we are not going to allow the Nazis to walk the streets of this country. We shall do everything to stop them.' He was asked repeatedly whether he condoned the use of knives, bottles, bricks and other offensive weapons by the demonstrators. Each time he replied that the National Front had to be stopped from building up a populist appeal. When a reporter said: 'In other words, Yes,' he did not reply.[15]

The *Daily Mail* reported Jefferys as saying:

> Since the police have no inhibitions about throwing bricks and using police horses and riot shields, intent on allowing the Nazis to march, we will use the means necessary to stop them.[16]

Stephen Jefferys and Chris Harman (who was joint author of the *Socialist Worker* report quoted above) had both been in leading positions in IS/SWP for some years. Jefferys, a thirty-one-year-old LSE history graduate, was one of those who went on to the shop floor after leaving university, and was a shop steward for a time at Chrysler's Linwood plant in 1972 before becoming a full-time paid organizer for IS/SWP. Chris Harman—whose earlier call for armed violence was quoted in discussing Grunwick on page 201—had obtained degrees at LSE and Leeds University before joining the staff of *Internationalist Socialist*. He later took over from Paul Foot as editor of *Socialist Worker*. All of these can be regarded as typical of the graduates who act as 'godfathers' to direct the activities of the SWP.

One, at least, of their West Indian demonstrators in Lewisham, however, saw more clearly than they did where the violence would lead. His anguished cry was reported by two newspapers: 'Don't fight the police. Please, no violence. That's what the Nazis want.'[17]

The *Daily Mirror* reported SWP's intention of using the same tactics in the Ladywood by-election in Birmingham the following week, where both NF and SWP candidates were standing:

We intend to crush the National Front. We will intimidate them off the streets. Of course there will be violence. And to achieve our object we will have to condone the use of every weapon that was wielded on Saturday.[14]

The Ladywood by-election

Deptford and Lewisham had a high coloured immigrant population, but the Ladywood constituency of Birmingham had the highest in the United Kingdom—no less than 40 per cent of the voters were coloured.[17] In the by-election on 18 August 1977, the ten candidates included one from NF—Anthony Reed-Herbert, and one from SWP, Kim Gordon, himself a coloured man who had been active in the Defence Committee for the Lewisham twenty-one and was one of those arrested in the rioting in Lewisham on 13 August. Both no doubt hoped to gain from the mutual fear of NF supporters and immigrants, and from the publicity resulting from conflict between them.

The occasion presented itself two days after the riot in Lewisham, when the NF were holding an election meeting in a school in Boulton Road. While the NF supporters (including the National Organizer, John Tyndall) went in by a back entrance, unnoticed, a crowd of SWP supporters attacked the police cordon outside the front entrance. The demonstrators, as predicted, used the same kind of weapons as at Lewisham. Of the 400 police on duty, fifty-eight (one in seven) were injured, six of them seriously.

This brought yet another dimension into the conflict, for it was an attempt to break up an election meeting of a parliamentary candidate. Kim Gordon, the SWP candidate, was reported as saying: 'Our intention is to frighten people from joining the Front. We want to intimidate them. I can understand black youngsters carrying weapons. They are not afraid. They are just more militant.'[20]

The effect of the violence on the voting was predictable in its effect on the National Front and disastrous for the SWP, as the figures showed:

	Votes	Per cent
Labour (J. Sever)	8,227	53·1
Conservative (J. Q. Davies)	4,402	28·4
National Front (A. Reed-Herbert)	*888*	5·7
Liberal (K. Hardeman)	765	4·9
Socialist Unity (K. Ahsan)	534	3·5
Independent (J. Hunte)	336	2·2
SWP (K. Gordon)	*152*	1·0
Others (three)	71, 63, 46	1·2

The NF (who had not stood in October 1974) increased their vote from 2·9 per cent in February 1974 to 5·7 per cent—putting them in third place ahead of the Liberals. The SWP candidate, with 152 votes, got less than either of the other two coloured candidates (Ahsan, an Asian and Hunte, a West Indian). The SWP claim to be the party that fought for the immigrants had failed. Their violence was rejected by the voters, white and coloured alike and, although it undoubtedly helped to double the NF percentage of the vote, 90 per cent of the voters voted a plague on both extremes.

The politics of hate

Eye-witnesses of the street violence of 1976 and 1977 were struck by the orchestrated element of malice and hate—especially against the police—which far exceeded that of previous years. Reading the issues of *Socialist Worker* during the weeks before these incidents (including Grunwick) gives some indication of the intentions of the 'graduate godfathers' who edited and wrote them. Most of those who reacted with violence against the police were young, and many (at Lewisham and Ladywood) were black. Some had criminal records already and others began them then. Some were unemployed, and became thereby likelier to remain so. The violence to which they were aroused did immense damage to community relations in these highly inflammable areas—undoing in a single night much patient work by community leaders of all races for the previous 364 days of the year.

Nothing could have been better for the National Front, who thrived on the provocation of white hysteria against black violence, and who were able to build up a clever image of orderliness and righteousness—under the Union Jack at that—in the eyes of a shocked public who saw their disciplined demeanour under bombardment on television, but did not read their inflammatory propaganda.

The numbers involved on both sides remained small— Bernard Levin's 1974 comment about 'rival gangs of totalitarians flexing their weedy muscles' was still valid—but the number of peaceful citizens affected, and alarmed and aroused by television coverage, was not so small. There were grim predictions that the rival gangs would emulate the Nazis and the Communists on the streets of Germany in the 1920s and 1930s, and reminders of where that had led. There were moves to revise or reinterpret the legislation governing public order. Politicians who consciously responded to this mood were loudly cheered. The threat was not so much to life and property as to the public tranquillity and tolerance on which the stability of a democratic society is based; and this was, perhaps, the one thing that suited both the 'rival gangs of totalitarians' equally well.

Their similarities were expressed in the terms 'Red Fascists' and 'Black Fascists' taken up by the press, but the pots on both sides continued to call the kettles black. *Socialist Worker* printed a photograph of NF slogans painted on the door of an Asian immigrant's home but on another page told a story of their own about how they intimidated a bus driver called Bunce from standing as a prospective NF candidate in Dundee.

> When we talked to Bunce we discovered that he hated being labelled as a Nazi. This prompted our members to step up the pressure. Last Sunday evening we sprayed the walls of his home with slogans in 2 ft high letters, 'Nazis live here' and 'Fuhrer Bunce is a Nazi'. The following week he made a statement to the press saying that he did not intend to stand because he was afraid that the scenes of Lewisham and Birmingham might be repeated in Dundee.[21]

The sickening parallel, on both sides, with the Nazis in Germany in the 1930s daubing the homes of Jews was all too clear.

PART III
Disruption, Reaction and Reform

18 The Forces of Internal Conflict

Revolution or reform?

British people enjoy certain blessings, in addition to environ-
mental ones. Despite their agonies, and unlike the Northern
Irish, the people of England, Scotland and Wales still live in one
of the least politically violent societies in the world. Historically
their record of non-violence has been unequalled over the past
one and a half centuries, epitomized by the viability of an unarmed police force. For a dozen generations, nearly three hundred years, they have had a stable political constitution, changing
by evolution but never by conquest, civil war or revolution. No
nation has enjoyed internal stability for so long. Looking at the
genocides and mass migrations, and at the upheavals and agonies
which revolutions inflict on millions of ordinary families, these
certainly are blessings. The explanation has lain in Britain's
ability to accommodate changing forces and to reform fast enough
to avoid revolution. The 'reformists' who disarm the explosive
force of revolutionary bitterness amongst the people were Lenin's
worst enemies. But Engels wrote ruefully in 1874 that the most
revolutionary body in Europe had proved to be the British House
of Commons.

This is one of the many reasons—though by no means the only
reason—why so many British radicals and revolutionaries now
speak in terms of change through the parliamentary process. The
fact that they also couple parliamentary with extra-parliamentary
action is quite in accord with the proper processes of a pluralist
society. Pluralism means nothing if it is not balancing of the
power of Parliament against the forces exerted by other institutions, parties and pressure groups.

But many forms of extra-parliamentary activity, if they are to
be effective, inevitably involve some disruption of the economy
and of the life of the community.

H

Sources of disruption in British society

The underlying causes of most internal conflict in Britain are economic ones—even if they are not in the precise form predicted by Marx. For over a century his forecast of a declining standard of living proved wrong. The standard of living persistently rose, though more slowly than in Britain's competitors, until 1974 when, as has been brought out in earlier chapters, it began to decline.

The causes of this decline are many and complex, but amongst them is the self-inflicted internal disruption of Britain's industrial society. Sometimes the disruption has been caused by selfish people out for money or power; sometimes it has been caused deliberately—perhaps for the best of motives—by those who believe that stability is stagnation and perpetuates privilege; and that progressive change can only come by making the existing system fail, so that it will crumble and collapse, at no matter what cost to today's generation, for the greater good of those to come.

Some who work for radical or revolutionary change believe that they can bring it about within the constitution without such a collapse. This is the contemporary policy of the 'Euro-Communist' parties, including the CPGB. It is also the claim of Labour Party Marxists, of two kinds: the orthodox Marxists, working for political power through industry: and the Trotskyist 'Militant' tendency, working mainly through the Labour Party's constituency and youth organizations. All of these (including the CPGB) believe that they can achieve power, and the changes they want, through a Labour Party controlled by people with their views and holding a majority in Parliament. Thus far, this aim is proper and constitutional; but it is over some of their techniques for gaining that control that ethical doubts must arise.

Other movements on the right of the political spectrum also have radical aims for changes in society—the National Front, the National Party, and the National Association for Freedom. NAFF —like the CPGB and the Labour Party Marxists—hopes to gain the power to implement these changes through Parliament. They work for a Conservative Party led by people like themselves.

There are other political parties and groups, however, which reject the parliamentary road to radical change, many of which have already appeared in the story: SWP, IMG, WRP, WSL, CPBML and CPEML—and a large number of smaller groups or factions. Their aims and methods will be briefly reviewed later in this chapter.

But not all the sources of conflict and disruption are in themselves political, though they can be exploited for political ends. Industrial disputes are one obvious example. But as well as the TUC and the CBI there are other institutions and concentrations of power, some of them too heavy for a healthy balance in the pluralist society; these too can be used to further political aims, both by those who wield the power of the institutions, and by those within them who use the opportunities available from the nature of their work to further their own political ideas: in the press, for example, in broadcasting and in the City of London.

It is also very easy to exploit racial, communal and nationalist tensions. Young people, too, are exploited, by those who want to use schools for social engineering or who believe that it will be easier and more effective to inculcate revolutionary ideas into children than into their parents; by those who hope to weaken the stabilizing influence of the family and exploit the natural impatience of teenagers to shake off their restraints; and by those who seek commercial dividends by harassing young people's urge for experiment and adventure along with the new-found affluence which those who have a job can enjoy. This affluence arises from the anomaly—unknown in China or Japan—of paying a person aged eighteen or twenty as much as his father for doing the same job, but with no family responsibilities on which he has to spend it.

The people who exploit these opportunities all thrive on conflict and tension, and many of them are prepared to inflict considerable disruption on the community to further their aims.

The Communist Party of Great Britain (CPGB)

By far the most effective of the political movements devoted to revolutionary change in Britain is the Communist Party, in association with its allies amongst the Labour Party Marxists. They have modelled their plans on the French and Italian Com-

munist Parties, both of which have established working arrangements with other parliamentary parties and will almost certainly
hold or share power during the next few years.

The CPGB still claim to be revolutionary; but to what extent
are they disruptive? They have for many years now had a published programme—*The British Road to Socialism*. This was
revised in 1977, and the new edition gives a very clear account of
how they plan to gain power and of how they would use it. Are
they, like the French and Italians, likely to do so?

There is little doubt about the sincerity of most of the members
of the CPGB. They believe that society as it stands is evil and
inequitable; that there is no cure other than to 'make a revolutionary change, end capitalism and build a Socialist society'.[1]
They claim that theirs is the only effective 'British Road to
Socialism'. And they are human enough to want, if their kind
of society comes about, to be amongst its leaders.

Most of them are also probably sincere in believing that this
can be achieved by gaining control (with the Labour Party
Marxists) of the *existing* structures of the trade unions and of the
Labour Party, and that parliamentary democracy can therefore
continue—though for how long it should continue is a matter
for some differences of opinion amongst themselves.

> We hold the view that all democratic parties, including those
> opposed to Socialism, should be guaranteed political rights
> and the right legally to contend for power in elections. That
> is, the struggle should proceed in conditions of political
> pluralism. The declared position of the Labour movement,
> including the Communist Party, is that it will respect the
> verdict of the electors, and that a Left Government will stand
> down if it is defeated in an election.[2]

The suspicious may detect loopholes: 'democratic' parties; 'political' (but not economic?) pluralism. But the reality of the freedom of other parties to contend for power in elections will depend
upon the control of the 'state apparatus'—and, more important,
of the media. The CPGB case is that these are all now controlled
by either big business or by a class-oriented establishment, so
that they themselves cannot fairly 'contend for power'. The fact
that the *Morning Star* (CPGB), *Socialist Worker* (SWP), *Socialist
Challenge* (IMG), *News Line* (WRP), and *Militant* (Labour Party

Marxist) are published freely along with *Spearhead* (National Front) and *Free Nation* (NAFF) does not in their view constitute a free press in that capitalist and Government advertising revenue ensure that the popular press will always have an overwhelming share of circulation. On the other hand, there has not so far been any established Marxist state which has permitted papers representing rival political parties to appear at all.

In the 1968 edition of *The British Road to Socialism*, the CPGB declared that when they, with a Left-controlled Labour Party, took power, the judges, chief constables, generals and civil servants would be replaced by others loyal to 'Socialism', and that the press would be taken over by 'the people'. This has been watered down significantly in the 1977 version. They would take steps to 'limit big business domination of the press and to open up the mass media to the working people'. They accept that, after 'winning the Labour Party' (an odd phrase which must have been chosen with some care), and the establishment of a Left Government with a Left majority in Parliament, much would initially remain unchanged:

> At this stage the armed forces, the police, the civil service, the judiciary etc.—that is, the state apparatus—would remain in the hands of the class representatives of capitalism. But the nature of the British constitution, under which Parliament has supreme authority, gives a Left Government the democratic right and the means, backed by the mass struggle of the people, to carry through drastic and necessary reforms in the state apparatus to correspond to the political change in the country expressed in the electoral verdict of the people. This will involve carrying further the steps outlined earlier in this section, including changes in top personnel . . .[3]

This may be saying much the same thing as before, and could be interpreted as either reasonable or sinister. Every revolutionary government has had, from sheer necessity, to use the 'existing apparatus of state' for a period at least. There is nothing unusual about requiring public officials to work loyally for the Government of the day. Those who publicly oppose its policies can expect to be censured or, if they persist, sacked by a Conservative or Labour Government, so why should a Communist Government not do so? The CPGB have, in their programme, kept their options open, and only time would tell how—and when—those options would be used.

Experience in other Marxist states is not encouraging. Lenin took power with a general election almost due. He let it go ahead, but the Bolsheviks got only 25 per cent of the vote. The Social Revolutionaries had a majority—in fact, with the Mensheviks as their allies, a very large majority. So Lenin sent in soldiers to close down the first session of the elected Assembly and it never met again. There is no Marxist Government in history which has ever, in the event, allowed itself to be ousted by parliamentary election. The CPGB admit this but claim that Britain, along with France and Italy, would be different. The voting in French and Italian elections in 1976–7 suggested that many of their people believed that. The CPGB vote of 0·1 per cent in the General Election of 1974 suggested that the British, as yet, did not.

There have also always been some CPGB members who themselves doubt the wisdom of this programme. In the 1960s one of their leading members, Reg Birch, broke away and formed a new party—the CPBML—in rejection of the idea of a parliamentary road to Socialism, and in July 1977 Sid French, a veteran Surrey Communist, rejected the ideas of the 1977 *British Road to Socialism* and formed his own New Communist Party.

For the time being, however, it is of more immediate concern to examine the means by which the CPGB hope to gain power, to 'win the Labour Party'. On this they have no doubts—it is to be through the trade unions, which provide 80 per cent of the funds and, with their card votes, control 88 per cent of the vote at the annual Labour Party Conference. The power of the Conference does not at present extend to the choice of the Labour Prime Minister and his Cabinet, but the CPGB and the Labour Party Marxists think that it should. If it did, trade union power over the Party and, if in power, over the Cabinet and the Government, would be complete. So CPGB and Labour Party Marxist control of the trade unions would provide the ultimate—and in practice probably irreversible—road to power.

Despite the 0·1 per cent popular vote, the CPGB's progress in the trade unions has been remarkable. In 1976, 15 per cent of the National Executive members of the biggest trade unions were CPGB members.[4] Roughly another 15 per cent were Labour Party Marxists who generally shared their aims.[5]

Contrary to popular myth, this was not achieved just by

ballot-rigging, but primarily by playing the rules to the full (with some gamesmanship), and by effective performance as nego-tiators. Communists are more concerned with power than with money and they are willing to work for it. They are ready to volunteer for the chores—usually unpaid—of being shop stewards, convenors and branch secretaries of their unions. Within their branch (and higher) union committees they form 'advisory groups' of CPGB members and Labour Party Marxists to discuss the agenda for meetings, and to plan their tactics in handling them.[6] In particular they arrange meetings at a time when a lot of union members will be doing other things, so that only the politically active will take the trouble to attend, and these often comprise 5 per cent or less of the membership of the branch; they conduct long and boring discussions, with much attention to procedure, for the first few hours of the meeting so that those who have other interests (such as watching a particular television programme or getting a drink before closing time) will drift away. They then count heads, and spring the really important votes—such as for election of members for committees or delegates for meetings—when they are sure they will win. Their model was created by Lenin himself at the London Conference of the Social Democratic Party in 1903, when he used just this method to gain editorial control of the party newspaper, *Iskra*.[7]

Nevertheless it would be misleading to suggest that even this 'gamesmanship' (still less the ballot-rigging) was the chief means by which the CPGB and Labour Party Marxists secured 30 per cent of the places on the big trade union executives, both at national level and lower down. The starting point is on the shop floor, and all depends on the confidence which the shop steward, the convenor and the union branch committee member earns from the men he represents; and for this there is no short cut, no substitute for hard work and effectiveness. As one of them put it to the author: 'It is a matter of finding out what the lads are really concerned about, then working to get it for them, and carrying on from there. They're not so interested in revolutionary doctrine or world history as in better bonus or overtime rates or a decent place for a wash. Get them what they want and you have their loyalty.'[8]

This particular shop steward worked a fourteen-hour day—eight hours at his job and six hours unpaid work as a shop steward—political, industrial and social. His unpaid work included studying the current problems on the job—and the rule book—so that he could successfully negotiate what his men wanted; lecturing to Young Communists and others; and—perhaps most important of all—welfare work. If a man lost his job it was he who went round in the evening to see what could be done, about the job and about the family. If a man went to hospital (or to prison), it was he who called in on the wife and children: 'Don't worry, we'll take care of you. Here's ten quid to go on with for tomorrow morning's shopping. I'll drop in again on Tuesday. In the meantime, if there's anything you want, you know where to find me.'

His men followed him, not because he was a Communist but in spite of it. When he stood in a Parliamentary election he got a derisory vote; but they would go to him with their problems, treat him as their negotiator and, if he said 'strike', they would strike. He earned their support because he served them well. What Communism gave him was what a religion can give—the strength and dedication to do two men's work.

Much of what a good CPGB union official or shop steward does to build his power base on the shop floor is wholly to be admired; how he uses his power is more controversial—and dichotomous. On the one hand, he wants to accelerate the collapse of the mixed economy by making private firms go bankrupt and nationalized industries fail, so that both will be handed over to the control of workers' co-operatives or trade union committees—both preferably under Party control; to do this, he needs to disrupt industries, public and private, to hit their profits. On the other hand, he knows that if his men form the opinion that his leadership is losing them money, by constant disruption of production, with lay-offs and, worse still, redundancies, he will lose their following.

A good Communist is, like Lenin, pragmatic. Subject to direct instructions from the CPGB Advisory Group in his Union Committee to halt production in accordance with a party line, he will, when there is a clash of priorities, do what will best retain his power base on the shop floor. The best way to do this is by *positive* results—a bigger bonus or better working conditions. But if his men are seriously worried about earnings, or about being sent to join the dole queue, he may temper his militancy with discretion—and sometimes even co-operate positively with management to increase production and earnings.

All the time, however, he will be aware that militancy can pay dividends in two ways; by persuading management that it will be cheaper in the end to make the concessions he demands; and by getting the rank and file 'involved in the struggle'. He knows very well that the majority of workers are not politically aware, and that (because they have wives and children) they have no great desire to sacrifice their pay-packets. On the other hand if, by confrontation, he can provoke the management into being high-handed—and especially if he can induce them to sack someone for disruption or supposed misbehaviour—the anger of a normally placid work-force can be aroused. Industrial history is full of examples of men heroically accepting privation out of loyalty to a fellow worker, with nothing in it for them. An effective militant shop steward will be able to handle a situation so as to arouse and harness this loyalty.

The same applies to violence. The CPGB strike leaders know well enough that the majority of workers dislike it, whether it is used against non-strikers or policemen. On the other hand, if a situation can be developed in which pickets are put in fear of their lives by hard-driven strike-breaking vehicles, or by the police appearing to use excessive force in clearing the highway or making arrests, this also gets moderate men involved in the struggle. As one shop steward put it: 'My lads regard the police as their friends. I have to convince them that they are enemies. There's nothing like a bit of violence to do that; provided that they blame the police and not me for starting it.'

The militant strike leader may be faced with a dilemma: if by his agitation he has aroused his men to a point of violent confrontation he cannot, without loss of face, hold back himself. A thinking CPGB leader will have to decide whether the damage done by the violence to his wider cause will exceed the loss in his own prestige and leadership if he were to 'chicken out' or to call cravenly for surrender when the men are steamed up for battle. If he is sensible he is most likely to give overriding weight to retaining or enhancing his shop-floor support.

The Labour Party Marxists

Most of the same considerations apply to Labour Party Marxists operating on the industrial front. They have a proper Leninist appreciation of the importance of leadership, of a tight organization and of getting their men aroused and involved. The only real difference between them and the CPGB is that they believe that they can achieve their aims more effectively within the Labour Party than outside it, in particular by building up the 'Left control' of the Party from inside, as advocated in *The British Road to Socialism.*

As with the CPGB, their most important avenue to that control is through the 88 per cent trade union card vote at the annual Conference, so their efforts are directed to extending their influence in the unions, and seeking to strengthen the power of the Conference and the NEC to direct the policy of the leader of the Labour Party in Parliament.

These are the 'orthodox' Marxists in the Labour Party. The Trotskyist Militant tendency works by 'entryism', aiming to control the constituency Labour Parties and, through them, the selection of Parliamentary candidates. They also hope to get the rules changed so that those candidates who become Labour MPs speak and vote as they would wish; in other words, to act as 'delegates' from the constituency party management committee rather than 'representatives' of the voters who elected them. These internal political challenges within the Labour Party will be discussed in Chapter 20.

The Socialist Workers' Party (SWP)

The SWP (formerly International Socialists, IS) was founded in the early 1950s. It was never a mass movement, though its membership, having hovered around 3,000 from 1973 to 1975, increased to over 5,000 in 1977. Its sources and methods of new recruitment were discussed in Chapter 17. It puts up some candidates for Parliament, but none have got more than a few hundred votes and SWP admits that the only aim of this is as a vehicle for publicity.

SWP aims to oust the CPGB as the focus for militancy on the shop floor, by organizing 'rank and file' movements on the shop floor as a challenge to existing union leadership, including CPGB leadership. It totally rejects the parliamentary road proposed by the CPGB,[9] and calls for mass action by the workers to seize control of the wealth created by them under capitalism and to destroy the system.[10]

The main appeal of IS (and now SWP) was always to university students. After nearly 20 years of student activity it had realized by 1973 that students have no political or economic muscle in their capacity as students (they can really only strike against themselves) and that they must somehow find a way of using students and graduates to direct activity on the shop floor. Attempts in the early 1970s by IS graduates to take manual jobs and become shop stewards sometimes succeeded because, being educated and middle-class, they made effective negotiators, but most of them were spotted and distrusted by other workers. One, at least, survived in the motor industry and is said to have claimed with pride to have been responsible for the loss of £30 million in production of British cars.

More widely successful was a plan to 'service' strikes by offering the kind of support that hard-pressed strike leaders welcomed. They ran a large printing works, which not only printed *Socialist Worker* but also had capacity for much outside work.[11] They were thus able to print and distribute leaflets for strike committees. They also provided transport and meal services for pickets and off-duty entertainment. This, apart from anything else, helped to fulfil a yearning amongst the students—male and female—for friendly and meaningful contact with members of a working class whose interests they felt they were fighting for but of whom they had seen very little. Many had earlier been rebuffed when trying to sell *Socialist Worker* at the factory gates, and these rebuffs had caused a considerable turnover of membership.

In the mid-1970s, they realized that there was growing potential for influence in the white-collar unions, and they tried (using the methods described above for the CPGB) to get control of branches of unions of teachers (NUT), civil servants (CPSA), local government officials (NALGO) and—perhaps most important—of journalists (NUJ) where they aimed also to institute a closed shop, including the editors. This, if achieved, would be their greatest prize, for it would give whoever controlled the NUJ effective control of the press. It has been in the white-collar unions that SWP have been most successful.

They have also, however, shown increasing realism in their efforts on the shop floor. When the two Shrewsbury pickets (Des Warren and Ricky Tomlinson) were imprisoned,[12] they learned that Tomlinson's union (TGWU) was paying his family substantially less than Warren's (UCATT). IS therefore paid Mrs Tomlinson £25 a week while her husband was in prison. This was an act of grace, and it also resulted in Tomlinson appearing on IS platforms when he came out.

It was after this that IS began its successful drive to recruit unemployed workers, as described in Chapter 17, and their activities resulted in a great deal more violence. A contingent of IS had been involved in Red Lion Square in 1974, but they played a smaller part than IMG. The violent confrontations with the police arising from the Right to Work March in 1976, and the Grunwick dispute and the attempt to stop the National Front march in Lewisham in 1977 marked the change in their character and composition, and reflected the change in their title from IS to SWP. Their attitude to violence can be assessed from pages 202 and 217 to 219.

They were not a serious political force in 1971–7, but they were a disruptive one and took part in some of the worst public disorders of the century. Their chief function was still to provide an outlet for students and graduates who wished to change society by extra-parliamentary means, but in 1976 they achieved what they had so long desired: a substantial working-class involvement. They did this by recruiting immigrants and unemployed workers, who had good reason to be bitterly disgruntled with society and had time on their hands. This created new problems, for a number of those attracted were inevitably people unlikely to get regular employment, sometimes with criminal records.

These violent confrontations did have the effect—which study of *Socialist Worker* suggests that they desire—of widening the breach between SWP and the main stream of the trade union movement, the Labour Party and the CPGB. And as in Red Lion Square, the violence at Hendon, Grunwick and Lewisham brought comfort and encouragement only to the far Right.

In the long run a more serious threat from SWP to the pluralist society may be in the intellectual field: in the civil service, local government, education, broadcasting and (through an NUJ closed shop) in the press.

IMG, WRP, CPBML, WSL, CPEML and Others

The only other two movements whose strength exceeds or has

exceeded 500 are the Trotskyist International Marxist Group (IMG) and the Workers' Revolutionary Party (WRP).

The strength of IMG has varied between 500 and 1,000 and it frequently splits. Though, like SWP, it claims to speak on behalf of the working class it has, unlike SWP, made few serious attempts to involve itself on the shop floor. Its support lies even more predominantly in the universities, with a fringe of older graduates in London and other cities, concentrating on the support of minorities (such as Gay Liberation, immigrant movements, Women's Liberation, etc.). Though of little political significance itself, IMG has proved adept at selecting issues for demonstrations for which large numbers of people will turn out (e.g. 50,000 at Grosvenor Square in 1968) and it can be extremely violent, as in Red Lion Square (see Chapter 13). A growing number of potential IMG members have, since 1975, been joining the Labour Party instead, in order to strengthen the Militant tendency in the Party, which shares its Trotskyist aims.

WRP (known until 1973 as the Socialist Labour League, SLL) was, until 1975, aggressively proletarian, rather despising intellectuals. It concentrated on young people, running successful summer camps. It thereby gained many young recruits, but they had a high dropout rate. It was reported that, of 20,000 'Young Socialist' recruits per year, only 5 per cent stayed in. There was, however, an unexpected by-product from these camps. Prominent show-business personalities with radical views attended to entertain the campers, and some joined the movement, including Vanessa Redgrave and her brother Corin. The WRP now also has a number of other actors, playwrights and producers from the stage and television, an important part of whose activity since 1975 has consisted of broadcasting plays with the organization's political message. Recent successes have been *Leeds United* and a series of four plays under the title *Days of Hope*. All of these set out to discredit both the trade union movement and the CPGB, as well as the more familiar targets. WRP also made a determined attempt in 1975 to take over control of Equity, the actors' union.

The Communist Party of Britain, Marxist–Leninist (CPBML) was mentioned earlier. Its leader, Reg Birch, is a veteran trade unionist (AUEW), who is convinced that the CPGB has joined the bourgeoisie and that change can only come by revolution. He believes that this is a long way off, and that his task at present is to educate the workers to reject social democracy. CPBML strength in 1976 was about 200, of whom only 20 per cent (to Reg Birch's sadness) were manual workers. The largest number were students and the next largest were teachers.

The Workers' Socialist League (WSL) broke away from IS in 1975, led by Alan Thornett, and operates mainly in British Leyland. It is small but highly professional in stopping production.

The Communist Party of England, Marxist–Leninist (CPEML) is a very small movement, avowedly Maoist, which was involved in Red Lion Square (see Chapter 13) and in a number of incidents at universities, as well as at Grunwick.

Apart from these, there are many other fringe movements, Marxist and anarchist, which form, publish papers, split and disappear. There are, in addition, a number of papers with a far-left bias, such as *Time Out*, but their primary motivation appears to be a commercial one, catering mainly for London's 'radical chic'.

The total membership of all the far Left parties in 1977, including SWP, was probably about 8,000. The CPGB had less than 30,000 members on paper, and many of these had not paid their dues.

The National Front (NF) and the National Party (NP)

The National Front (NF) was formed in February 1967, an amalgam of neo-Nazis and nostalgic British Empire loyalists. Coloured immigration in the 1960s had been enormous and the confirmation of the Labour Government in office in 1966 suggested that the door would remain open. This, the fear of 'creeping Socialism', a general disillusion with 'soft politicians', and a yearning for a strong leader provided the impetus.

The NF is a populist party, recruited almost entirely from manual workers or small-scale self-employed—shopkeepers and others. Its appeal to unskilled workers is different from that to the skilled or self-employed. Its unskilled workers resent black job competition and, feeling themselves inferior to the rest of society, need someone to kick—rather as in the nineteenth-century USA the Anglo-Saxons kicked the Irish and the Irish kicked the blacks. On the other hand, the skilled and self-employed resent their declining status and pay differentials, and particularly envy the prosperity of some of the Asians who are willing to work a fourteen-hour day to build up a family business.

A large proportion of NF members are middle-aged—many fought in the Second World War and feel cheated—and some of these have considerable confidence and organizing ability. They are able to recruit an increasing number of white boys, not averse to bashing blacks and Asians physically, and happy to support a party which does so politically. The boys are also attracted by a cause with which they can identify and to which they can be aggressively loyal; the terraces at Manchester United or Chelsea are more likely to provide recruits for the NF than for the CPGB —though they would probably rally as readily to any strong leader, fascist, nationalist, populist or Marxist, if they sensed that he held the power.

Other breeding grounds are the schools with high immigrant ratios. So are some of the Borstals, particularly where there is a 50–50 balance between blacks and whites. In some of these the West Indian boys are well organized in the intensely racist Rastafarian movement,[13] and establish 'no-go' areas for themselves—the best washrooms and toilets, etc.—'Rastas Only, White Trash Keep Out.' There is not much doubt where the white boys will turn when they get home.

By 1970 NF candidates were gaining up to 10 per cent of the votes in municipal elections. General Amin's flood of Ugandan Asian immigrants in 1972 gave them a fillip, but their best and most lasting boost came from the IMG in Red Lion Square in June 1974. This had all the ingredients they needed: hairy intellectuals siding with the blacks and the Reds; pampered middle-class students attacking working-class policemen; NF pride in their order, discipline and respect for the law contrasted with disorder and violence by the students; and the publicity, hostile to the students and therefore indirectly favourable to the NF—but, above all, publicity for their existence and their aims.

So in the second half of 1974 recruits poured in—though many poured out again when they found out what they had got into; membership reached 12,000, and as many as 20,000 were NF members at some time or other during 1974.[14] In the October 1974 election the NF candidate at Hackney and Shoreditch took 9·4 per cent of the vote, their highest yet in a General Election, and remarkable in view of the intensity of the Labour-Conservative contest which drew most voters away from the splinter parties.

In December 1975 the NF split, about 20 per cent moving to a new National Party (NP), which rejected the marching and flag-waving image but was, if anything, more racist than the NF. The split, however, did little to check the NF's momentum. In the local elections at Leicester in May 1976 the NF took 18 per cent of the vote, and at Deptford in June the NF/NP vote totalled 44 per cent—higher than for the Labour candidate, who only got in because of the NF/NP split. So it was no surprise when the NF selected Deptford Town Hall for the start of the Lewisham march in August 1977 and, like IMG in 1974, the SWP provided the answer to their prayer.

In three Parliamentary by-elections in 1977, the NF candidates moved into third place, ahead of the Liberals. The voting pattern made it clear that they were drawing most of their new voters from those who had previously voted Labour, not Conservative. Like Hitler's National Socialists, NF dislikes the Establishment and regards the City of London and the EEC as sinister manifestations of the international conspiracy of Jewish financiers. They despise the Conservative Party—especially since Enoch Powell left it.

Nevertheless, if the country seemed to be heading for really alarming chaos and economic collapse and the Conservative Party threw up a strong leader promising order and national revival—a de Gaulle—the kind of people who join the NF would probably rally to his lead.

The National Association for Freedom (*NAFF*)

The National Association for Freedom was, at its inception, very different from the National Front. It was founded by people who would feel very much at home amongst the Establishment, or amongst the leaders of the right wing of the Conservative Party. But NAFF's membership became much more broadly based in 1976–7, when it captured the mood of a substantial sector of opinion in the country with its challenges to bureaucrats and trade union power. This led many more manual workers to join it and it consciously set its sights on a populist appeal.

NAFF was formed in the summer of 1975 and was publicly launched in December 1975 just after the murder by the IRA of Ross McWhirter, whose twin brother Norris was one of the founder members of its Council. It was dedicated to the principle of *laissez-faire*, including freedom from interference in running a business, freedom to choose a school or a doctor or a hospital —and freedom to strike. Amongst its declared targets are the powers of the bureaucracy and of the trade unions, and the closed shop.

It has concentrated with some success on legal action, such as obtaining a High Court injunction to release cars stranded on a ferry by a strike, and to permit the Conservative Tameside Council to retain its grammar schools. It first hit the headlines in November 1976 when Tom Jackson, UPW General Secretary, drew back from blacking Grunwick's mail in the face of a High Court action prompted by NAFF director John Gouriet. Gouriet had a further success in January 1977 with an injunction to stop the UPW boycotting mail and telephone services to South Africa. This success had a piquant flavour because the Appeal Court decided that Gouriet had a right as a private citizen to launch the case in defiance of the Attorney General. Though this was later overturned by the House of Lords, NAFF gained much prestige and publicity as the defenders of the individual against the power of the state. They claimed to be receiving £1,000 per day in donations after this, and their membership doubled to 15,000, overtaking the National Front.

Then, during 1977, the Grunwick dispute gathered momentum, as described in Chapter 16. NAFF's fortunes ebbed and flowed in the High Courts, Appeal Courts and House of Lords, but every case brought more publicity and, as in Red Lion Square, the violence of the fringe groups around the Grunwick factory played into NAFF's hands.

NAFF claims to be non-political, but John Gouriet has said: 'While many people are talking about opposing Socialism, we are one of the few bodies that does anything about it.'[15]

Their real aims are best revealed by their choice of victims. In picking Tom Jackson (UPW) and Roy Grantham (APEX) as their 'fall-guys', they have been happy to humiliate two of the leading moderates in the trade union movement. This is the very reverse of the attitude described on page 103 by a Minister in the Heath Government: 'If you're going to help the moderates they've got to be seen to be fighting like tigers.' That is why NAFF is cold-shouldered by the more liberal Conservatives like Edward Heath, James Prior and Peter Walker, who seek the kind of

Government/trade union co-operation so successful in Germany. NAFF is clearly more concerned to discredit the unions and their leaders, moderate and militant alike, rather than to seek their co-operation.

NAFF can argue[16] that they fight principles and not personalities and that, as a matter of tactics, they must seize their chances (like Grunwick) when they arise. Actions and successes are what give the movement its momentum; if the casualties are moderate trade unionists, they say, that is their bad luck.

These, however, are the arguments, not of people who wish to bridge the divisions in British society, but of political activists —which is what NAFF really are.

Others on the Right

The Right—in politics and economics—has as many varieties as the Left. Some concentrate purely on industry, like the Economic League, run by subscription from private firms to keep management informed about disruptive movements in the unions and on the shop floor. Aims for Freedom and Enterprise does this too, but has also published political pamphlets and advertisements. Its director, Michael Ivens, is also a member of the Council of NAFF.

On the populist Right is General Walker's movement, mentioned in Chapter 10. And there is also a lunatic fringe of far Right movements which form, split and dissolve as fast as their opposite members on the Left.

Finally there are two movements which defy classification, since they are actively anti-Communist, but work within the trade union movement and the Labour Party. The Movement for True Industrial Democracy (TRUEMID) was formed in 1975 by militantly industrial (rather than militantly political) trade unionists to counter the takeover of the unions by the CPGB and Labour Party Marxists. The Industrial Research and Information Services (IRIS) publishes data about the candidates in union elections, saying in particular which are supported by the CPGB, and has traditionally had as its President a distinguished senior member of the Labour Party or trade union movement, such as Ray Gunter. TRUEMID and IRIS cannot be described as disruptive or right-wing, and serve to illustrate the breadth of the political spectrum to be found within the Labour Party.

The price to pay for disruption

Disruption is an escalation of dissent. It can, within reason be a stimulus, a necessary force for progressive change. Too much of it is a luxury, from which only those who exercise it benefit, at the expense of the rest of the community. The question is how much disruption Britain, in a state of economic siege, can afford.

Pluralism thrives on dissent. A democratic society without dissent stagnates. Refusal of the majority to tolerate minorities or to accommodate dissent leads to explosive pressure. It is no coincidence that the two longest-lived constitutional systems— Britain (1688) and USA (1776)—are the two which have most consistently permitted and responded to dissent. No society which consistently suppresses dissent has yet reached the age of three-score years and ten without at least one violent internal upheaval, and none are likely to do so unless they do begin to accommodate it.[17]

Dissent cannot be effectively expressed without at least some disruption, even if only of the traffic. But how much disruption, damage and injury should the rest of the community have to bear? Even quite a small strike, like that of the British Airways maintenance engineers over the 1977 Easter holiday, cost the taxpayer £31 million—and lost the country that much too in its balance of payments. Was this too high a price to pay over such a small issue on behalf of so few men? And how many Saltleys, Shrewsburys and Red Lion Squares will people stand before turning in exasperation to an equally disruptive reaction? Was Grunwick a warning light or a flash in the pan?

There are many forces of disruption and of reaction to them, as described in this chapter. In a democratic society, their excesses can only be legitimately controlled in two ways—by the rule of law and by the political process. Are these adequate for the task? This question is the subject of the next two chapters.

19 The Rule of Law

Political violence and the law

The law in relation to terrorism, demonstrations and industrial disputes has been discussed in context in the appropriate chapters.[1] The purpose of this chapter is to pick out some of the aspects of the law which most need to be kept under review, or changed.

Because of the universal public dislike of political violence, the laws covering it can be changed more quickly than most. In the wake of any spectacular political violence, Parliament can be confident of a consensus, both inside and outside the House. The Prevention of Terrorism (Temporary Provisions) Act became law within a week of the Birmingham bombs in 1974. In July and August 1977, after the violence at Grunwick, Lewisham and Ladywood, it would have been equally possible to pass draconian legislation about demonstrations. But laws should not be drafted hastily, so the Government should maintain contingency legislation in draft and updated in readiness for presentation to Parliament in emergency.

Terrorism

Though legislation can be protective in making it more difficult for terrorists to get weapons or explosives, or to move or to mount attacks, the only lasting protection against terrorism is to prevent it from paying.

This is very easily done in totalitarian societies, partly because there is no avenue for public challenge to Government actions, and secondly because with a controlled press, the terrorists can be denied any publicity. The Security Officer of a famous soft drinks firm has said that the countries in which he had fewest anxieties were those behind the Iron Curtain—but that he would hate to live there.[2] Soviet officials and citizens face little risk from terrorism, but they have to live with other and more disagreeable restrictions and threats to their personal liberties.

In a pluralist society the determined terrorist can always kill or destroy, and the art lies in keeping his activities within bounds at a tolerable price for the rest of the community to pay. That price can best be paid by efficient police work, which means spending enough money on the police to attract high-quality recruits and to avoid the lures of corruption; and for the police service to build up the confidence, and hence earn the co-operation, of the public. The British police service qualifies for all those except for the pay, and it has to maintain its quality and guard against corruption by being highly selective, at the cost of severe undermanning. This is a dangerous situation which needs urgent action.

When efficient police work alone proves not enough to keep the threat within bounds, then emergency legislation involving some curtailment of civil liberties will be accepted by the public. If the police and the legislation still prove inadequate, then there is a risk of unauthorized members of the public—vigilante groups or assassination squads—taking the law into their own hands.

The most effective example of efficient police work against terrorism was the virtual defeat of hijacking in the United States by the introduction in 1973 of a 100 per cent search of all passengers and baggage at the boarding gates.[3] And the most successful emergency legislation has probably been the British Prevention of Terrorism Act of 1974.

Legislation which was not then found necessary, but should perhaps be kept in readiness for emergencies, includes tighter passport control; identity cards, if necessary incorporating magnetic data; lodging registration, for private lodging as well as hotels; an extension of police authority to retain personal records (fingerprints, etc.); and tougher punishments—if necessary including the death penalty.[4] If the intimidation of witnesses and juries were ever to become as widespread as in Northern Ireland, it could become necessary to introduce something like the Northern Ireland (Emergency Provision) Act 1973, modifying some of the procedures for giving evidence and suspending trial by jury for terrorist offences. All of these things would be a curtailment of much-valued liberties and, if introduced when not absolutely essential, would make the society they aim to protect more brittle and vulnerable. But if, suddenly, there were a huge escalation of indiscriminate bombings and terrorization of the population, such measures would be the better for having been thought out in advance.

The greatest deterrent against terrorism, however, is the likelihood of being caught. Terrorist attacks are, in any case, crimes under existing laws. The greatest value of emergency legislation will be in its effectiveness in helping the police to catch the terrorists and to secure evidence for conviction.

Political demonstrations

The fundamental right to demonstrate peaceful dissent should not be denied to the majority because of its violent abuse by a minority unless this becomes absolutely necessary to prevent intolerable disruption, injury and death. The Public Order Act of 1936 was introduced to contain street violence between two very tiny political movements—the Fascists and the Communists. It is still on the Statute Book, and probably contains all the powers which the police might need to ban processions or to control their routes. If a chief police officer 'has reasonable ground for apprehending that the procession may occasion serious public disorder', he may direct those organizing or following it to take a prescribed route, or he can prohibit them from entering specified public places.[5] If he thinks that these powers are not 'sufficient to enable him to prevent serious public disorder', he may ask the Home Secretary (through his police authority if outside London) to ban the procession for up to three months.[6] These powers could have been used to ban the marches in Red Lion Square or Lewisham if the Commissioner of Police and Home Secretary had thought this wise; and the police did direct the route, in both cases. In his Report on Red Lion Square, Lord Justice Scarman recommended that the route approved should be specified in writing, and it has become customary to do this.

Scarman also noted that, while the senior police officer on the spot could redirect a march if he judged this necessary in the interest of public order, this power should be made statutory.[7] Scarman did not, however, support a proposal by Sir Robert Mark that it should be an offence to organize a demonstration without giving prior notice to the police.[8]

These powers, however, apply only to marches, not to meetings. No doubt with Red Lion Square in mind, the SWP did not organize a march in Lewisham, but merely called upon their members (through *Socialist Worker*) to gather at the advertised starting point of the NF march (Clifton Rise).[9] They also took over a house with windows overlooking it (from which missiles could be thrown) and notified their members that they had done so.[10] There is nothing in the Public Order Act which gives the police the power to prevent people gathering at some particular street corner. It would be difficult to devise legislation to do this, and probably not desirable in a free society unless the situation had so deteriorated as to necessitate a curfew.

The danger to society, however, does not lie in the fact of people marching or assembling but in the violence, disruption or damage which they do, or which they provoke. It is these which must be deterred and, as with terrorism, the best deterrent is the probability of detection and conviction. The best and fairest way is to identify and convict the man who actually uses the violence or intimidation personally for an individual offence.

The range of offences which individual demonstrators or counter-demonstrators may commit includes assault, affray, obstruction (of the police or of the highway), criminal damage, intimidation, threatening or insulting behaviour or conduct likely to cause a breach of the peace.

It is, however, not always easy to identify individual attackers with sufficient certainty to secure a conviction. When the Right to Work marchers at Hendon (Chapter 17) first attacked the eight police officers escorting the march, they inflicted the most serious injuries during the first minutes before any other policemen arrived on the scene. One of the marchers struck a police sergeant from behind with a heavy metal loud-hailer, inflicting serious head injuries. Only one other police officer was near enough to see the man who did it, but the judge ruled that identification by one person was insufficient. Although only one man was seen to be carrying a loud-hailer, there was no proof (apart from that one policeman's evidence) that he had not temporarily handed it to someone else to strike the blow, so the judge decided that there was no case to answer and the jury were not asked to give a verdict. The answer probably lies in taking more photographs—including film—but it costs money to deploy photographers and, while this can be foreseen when one or more groups plan a confrontation at a fixed point such as at Grunwick, Lewisham or Ladywood, it provides no answer when the marchers unexpectedly turn on their police escort, as at Hendon. Here it was the organizers of the demonstration who had deployed their own photographers around the spot in readiness, it seemed, for a planned publicity exercise. The best practical answer for the police may be to give every assistance to the normal press and television cameras to get pictures, and supplement these with their own.

Collective offences may be easier to prove, but are less satisfactory. *Affray* can be an individual or a collective offence and involves using violence or displaying force 'in such a manner that reasonable people might be frightened or intimidated'.[11] Affray can be proved by describing the actions of the accused, and this is easier than proving that an individual committed a particular assault.

An *unlawful assembly* must be of at least three persons, assembled with a common purpose to commit a crime of violence or to achieve some other object, whether lawful or not, in such a way as to cause reasonable men to apprehend a breach of the peace. It becomes a *rout* as soon as some act has been done 'moving towards' the execution of the common purpose, and a *riot* when some act is done in part execution of that purpose.[12]

The disturbances at Lewisham could certainly have been described as a riot, but there is a practical snag. If a disturbance becomes classed by the police as a riot, damage is not covered by insurance, and compensation can be claimed from the Police Rate. The Police (and local authorities) are therefore reluctant to charge people with rioting. There is some ground for amending the Riot (Damages) Act 1886 to overcome this.

Paradoxically, the charge of 'incitement to riot' produces fewer problems, since it is not necessary for the riot to have taken place. This may enable the organizers, or those who maliciously inflame others to use violence, to pay the penalty, which they probably deserve more than the people whom they launch into battle.

The blanket charge of conspiracy in this context is not satisfactory and is under review. It is unlikely to be used again in the way it was used at Shrewsbury.

The biggest practical problem, as was discussed in Chapter 5, may lie in the trial of a large number of people for a large number of charges of assault and other individual offences. This costs money, risks prejudice and ties up a lot of police giving evidence. Yet in view of the serious damage that organized political violence does to society, the problem must be solved. Natural justice is better served by individual than by collective convictions, and if this needs higher manning levels for the police, then that may in the end be more effective than amending legislation.

Judges and magistrates do, however, need to be empowered and encouraged to give far heavier penalties than they do for offences against public order, and particularly those involving violence and intimidation, for they strike at the deepest roots of liberty.

This was well put by Lord Scarman in concluding his Report on Red Lion Square:

> The overall lesson for demonstrators is clear: co-operate with the police. (The law and police practice must of course be such as to convince fair-minded people that the police are not politically motivated but concerned only to maintain or, if need be, to restore public order.) Demonstrators should, whenever possible, give notice to the police and accept limits upon the time and routeing of their demonstration as a necessary condition for the protection of their right to demonstrate. Within the Metropolitan Police District alone the police have to handle some 500 demonstrations each year: the burden of this work imposes very great strain on the police, and it would be unrealistic to imagine that demonstrations in this sort of number could be handled by the police without the co-operation of the demonstrators. If demonstrators do not co-operate they have only themselves to blame if the law loses its present freedom and becomes more restrictive, less flexible.
>
> Finally, I would emphasize that demonstration is only one of several purposes to which our streets may be put; and, perhaps, not the most important. It is a means of protest, not a substitute for political discussion or parliamentary debate. The streets are not the place for carrying on the discussion necessary for democratic government, though they can accommodate the voice of protest provided public order and the right of passage are not endangered.[13]

Violent picketing

It is not necessary to rehearse the laws of picketing, which were covered in earlier chapters, because charges in breach of these laws themselves are very rare. Most charges are for other offences which are criminal in any context, such as were listed above, under demonstrations. One of the aims of the laws relating to picketing should be to minimize the incidence of these other offences and to ensure that the law provides no loopholes for them if they are committed.

The loopholes most commonly used arise from immunities from prosecution enjoyed by pickets under the Trade Union and Labour Relations Act, and its predecessors. These, however, should not and were never intended to cover crimes but only torts; they should never excuse violence or intimidation; nor should they override the prior right of others to use the public highway; nor the right of others to work if they wish, since there may well be family or other reasons for this, quite apart from industrial ones.

It is reasonably argued that picketing cannot be effective unless pickets are given the opportunity to persuade. This being so, that opportunity should be provided by the police who (to prevent abuse by either side) should be left considerable discretion in providing it. No picket should be empowered to stop a vehicle, but a policeman should be so empowered. For, say, the first week of a strike, the driver and passengers in a vehicle could be obliged (by the police) to stop for, say, five minutes, and the pickets given access to them for that time. After the first week, the police should still stop them, but should not oblige them to wait unless they agree to do so, since it is reasonable to suppose that most if not all those attempting to pass the picket will by then be aware of the issues involved in the strike.

It is also essential to differentiate between pickets and demonstrators. It is not difficult to judge what is a reasonable number of pickets and this should be specified in the law—perhaps six for each line of traffic (e.g. twelve for a two-way road) and six for each separate pedestrian entrance. These pickets, in order to enjoy their privileges and immunities under the law and the co-operation of the police in giving them the access described above, should carry and display official authorization from their trade union.

Anyone else present is not a picket but a demonstrator.[14] To minimize the risk of disorders, demonstrations within 100 yards of an authorized picket should be unlawful—just as it is unlawful to demonstrate in a law court or inside or in the vicinity of Parliament.

People demonstrating in connection with an industrial dispute should in other respects have the same rights and obligations as any other demonstrators. They should have no claim on the privileges and immunities of pickets.

Mass picketing is not picketing and cannot be treated as a lawful assembly. Since its declared (and indeed its only) purpose is to obstruct, it is clearly unlawful. If a law is not enforced it breeds disrespect for the rule of law as a whole. Merely condemning the breach of it in Parliament is weak and inadequate. Parliament must ensure that the terms of the law give the police and judiciary the ability to enforce it in practice.

Picketing of premises by people not involved in the dispute was never intended in any legislation, but it is not specifically unlawful. It should be. If it is lawful for some, then the law cannot discriminate and it has to be lawful for all—for teachers who want to close the power stations or civil servants who want to close the airports, on the grounds that closing their schools and their offices does not give them the leverage to win. The public would clearly not wish this, and if the public does not wish it it should not be either legalized or condoned.

The blacking of goods coming from or destined for premises in dispute is a grey area. TULRA as amended in 1976 did make it lawful, but this does open the door for abuse of power and should be watched carefully by Parliament.

After the worst week of mass picketing and violence at Grunwick, Lord Robens—a former Minister of Labour and member of the Donovan Commission—recommended that the definition of 'picket' should be confined to those picketing their own place of employment or prior place of employment (to allow dismissed strikers to take part). Lord Robens added:

It would enable peaceful picketing to actually take place, it would assist the police to perform their function, and prevent

the 'rent-a-picket' and others from turning peaceful picketing
into mass intimidation.

It would seem to me that this would allow the trade union
movement, the Secretary of State for Employment and the
police to perform their function in a much cooler atmosphere
than is presently the case, with possibilities of agreed settlements in a much speedier time.[15]

Public interest and personal options

The right to strike was enacted to give collective power to wage-
earners to apply pressure on private employers or the shareholders of companies by hitting their pockets. In the majority of
serious strikes now the employer is the public. Of every £100
million lost in output by British Leyland, £95 million can be
found from one source only—taxation, that is, either by raising
more taxes or by diverting more public money away from other
services. The same applies to every extra £100 million paid in
wages and salaries in publicly owned industries and public services. The public also suffers indirectly from losses to the balance
of payments by the dislocation of both public and private industry, whether caused by strikes or by denial of public utilities.
And, of course, the families stranded in the airport lounges at the
cost of their Easter and August holidays in 1977 by the small
numbers who chose those moments to strike suffered very directly
indeed. So, in a complex industrial society, every strike is wholly
or partly a strike against the public.

Nevertheless, to deny or unduly restrict the right to strike on
these grounds would be incompatible with pluralism, and would
be only one step from the totalitarian concept of giving all power
to the state, in the name of the people, against whom no strikes
are permitted.

There is, however, some justification for restricting the right
to strike in certain public services on which life and public health
depend. This has long been recognized in some public services,
such as those concerned with national defence and the police,
and to a limited extent in others, such as the postal services.
People choosing to work in these services are well aware of the
restrictions and, in the overwhelming majority of cases, recognize
their necessity and abide by them. Many, in fact, are attracted to

join by the knowledge that their work will not be subject to disruption and that they will not be faced with an agonizing conflict between loyalty to a union and loyalty to the public. There is, however, a need for legislation to codify these restrictions more clearly. There are two ways in which those who accept the sacrifice of a power enjoyed by others might be compensated for that sacrifice: first, by a 'no right to strike' increment to their incomes, to be paid independently of any wage settlement: and secondly by the guarding of their interests by a Pay Review Board, required by Parliament to base its review on the cost of living and on comparable incomes in other industries and services. This is already done for the armed forces and for the police, though it has not always kept up with its task.

Other vexed questions which often poison industrial relations include the closed shop, union recognition and the right to join or not to join a union.

The closed shop can be enforced only if both the unions concerned *and* the employer agree, formally or informally, to this arrangement.[16] This condition of agreement must clearly be retained, and all concerned must be protected from coercion into an 'involuntary agreement'. Closed shop agreements have considerable value to both sides in small firms but can be abused in large firms. The law should not permit them to apply to industries or services as a whole, since this invites the abuse of industrial power for political purposes, thereby further eroding the balance of the power of Parliament.

The right to join a union must be recognized but so must the right not to join a union. TULRA needs to be more flexible—for example, the right to opt out of a closed shop only for 'religious' reasons is not enough. The application of this, and of the laws regarding unfair dismissal and trade union recognition are best left to the good sense of ACAS and the industrial tribunals, provided that both retain a fair balance of members from trade unions and employers. Both work well in practice. But adjudication by an 'independent review committee' set up by the TUC, as for considering appeals from people who have been sacked by their employers because they have been expelled from their trade union,[17] is unfair for obvious reasons, as it would be if the appeal committee were set up by the CBI.

There is a strong case for legislation to oblige unions and unofficial strike leaders to exhaust certain specified conciliation and arbitration procedures before calling a strike, and then to give a specified period of notice before doing so. This is the case in most industrial countries, including Germany, where collective agreements are legally binding, 'sympathy' strikes (i.e. those not affecting the strikers' own pay or conditions) and strikes for purely political purposes are illegal, and strikes must have the support of 75 per cent of the work-force.

The biggest problem lies in balancing tolerance with the public interest. For every working day lost by strikes in Germany in 1972, 183 were lost in Britain. Yet in Germany, despite her prosperity and industrial performance, there is far more violence than in Britain. Perhaps Germany and Britain both have the balance tipped too far in their opposite directions.

Violence springs from frustration, and frustration comes from lack of personal options. An unemployed man on the dole does not have many options; nor does a man who cannot get a job because he has been expelled from his union; nor does a man whose pay or working conditions are dismal but who dare not do anything about it for fear of being thrown into the pool of $1\frac{1}{2}$ million unemployed.

The law should allow the maximum possible scope for personal options. One of these options must be the right to strike, even if the reasons may sometimes be irrational. The consequences of being unable to exercise this option may produce frustration which can be even more damaging to the public interest—either by exploding into violence or simply by inducing sullen apathy and non-co-operation, which can be the most damaging of all to production and prosperity.

But the law must be sophisticated and shrewd in making it difficult for cynical men to exploit this frustration with political intent, which is in the interest neither of the public nor of the individual.

20 The Political Process in Britain

What people want

Most people want stability and confidence in the future more than they want radical political change. They still see around them societies where, at a knock on the door, members of the family can vanish without trace and with no means of redress. They fear that a collapse of the fabric of society would lead to this, and the majority would rather settle for what they have. But they do seek confidence that there will be work of the kind which they and their families can do, and enough to live on next week and next year; confidence that their possessions will not be taken away and that their savings will not become worthless; confidence that they will not be driven out of their homes; and confidence that their lives will not be disrupted by violence on the streets.

For these reasons, 80 per cent of people belong one side or the other of the political centre, that is, they prefer moderate social democratic, progressive conservative or liberal philosophies. Not more than 10 per cent at most, would opt for the radical solutions of the authoritarian Right, and if anything, less than 10 per cent for all the Marxist parties combined including the Labour Party Marxists. The political activists of left and right have for years tried to persuade people that radical solutions will be better for them in the end, but the majority have preferred to play safe —and the instinct of the majority has more often proved right than wrong.

But no country in the world has yet found an ideal political process which ensures that the free choice of the majority prevails. In Britain, the power of Parliament, as pointed out at the start of the book, has been overtaken by the power of functional groups and pressure groups. These are responsive to their own interests, which they may identify with what they judge to be good for the public.

Most people are neither saints nor fools. What any individual wants is an amalgam of what is in the interests of himself and his family, what he believes to be reasonably fair to others and what he conceives to be for the public good—which is itself in his interest because the stability he longs for can only come if the aspirations of the majority are not frustrated. Everyone is selfish up to a point, but most people are not blinkered. Where the wishes of the majority of individuals—with all those amalgams— coincide, it is only the politically arrogant who insist that they know better.

So the problem is to find a reliable way of assessing what the majority want and then to find a way of providing it—in other words to give real power to the people.

Parliament evolved with this aim in mind and, with universal male suffrage since 1884 and female suffrage from 1918, many thought we had achieved it. But for many reasons—partly because of its being swamped by functional and pressure groups— it has not. So what can we do to restore power to Parliament and, through Parliament, power to the people?

Many people now have doubts about the two-party system, which is the product of our first-past-the-post electoral process. For over a century it was effective and progressive—as even Engels was ready to agree.[1] But is it still adequate for a world very different from the world of Engels, Marx, Gladstone and Disraeli?

The Labour Party

Defenders of the two-party system point out, correctly, that each of the main parties is itself a coalition of the followers of at least two separate philosophies. This especially applies to the Labour Party. Its two main groups, the Social Democrats and the Marxists (the heirs of the original Menshevik–Bolshevik split) are themselves subdivided: the Social Democrats into those who follow the contemporary European model and believe in a mixed economy; and the Libertarian Socialist (typified by Michael Foot) who believe that total public ownership is possible without having a totalitarian society. The Marxists, in turn, are split between the orthodox, who are currently working through the trades union movement to power, and the Trotskyists, who are concentrating on the constituencies. The rings into which they put their champions to fight—the annual Conference, the NEC and the Parliamentary Labour Party—were discussed in Chapter 18. And the framing of the Party rules to resolve which winners in which rings shall control the Leader and (when in power) the Cabinet, is the subject of continued debate in Parliament and of anxious interest to those who would be subject to their rule.

All the evidence suggests that the great majority of those who vote Labour are voting for European-style social democracy. This is reflected in the make-up of the Parliamentary Labour Party. About 230 (75 per cent) of the Labour MPs accept the idea of the mixed economy for the foreseeable future. Of the Tribune Group, about fifty (15 per cent) are Libertarian Socialists and thirty (10 per cent) are Marxists—mainly orthodox. In the rare cases where Trotskyists have been selected as Labour candidates, the voters have not elected them.

In the short term, the Labour Party would undoubtedly have gained more votes if it had split, disowning its Marxist wing, and declaring that it intended to govern as it believed the majority of the people wished to be governed; that is, as a modern social democracy as exemplified in Germany and Sweden—two of the most successful economies in Europe—rather than one based on the philosophies of Marx and Engels which, whether relevant or not in the nineteenth century, were not relevant now.

The moment of truth was probably in the summer of 1974. Had the Labour Party split then and gone to the country on a Centre Party platform, it would almost certainly have taken 400 seats—even though it would have had to campaign with a mere skeleton of its constituency organization where the work, as in every party, is inevitably done by political activists[2] (few others are willing to give up the time). In the Labour Party these also include a majority of the intellectuals in the party—the archetypal Labour Party canvasser is not a bricklayer or a boilermaker but a teacher, a lawyer or a journalist—probably a graduate. Had there been such a split, many of these would have moved out with the Tribune Group to form the new 'Left-Socialist' party, but the main stream of the Labour Party would still have gained a large majority of the seats from a public longing for social harmony and fed up with confrontation.

Whether or not the Labour Party would have wished to do so,

I

by 1976 it was probably too late; first, because the Government was so unpopular that it would not have been re-elected in any form; and secondly because the NEC had by then fallen firmly into the hands of the Libertarian Socialist and Marxist wings, so that the Party's organization and funds might have fallen into their hands rather than those of the Social Democratic wing—and a new party based on Libertarian Socialism and Marxism would certainly have had no chance of election.

Such a split, however, was never really likely. The Left know well that their chances really depend, not on being a small radical splinter party, but on capturing the leadership of the mass-based Labour Party from within; and many of the Social Democrats would be reluctant to lose their Marxist wing, which they feel supplies an essential ginger group and fund of ideas without which the party would cease to be progressive. They also look at the history of similar splits of radical parties in the past. When the Liberal Party split early in the century, its radicals moved to the new Labour Party and the 'moderate' Liberal Party had only fifty seats by the 1930s, falling to a miserable six by 1951. Again, when Ramsay MacDonald took the official Labour Party into the National Government in 1931, it was the radical wing which opted out of MacDonald's deal—then a mere seventy Labour MPs—which survived, to join Churchill's wartime coalition in 1940 and capture power with 393 seats in 1945. MacDonald's National Labour Party had by then virtually vanished without trace. Labour's moderates are convinced that if they split now, the same fate would await them. So, in practice, the Labour Party will probably remain as it is, and the internal battle for its control will continue.

The Conservative Party

The amalgam within the Conservative Party is between the *laissez-faire* philosophy of which the leading proponents are Sir Keith Joseph, Airey Neave, Angus Maude and John Biffen, and the liberal or co-operative philosophy expounded by Edward Heath and Peter Walker.[3]

With the election of Margaret Thatcher to the Party Leadership in 1975, the *laissez-faire* philosophy prevailed, though she herself probably sees herself—as Harold Wilson did—as a bridge between the two. Just as Wilson took people from the various wings of the Labour left as ministers, such as Michael Foot, Judith Hart and Eric Heffer, so Mrs Thatcher has retained Heath supporters such as William Whitelaw, James Prior and Douglas Hurd in her Shadow Cabinet—but not Heath (who declined) nor Walker.

The Heath–Walker philosophy is based upon Disraeli's declared purpose of fusing Britain's divided society into one nation. It is a Centrist philosophy built around the idea of a state run in co-operation between the Government, the City,[4] industry and the trade unions, as has been done so successfully in Germany and Japan.[5] This was what Heath tried and failed to do in 1971–4, as described in the first part of this book. His philosophy included giving greater power and influence to the trade unions in exchange for their accepting a wider democratic participation in the election of their officials and the recognition not only of the right to join but also the right not to join a union; and an extension of individual democracy, worker participation in management at all levels, profit-sharing and workers' co-operation. Some of these are further examined later in this chapter.

The *laissez-faire* (Keith Joseph) wing of the Conservative Party echoes the 1951 call to 'set the people free'. Its adherents reject the idea of the corporate state, contending that decisions taken at the top cannot take account of the varied conditions in individual industries and other activities. They believe that social services can only be provided for by creating more wealth, not by higher levels of taxation, and that this wealth can best be created by allowing free enterprise to develop, with incentives both for companies and for workers; if productivity increases, earnings will increase and then taxation rates can be lowered, since greater earnings will produce as much money in tax at the lower rate. They believe in reducing Government and bureaucratic controls, increasing parental choice in education, reducing the rate of immigration and selling more council houses for owner occupation. They want to strengthen the police and get rid of the 'wreckers' in society. They would treat confrontations by the miners and others as confrontations with the public, not with the Government, because it is the people who pay the miners and pay the cost of coal, and the people who are actually the losers when strikes cause British Leyland and British Airways to lose £30 million of business to foreign competitors.[6]

More than half the voters for the Conservative Party in a General Election must come from among manual workers and less than half from professional people, managers and white-collar workers. Unless at least $6\frac{1}{2}$ million manual workers, that is, one in three, vote for them, they do not hold power—nor, it can be argued, would they have any right to do so.

If every Conservative MP, candidate and constituency worker had a reminder to that effect hung up in his office, their chances of election would be increased—just as their Labour opposite numbers would gain from a reminder that most of their voters actually prefer a mixed economy to a Marxist one.

Winner take all

The two-party system normally ensures, better than any other, that the party which wins a General Election will govern without having to compromise with other parties.[7] The electors therefore know what they are voting for and can, in theory at least, hold the party to the promises it made in its manifesto.

One of the disadvantages is that never, since the three-party National Government re-elected in 1935 and the subsequent wartime coalition from 1940–5, has any Government in Britain ever enjoyed the support of a majority of the electors.[8] The highest percentages were 49·7 per cent for the Conservatives in 1955 and 49·4 per cent in 1959—both higher, surprisingly, than Labour's 48·3 per cent in 1945. The lowest were Labour's 37·1 per cent in February 1974 and 39·2 per cent in October 1974.[9]

This means that every Government since 1945 has known that more than half the country does not want it. Its opponents and the public both know this too, so its authority has been danger-ously weakened.

A more serious disadvantage, in practice, is that the party which wins gets *all* the fruits of office, while the loser gets none. The average number of seats won by the winning party since 1945 has been 337. Of these, approximately 100 (one in three) get some kind of Government office, from Cabinet Minister to Parliamentary Private Secretary. Ministers have salaries, offices, personal assistants and large departmental staffs. They have cars when they want them. They have power, so when they travel they are met and treated with deference by people who want to keep in their good books—'Yes, Minister. Of course, Minister.'

Perhaps the saddest disillusion for the reader of Richard Crossman's Diaries[10] was that a man whom so many respected for his intelligence, sincerity and courage, should appear to get such petty satisfaction out of these little pomposities of office-holding.

Yet it is only human that a back-bench MP, after years on a dismal salary with no office to work in and a half share of a low-paid secretary, should relish the fruits of office. He will probably have become an MP in the hope of one day being a Minister, and every year in opposition is a year largely wasted. He desperately wants his party to win the next election—more than anything else in the world.[11]

This means that, while in opposition, he has a burning desire to see the Government in power fail and be discredited, so that his lot, not theirs, will get the jobs next time. From discrediting the men in power, to trying to instigate public non-co-operation with them, are but a short step from trying to *make* the Government fail, by fomenting strikes or exacerbating inflation. Actually being seen to encourage violence would be so obviously counterproductive as to rebound, so there are some self-imposed limits. But in an industrial country so complex to govern, and with such a knife-edge economy, so vulnerable to erosion of international confidence, it can hardly be an ideal system which gives nearly half the professional politicians in Parliament a powerful incentive to cause the running of the country to fail.

The two-party system evolved in an age when being an MP was a voluntary unpaid public service, like being a local Councillor today. The Cabinet contained very few Ministers and most MPs genuinely felt that the good of the country came before the party and usually acted accordingly; certainly if they were detected doing otherwise it was politically fatal for them. Today it is otherwise.

So has the two-party system, which was once world famous and is sometimes still envied for providing decisive and stable government, outlived its usefulness?

If so, what are the alternatives? If the Conservative and Labour Parties were to split, a Grand Coalition—commended by so many in the late 1950s as 'Butskellism'—would be perfectly feasible; but two such splits are unlikely and, in any case, Grand Coalitions have a bad record; they lead to the growth of extremist politics on both wings, and of extra-parliamentary disruption and violence by the 10 or 20 per cent who feel themselves denied a voice. At least the Labour Party Marxists today feel that they can influence the Party and, therefore, the Government; that is why they stay in the Labour Party.

The only other alternative is one which would compel compromise and coalition, the system now used in one form or another in the great majority of democracies—proportional representation. The majority of the public want it. The majority of politicians do not.

Proportional representation

There are many systems of proportional representation (PR), but one system seems eminently suitable for Britain—that used in the Federal Republic of Germany, where it has proved its effectiveness. There have been Conservative and Socialist Governments, once in Grand Coalition together, but otherwise each in turn has been in coalition with the Free Democrats. The result, which has confounded many of the prophets, has consistently been to produce the most stable and successful Government in Europe.

The German system works roughly like this: of the 496 seats, 50 per cent (248) are held by constituency members who win by being first past the post. The remaining 50 per cent are 'list seats' filled from the pool of other candidates who did not win constituency seats. They are allotted in such a way as to bring the *total number of seats* held by each party (constituency plus list seats) to the exact proportion of the *total vote* that party received, nationwide. There is one proviso, designed to avoid a plethora of splinter parties: no party gets any list seats unless it gains at least 5 per cent of the total national vote.

In Britain, one variation would be essential; the Scottish Nationalist Party (SNP) would receive list seats to give it representation in proportion to the total vote in *Scotland*, provided that it got at least 5 per cent of the *Scottish* vote. The same would apply to Wales and Northern Ireland.

If this method had been applied to the British General Election of October 1974, the result would have been approximately as follows:

Party	Percentage of national vote	Seats won under present system	Seats won under PR system	Remarks
Labour	39·2	319	249	
Conservative	35·8	277	227	
Liberal	18·3	13	116	
SNP	2·9	11	22	(30·7% of Scottish Vote)
Plaid Cymru	0·6	3	4	(10·8% of Welsh Vote)
NI: Unionist		11	12	(66% of NI Vote)
,, SDLP	2·7	1	4	(22% of NI Vote)
,, Alliance		—	1	(6·4% of NI Vote)
National Front	0·4	—	—	
CPGB	0·1	—	—	
Total	100·0	635	635	

There would undoubtedly have been strong resistance to this system by existing Labour and Conservative MPs. First, 71 Labour and 51 Conservatives would have lost their seats. Secondly, the number of constituents which each constituency member would represent would be doubled. Thirdly, those who did *not* represent constituencies might feel themselves to be second-class members.[12] Fourthly, if there were, say, a Lib–Lab coalition, supported by 249 Labour and 116 Liberal MPs, the Government posts would presumably go in proportion to, say, 68 Labour and 32 Liberals instead of all 100 to Labour. And both Labour and Conservative—members and party workers alike—would know that there would probably never again be a wholly Labour or wholly Conservative Government.

It can also be argued that the Liberals would invariably dictate the policy of whichever Government were in power, since it could threaten to form a coalition with the other. But this has been the position of the Free Democrats in Germany and they have not, in practice, dictated the policies of Adenauer, Brandt or Schmidt. Another possibility is that the Labour Party would split, having less incentive to remain united—and conceivably the Conservatives too. This might, over the years, change voting patterns in such a way that all parties would tend to compete for a wider range of voters than they do now, getting away from the traditions of narrower class interests, which could only be beneficial for national harmony.

One common criticism of a system which leads inevitably to coalition is that parties could promise the earth in manifestos, knowing that they would always have an excuse (their coalition partners) not to carry them out. On the other hand, the public would soon get a nose for this and there might well be some advantages over the present system, whereby the political activists in the Party HQs have a dominant voice in drafting manifestos which then become a millstone round the necks of elected Governments faced with the realities of managing the country. Both the Conservatives in 1971–4 and Labour in 1974–7 had to go back on their manifestos. Perhaps it would have been better if they had been elected on a broader platform and then governed pragmatically, knowing that they would anyway be accountable within five years.

21 Power to the People

Public opinion

The reform of the political and electoral system will not alone bring power to the people. While the restoration of sovereign power to Parliament is an essential part of the process, better use must also be made of the means now available to be responsive to public opinion, and to ensure that the majority of the public are not deprived of what they want by the functional and pressure groups, by the new élites in these groups which can abuse their power and by the use of political violence.

To protect itself from these abuses and to assist majority opinion to prevail, British society has been slow to recognize the support and authority which can be obtained by using modern techniques for testing public opinion; slow to come to terms with the increased power of the media, and especially of television; slow to extend the proper democratic processes from Parliament to industry, both in the trade unions and in management; and slow to appreciate and counter the dangerous poison of political violence.

The traditional method of sampling public opinion is the referendum, and this is widely used in Switzerland and in some other countries. On the other hand, referenda have a bad name because historically, dictators have abused them by asking loaded questions, by exploiting public emotion or simply by rigging the vote, to obtain a bogus legitimacy. Referenda are, moreover, expensive, protracted and unpopular.[1]

On the other hand public opinion polls are relatively cheap and have now produced sufficient evidence of their accuracies and inaccuracies to make it feasible at least to consider their *official* use—with safeguards—as an alternative to referenda.

Modern sampling techniques, if properly monitored, can be remarkably reliable, and a sample of 2,000, scientifically selected, should ensure that the *sampling* error[2] does not exceed 2 per cent. Maverick results have become very rare in recent years and can be guarded against by stringent monitoring, by avoiding haste and by carrying out multiple polls.

If it were desirable to sample public opinion *officially* on an issue, the best way would be to engage three established polling organizations (Gallup, NOP etc.), commission them to conduct three independent polls and to accept the result only if all three pointed the same way; if all three were not less than the maximum statistical margin of error above 50 per cent, and if the average of the three were not less than *twice* this margin of error above 50 per cent. Parliament would set the precise rules.

Supposing that the statistical margin of error were plus or minus 3 per cent, the poll would be discarded if *any* of the three polls showed a vote of less than 53 per cent in the same direction, or if the average of the three was less than 56 per cent. If, for example, the percentages saying yes were 52, 58 and 60 per cent (one under 53 per cent) or 53, 54 and 58 per cent (average under 56 per cent), the answer would be discarded as indecisive. If they were 53, 57 and 58 per cent (average 56 per cent) it would be accepted as a valid indication of majority opinion. (There would be nothing, of course, to prevent Parliament demanding, say, a two-thirds majority rather than 56 per cent on any issue if they chose.)

The whole poll should be supervised by an independent body —selected, probably, from the judiciary or from the Electoral Reform Society—which would also specify the sample and sampling methods to be used.

A poll, however, depends a great deal on the framing of the question and on the degree of understanding of the two sides of the argument by the people questioned. Much was learned from the EEC referendum, where each side was given a specified number of pages, with identical formats, in which to put its case and the two resulting leaflets were simultaneously delivered to everyone on the electoral roll. For an official poll of public opinion it is suggested that each person selected (and agreeable) for questioning should be given, one day in advance, a piece of paper on which the two sides concerned would have put their case, one on each side of the paper. Where the poll was on an issue in which there was a clear division in Parliament, it would be normal for the Government to draft one side and the Opposition the other; though on other occasions (as in the EEC referendum) cross-party groupings could be made responsible for the drafting. If the issue was a demand for a major pay rise in a nationalized industry which the Government wished to reject, the case for the rise would be put by the union or unions concerned. In any event, the choice of the bodies responsible for drafting the two sides of the case would be subject to the approval of the independent supervising body.

On one side of the paper would be the question, in heavy type, followed by the arguments for answering 'Yes'. On the other side, in heavy type, would be a comment of up to 50 words on the wording of the question (or longer if the question itself were longer) followed by the argument for answering 'No'. Each case would be limited to one side of the sheet of paper and it would also be necessary to impose a ban on press or broadcast commenting on the subject from the day of issue of the paper until polling was complete (probably two or three days).

Parliament would decide whether the subject justified a poll and was suitable for it. Where very large sums of public money or a major dislocation of public life were involved, it would be proper for the Government to seek a mandate in this way. The method should be used sparingly and it could, of course, be abused. The decision to use it would, however, be left to the good sense of Parliament and to the strictures of public debate. If the method were used illiberally in Britain there would, fortunately, be no shortage of people ready to say so. The aim would not be to replace the powers of Parliament but to support and confirm its authority—and to give it more of the power that it needs to match the currently disproportionate strength of the functional and pressure groups.

The media

Parliament and politicians have been slower than the functional and pressure groups to appreciate the dramatic change which television has made in politics.

In the great age of Parliamentary debate, from Burke and Fox to Gladstone and Disraeli, there was no popular press. The first dramatic changes came in the closing decades of the nineteenth century, from two sources; the extension in 1884 of the suffrage to all adult males, by then largely literate; and the appearance of a popular press, pioneered by Lord Northcliffe in 1896 with the *Daily Mail*. Radio, from the 1920s, was no more than an extension of this. But television added a totally new dimension.

The new dimension of television is that the individual viewers —in millions—are not only better informed, but they can also make their own judgements as to whether their leaders are lying, or covering up, and whether they are really confident or not.[3] Aided by the art of a really able interviewer (an abrasive or bullying one is self-defeating) the viewer can *see* the flicker of the eyelash, the wobbling of the Adam's apple, the mean or cunning look—and judge by his own experience, from his years as a boy and as a man, dealing with honest men and liars, with the candid and the sly, with con-men and bullies, what is really in the man's mind. He may be wrong, but that is how he forms his opinions and develops his trust or contempt, for good or ill.

This places a premium on politicians who can cope with the strains of television. Heath was too wooden. Wilson was too clever and many viewers found it hard to believe him. Margaret Thatcher's elocution courses have prejudiced acceptance of her sincerity. Callaghan and Macmillan have been the best.

But enormous power is placed in the hands of television programme makers: producers, presenters, reporters and researchers. On any controversial issue, both sides will almost always feel that the programme makers had a bias towards the other side. One shot of a policeman being rough in making an arrest will enrage the law-and-order lobby; a cruel shot of a picket or a National Front marcher, or the shot of PC Wilson's blood flowing from his head at Grunwick, will provoke cries of 'unfair' from the demonstrators.

The same applies more widely, too. Many middle-class, middle-aged viewers think that all programme makers are 'trendy lefties', while many 'trendy lefties' are convinced that the BBC is the arm of the Establishment and ITV of Big Business, and that the whole process is part of a 'high conspiracy'—part of 'repressive tolerance'—to con the people into accepting the *status quo*.[4]

Both are wrong. It is true that the ambition of many of the brightest radical students, or graduates, is to get into television, where they can influence men's minds. Some do—though many more have to be content with becoming pressmen (provided that they first endure six months' probation on the Puddlecombe

Advertiser) or teachers or lecturers. But, as in other professions, they are balanced by those who hold more conservative views and by their older brethren who were once radicals but have grown out of it. And the average TV producer, whatever his political views, is motivated mainly by the desire to achieve high audience ratings.

This is not only because of his professional pride but also because, if his programmes cause ratings to rise, he will be given greater opportunities, whereas if his programmes drive viewers away he will be relegated to drearier and drearier assignments, at off-peak hours, exerting less and less influence on public opinion. It is true that some programmes openly have a left-wing political commitment (The Annan Committee named *World in Action*, and certain drama series). There are more which, directly or indirectly, reinforce the *status quo*. Since most viewers themselves prefer the *status quo* to radical change, this is not only fair but is generally in accord with what they want. But if a programme maker uses his power to propagate his personal political views, this soon becomes apparent and his ratings drop. In practice, few try it very often and if they do, they have to be remarkably good to survive.

For all their faults, a commercially owned press and ITV, and a BBC with constitutional freedom from editorial interference by the Government, are probably the best insurance against excessive political exploitation of the media. In the USA, where commercial freedom is unbridled and politicians can buy time on the air, television tends to unbalance the political process unhealthily—and to produce bad programmes. In the great majority of countries, including all Marxist countries and most of the third world, television is editorially, if not wholly, controlled by the Government, which is far, far worse.

The media in Britain can be influenced (rather than used) by people who make conscious efforts to help them to get access to what they want—be it news, facts, personalities or pictures. Reporters are human enough to show some sympathy to people who help them, and to want to encourage them to give similar help in the future. Members of small extremist groups try hardest to exploit this because they know that they have no other way of attracting attention. Public officials (and, in the case of violence, policemen) are, however, far better able to give practical assistance to reporters and cameramen in advising them of where to go and giving them access; they are nevertheless wary of giving information themselves for fear of being accused of breaking the rules by expressing political opinions in public; and in the case of the police, they do not want to risk prejudicing a prosecution. The Army in Northern Ireland has, perhaps, given the best model of how this can be done; since 1971 they have permitted, even encouraged, soldiers of every rank to talk in front of the camera about whatever is happening on the spot (though they are told to avoid discussing policy). Young corporals in command of patrols have come through particularly well on the television screens, straight into people's homes—cool, confident and sensible; not like the 'pigs' their enemies try to depict, but like the kind of twenty-four-year-old brother that most people would want to have. It is a pity that the problem of prejudicing prosecutions usually precludes young policemen from being allowed to do the same.

In a conflict, the TV camera is like a weapon lying in the street, available for either side to pick up and use. It is the most powerful of all weapons in such an encounter. A major part of government, in seeking to resolve these conflicts and keep the peace, lies in learning its power and how to live with it.

Industrial democracy

For over a century, the boards of big industries had tremendous power, not only over their workers but also over the economy of the country. This power has been curtailed, but rather by Government intervention and control than by the extension of industrial democracy.

The power of trade union leaders—both official and unofficial —has greatly increased, but Governments have proved unable to contain the growth of their power, and the democratic control of trade union leaders falls far short of the standards observed in politics.

British industry would gain a great deal from an extension of industrial democracy, both in trade unions and management. Most people want economic security for themselves and for the country, and they know that this depends on maintaining industrial production and consumption of the output, which depends on competitiveness and on meeting delivery dates, which in turn depend on investment. Few people want to see their work disrupted, both for this reason and also because they do not want to lose their family incomes and want still less to see their jobs fold up. Every shop steward knows how difficult it is to get people out on strike. Yet it is only human to want more money and to believe that one's own job, of all jobs, is undervalued.

The most intractable problem is how to avoid a situation where only militancy and industrial blackmail is rewarded. If shop-floor workers observe that moderate trade union leaders always get less for their members than militants (from whatever motives) then they will follow the militants. If, however, in order to make responsible trade unionism be seen to pay, the Government and employers concede uneconomical pay rises to everyone to match what those which the more militant and the most muscle get by blackmail, the rises will be meaningless and the result economic ruin.

The first line of attack must be better public information about what militancy costs; what a stoppage of work will cost the workers concerned, directly or indirectly; and what it will cost the public—who in the end pay for everything. The second line of attack must be to make union privileges conditional upon union democracy. Unions have immunities from damages for disrupting production and immunities against prosecution on picket lines. It is these privileges which make union leaders more powerful than elected members of Parliament, and a union with a monopoly of an essential public service is more powerful than Parliament itself. Yet the men wielding that power are often elected by less than 5 per cent of their members, on whose loyalty they can call for a strike, and in whose name (and with whose numbers) they can swing the vote at the Labour Party Conference.

The power should be conditional upon their being elected by an independently conducted secret ballot, in which a majority of their members vote. Such a poll would be easier to conduct than a General Election, since it could be conducted at the factory gates—or, as already done by NUM, at the pithead, where a very high turnout is normally recorded. This is asking that the members of the executive of a trade union should, in view of their power and responsibility to the public, subject themselves to an electoral process no more stringent than MPs and Ministers do.

Those who want to use the trades union machinery for political rather than industrial aims oppose this, because it would deny them the opportunity to manipulate this machinery in the way described on pages 230 to 234. Their plea for 'no vote without participation' means that a union member should not be allowed to vote unless he has first sat through as long a branch meeting as those organizing the vote shall decide. There would be a considerable outcry if citizens were ordered to attend long and compulsory constituency meetings as a condition for exercising their vote in a General Election.

Industrial democracy in management is equally important. This is opposed by some managements and also—not surprisingly—by those same trade union leaders whose motivation is political,[5] because they perceive that their route to power is not by co-operation but by conflict with management. They appreciate that a decision or production plan in which workers' representatives have participated will be harder to challenge.

Worker participation would be beneficial to industrial output provided that two conditions were incorporated. First, the decisions reached with worker participation at shop, plant, works and board level should not only bring more pay to the workers where they succeed, but also less where they fail, as is done in the self-management scheme in Yugoslavia; this ensures that they have not only an incentive to increase production and competitiveness but a fair share of the profits if they do. Secondly, the workers should elect their representatives at every level by secret ballot, directly, and not through a trade union. This will not only be more democratic but will leave the union free to pursue collective bargaining with the management, which they could hardly do if they were themselves members of it.

George Goyden, himself a managing director for over thirty-five years, has suggested an interesting system of industrial democracy in which not only the shareholders and the workforce but also the consumer (i.e. the public) are represented.[6] But his main theme—as the title of his book *The Responsible Worker* implies—is to get workers not only involved in decisions which affect their earnings and working conditions, but also to share the responsibility for them. This already happens in many small factories where the work-force—managerial, technical, clerical and manual—can see for themselves that their present and future prosperity depends precisely on the output and marketability of their product. Though the CBI and the TUC can give a lead, it is on the shop floor that this realization of a common interest in productivity must develop, and with it the joint determination not to allow a minority to disrupt it at the expense of the earnings and job security of the others. In large firms, this means more devolution to plant and shop level, and personal involvement of management at the dirty and noisy end of the job as much as of workers in the board room. This is to be seen in most successful German and Japanese firms, and in some British ones, but is horrifyingly absent in others. That may sometimes be because politically motivated trade union officials deliberately try to maintain a barrier between management and workers, but management itself is often to blame.

As with the parliamentary process and with trade union organization, we can look with advantage to the successful experiments with industrial democracy in Germany. The British, in fact, played a major part in founding all of these processes during the rehabilitation of German democracy and trade unionism during the years immediately after 1945. These have been well described by Peter Walker in *The Ascent of Britain*.[7] The Germans have a supervisory board, on which workers are represented, and a management board, which takes day-to-day decisions, and most German industrialists say that the system has been wholly beneficial.

There are, nevertheless, some impressive British examples closer at hand. The John Lewis Partnership is one. While a firm running a chain of retail stores does not face the same problems as a giant manufacturing concern, many of its lessons are widely applicable. Since it is made up of individual stores, the management at working level is very personal; and this has been achieved in many giant firms by splitting their plants into small units with a high degree of autonomy. This is the starting point for the John Lewis type of self-management to succeed.

The John Lewis Partnership employs about 12,000 people, all of whom are partners in the firm; there are no shareholders; any distributed profit is shared *pro rata* amongst the workers and they elect the 150-man council which decides how much of the profit is distributed and how much reinvested. The council consistently votes for a high rate of reinvestment and expansion, rather than for distribution of cash. It appoints the chairman (who is also managing director) and can dismiss him—though it has never done so. He, once appointed, selects his executives and

managers and decides upon their salaries. The council approve
his decision by approving the accounts and, if they disapprove,
their remedy is to sack him. In practice, however, their tendency
is not to cavil at the salaries but to urge the chairman to pay more
to attract the best managers.[8]

This last point will help to explode one of the biggest myths—
and fears—about worker participation. Provided that the workers
gain by success and lose by failure, they will be ready to pay the
going rate to get a good manager; they will no more want to
skimp on this than the supporters club of a top football team
will grudge the payment of a high fee to get a star player, nor of
the right salary to attract the right manager to lead them to the
Championship. With pay differentials as low as they are in
Britain, working managers have little to fear on this score.

The more the workers are involved in the decisions affecting
their own prosperity, the more sensible and constructive these
decisions will be, and the more loyally they will support them.
The benefits, to the workers, and to the profitability and competitiveness of British industry, will follow.

Political violence and the police

Just as democratic participation works for harmony and efficiency
in society and industry, so political violence injects the most
virulent poison.

People who use violence for political ends are generally more
vicious and more arrogant than those who use it for personal,
criminal gain. In the Republic of Ireland, a Dutch factory manager, Dr Herrema, against whom the IRA had no conceivable
reason for a grudge, was kidnapped and held hostage by two IRA
terrorists. They lived with him, within a few feet, for five weeks;
during the whole of that time one of them, Marion Coyle, said
not one word to him, nor acknowledged any word he said to her.
That any human being could become so inhuman is an awe-
inspiring example of what political fanaticism can do.

And the hatred and viciousness of the violence in Red Lion
Square, Windsor Park, Hendon, Grunwick, Lewisham and
Ladywood was in sharp contrast to that at Saltley where (apart
from some of the leaders) the miners were fighting for money
rather than for power.[9]

Yet British courts remained puzzlingly lenient in punishing political violence. Of 105 people convicted of assaults on police officers in demonstrations in London in 1972–4, in which 297 policemen were injured, only ten actually went to prison, and none of these for more than three months. The others were given suspended sentences or fines.[10] And after the Right to Work march at Hendon, where three of the forty-one injured policemen were injured seriously, only one of the twenty-five people convicted[11] went to prison, and he for only three months. Suspended sentences and fines have little effect on political fanatics (or on people they employ to do violence for them) as they convince themselves that violence is justified by their cause—and in any case their political movement will pay their fines and costs for them out of its 'defence funds'.

These people are in fact exploiting the tolerance of the free society in order to destroy it. For people convicted of deliberate and politically motivated violence, such sentences are betraying the policemen who endure the battering on behalf of the public. And there is no doubt about where the sympathies of the public lie.

Between 1972 and 1975, Dr William Belson, then head of the Survey Department at the London School of Economics, carried out a three-year survey of public attitudes to the Metropolitan Police, based on questioning a scientifically selected sample of 1,200 adults and 500 teenagers in much more depth than in a public opinion poll. (The adults were asked about 300 questions each.) The results astonished the police themselves. Amongst adults, 98 per cent 'respected' the police, 73 per cent of them 'a lot'. 90 per cent 'trusted' the police, 30 per cent of them 'completely'. 93 per cent liked the police, 31 per cent of them 'very much'. And 96 per cent were 'satisfied' with the police, 61 per cent of them 'very satisfied'.

Teenagers (aged thirteen to twenty) gave surprisingly similar answers. 94 per cent 'respected' the police, 83 per cent 'trusted' them and 85 per cent 'liked' them. The teenagers were not asked if they were satisfied but whether they were scared of the police. 86 per cent were 'not at all' or 'just a bit' scared, 12 per cent 'fairly' scared and 2 per cent 'very' scared.[12]

The public support the police because, even more than economic stability, they want tranquillity, for themselves, their families, their homes and their possessions; because they want protection from fear, coercion and robbery by men of violence, whether motivated by criminal greed or politics—and protection if needed from officials acting in the name of the state. The police act in the name of the law, not of the state nor even of Parliament, except in so far as Parliament may change the law. So do the independent judiciary and magistracy—so that when they fail to uphold the police they are betraying the people rather than the state.

For all of these reasons, the public would support a 'special case' for paying more for the kind of police they want. If this were the subject of the kind of multiple-poll test discussed at the beginning of the chapter, there is little doubt which way it would go. In London, there are only three policemen to the square mile, and one of these is likely to be in Court giving evidence, leaving two. At night, there may be as many as 50,000 people depending for security on one policeman. When political extremists decide to use force to try to solve an industrial dispute at Grunwick, or to fight each other in the streets of Lewisham, one in six of London's policemen had to turn out to keep the peace. And the injury rate—one in fifty of London's policemen during 1977 alone, 100 on a single day at Grunwick and 58 out of 400 protecting one by-election meeting in Birmingham—was such as no trade union would tolerate for its members.

This raises the question of whether the police should make more use of special equipment or form special riot squads. As far as possible, the answer to both should be no.

The police have already had to use shields to protect themselves from the bricks and bottles whose use the people who instigated the 1977 riots openly defended. If the use of ammonia or acid became more widespread, it would be necessary for policemen on riot duty to wear visors, as in Northern Ireland. Policemen can already wear cricket 'boxes' and shinguards, and can use their truncheons—and use them only—in self-defence; but body armour (like special helmets) presents a different image and there is a price to pay for this, both in terms of escalation and of a subtle erosion of public sympathy. Ironically, the very vulnerability of the police increases this sympathy and arouses disgust against the rioters.

All of these things are defensive—to protect the individual PC from injury. The use of 'offensive' equipment—water cannon, CS gas, rubber bullets, stun bags etc—would be counterproductive for the same reasons and no police officer is likely to want even to consider using it in England.

Nor is there any case for forming a special riot force, like the CRS in France. Such forces generate hostility and this soon becomes mutual. The British method depends on the use of relatively large numbers of normal policemen, in familiar uniforms. The policemen pay a heavy personal price in terms of injuries but they gain more in the long run from their unique relationship with the public.

Public anger after such violence as was seen in Red Lion Square, Grunwick and Lewisham usually leads to suggestions that the Army should be called out to support the police in maintaining public order. This, however, would be both unnecessary and unwise, except as a last resort; unnecessary because this is a task for unarmed policemen, not armed soldiers, and the police reinforcement system can provide the numbers required without calling in the Army—in 1968 they concentrated 9,000 policemen for the Grosvenor Square demonstration. The situation in Northern Ireland, where the decision was taken to bring in the Army in 1969, was in no way a parallel for two reasons: large numbers of the rioters (and the RUC) were armed; and a substantial proportion of the Northern Irish public did not accept the validity of the laws nor the legitimacy of the RUC. Neither of these considerations apply, nor are they likely to apply, in Britain.

The use of the Army to maintain essential services is quite different, and is accepted by both the trade unions and the public, provided that it is confined to services which clearly are essential, as was brought out in the UWC strike (see Chapter 11); but the deployment of soldiers on essential services does carry a risk of their becoming unintentionally involved in a public disturbance. Although they do not carry arms in an essential services role, a confrontation between uniformed soldiers and strikers or demonstrators would not help the police in any way.

The use of soldiers to combat armed terrorists is, of course, both necessary and welcomed by the public. They have been deployed in this role on a number of occasions (e.g. at Heathrow in 1975) but have not had to open fire in Great Britain since 1919.

Public order, however, must remain the responsibility of the police, and for this their greatest asset is the sympathy and support of the public. Anything which erodes that relationship—be it special equipment, special riot squads or the use of troops—is likely to be counter-productive.

Revival or relapse?

If the aim of legislation is to bring 'the greatest happiness to the greatest number',[13] the art of government is to give scope and power to the desires of that greatest number so that what they want is brought about. The greatest number want industry to prosper and Britain to break out of its agony. They want to recover their pride. The depth of this feeling was demonstrated to a degree which astonished the most euphoric as well as the most cynical in the Jubilee celebrations in 1977. The mood was an indication of the power that is there to be mobilized by any Government which can find the way.

German workers are more prosperous than British workers because, out of the bitterness and chaos of defeat, their leaders were able to call upon them unashamedly to work together for the recovery of Germany, and the people responded to their lead. The Japanese did likewise. The greatest number would respond to a similar lead in Britain. If the lead fails to come from legitimately elected politicians and trades union leaders, then the danger is that people will turn in desperation to more authoritarian solutions, wherein the main threat to a pluralist society lies.

Some of the possible approaches for such a lead have been discussed in this book: by restoring the sovereignty and authority of Parliament; by learning to live with television; by industrial democracy in unions and management; by changes in the laws governing political violence and by firmer judicial support for the police in enforcing them.

Those who wish to bring about political change by *constitutional* means, by extending their influence in the trades unions or in the Labour or Conservative parties, act legitimately, even if they play the rules to the limit, provided that they keep within the law. If they achieve their results by working a 14-hour day, then it is up to their political opponents to match their efforts or lose by default. If the rules leave room for abuse of the democratic process within the existing law, then it is in the power of Parliament to change the rules.

People who carry this to the extent of working positively to make Britain fail—by *disrupting* industry and the economy for political ends—need to be more positively identified and their motives exposed. Many of them are people of ability, sincerity and dedication, and they believe that the public rejects their ideas because it is misled. A realization that the public is not so gullible, and that its rejection is real and deep, could induce at least some of them to redirect their powers of leadership for the benefit of the British people rather than to impoverish them.

But for those who use political *violence* to further their ends there should be no quarter—and political violence should be treated more seriously than criminal violence, not only because it has a more arrogant motivation, but also because it affects the lives of more of the community.

Crimes of violence have increased alarmingly and, for robbery with violence and rape, the courts will send a man to prison for several years. But some magistrates seem to regard political violence as morally more forgivable than violence for personal gain. They are wrong, because apart from the few big-time professionals, most criminals have suffered some deprivation, whereas those organizing political violence are more often people who have many other opportunities open to them. They are arrogant in their belief that they know better than the majority what the majority ought to want, and cynical in their resort to violence because they know that the community would never voluntarily accept their views. Their exploitation of those who really are deprived, whether by unemployment or by racial discrimination or both, makes their actions all the more despicable.

The last word can appropriately be left to Sir Robert Mark, who said in a television interview shortly after his retirement as Commissioner of the Metropolitan Police, in 1977:

> I do not think that what we call 'crimes of violence' are anything like as severe a threat to the maintenance of tranquillity in this country as the tendency to use violence to achieve political or industrial ends. As far as I am concerned, that is the worst crime in the book. I think it is worse than murder.[14]

Postscript

Autumn 1977 saw the revival of hopes that Britain was pulling out of her agony. Contrasting with the earlier 'days of hope' in 1973 and 1976 (pp. 96 and 179), the ticking of the time bombs seemed to have subsided—though it was still in the power of the 'godfathers' of either side to ignite another explosion like those at Lewisham or Grunwick.

As so often, the miners played a crucial role. After an aggressive campaign led by Arthur Scargill, a pit-head ballot rejected a productivity deal which would have brought some underground workers an extra £23. This later rebounded, however, and the NUM executive agreed to a demand by individual pits or areas to negotiate their own productivity deals. Nevertheless, had Scargill prevailed, the miners were well placed for a winter strike as two years of poor productivity and high absenteeism had brought coal stocks very low.

Public sympathy for the miners, however, was running out. A Gallup poll on 10 December 1977 showed only 20 per cent supporting a 'special case' for miners, compared with 63 per cent for the police, 62 per cent for firemen and 60 per cent for nurses and doctors. A November poll had shown strong support for the Government's pay guideline, and over 75 per cent were prepared to endure 'a miserable winter of strikes and power cuts' rather than give the miners preference over other workers.

Grunwick seemed to be settling down for the winter. Mass picketing had reversed the public estimate of who were the bullies and who were the victims, and had therefore lost favour in the unions—perhaps one of the few real gains from Grunwick—but the prospect remained of a resumption of violence in the 'holiday snap' season.

SWP remained impenitent about violence. Ten pages of the September issue of *International Socialism* were devoted to a justification of the violence at Lewisham. Meanwhile the NF basked smugly in the after-glow helped by ten minutes of television publicity in a controversial Labour Party political broadcast. The exploitation of racial strife for political purposes, by both extremes, remained the likeliest of all causes for further political violence.

The undertow of hope, however, lay in rising investment and productivity and an improving balance of payments as North Sea Oil came onto full stream; also because the Government seemed determined to defend this recovery (e.g. in their resistance to the firemen's strike) by keeping the overall rise in earnings, if not at 10 per cent, at least within 15 per cent; and there was hope that incomes would again—at last—outstrip inflation.

They were conscious of strong public support for their firmness —despite pressure within their own NEC to give way. Public opinion polls suggested that Callaghan's 'window' for an election (p. 190) might be in sight. To this the temporary Lib-Lab pact had contributed, for the Government had been anchored to the centre and had clearly benefited from it.

The Conservatives displayed their own wide spectrum, from Sir Keith Joseph to James Prior, who revived the philosophy of the government-industry-city-union team. Mrs Thatcher led from the centre, flying a kite about referenda to let the public decide major industrial and other confrontations. The Conservatives' chief worry was that Labour had 'stolen their clothes' as what the *Financial Times* described as the best 'conservative' government Britain could have.

The prospect of Labour catching the tide depended much upon whether they could redress the left balance of their NEC before writing the manifesto for the next election. Each party hoped to drive its opponents into the hands of their extremes—NAFF and the Marxist wing—away from the centre of the channel where the tide ran strongest. Each knew that whoever won the next election would have—with North Sea Oil—a spring tide under them. Each knew that if wild men of either extreme—left or right—were blamed by the public for provoking violence, this would help the other.

The British people yearned for a Government which would work for a consensus; which would deal firmly with those who sought to impose minority views by industrial disruption or political violence, and would make the disrupters more answerable to the public and those using violence more answerable to the law. The election of a Government dedicated to these things would decide whether or not historians would be able to record that Britain really did emerge from her seven-year agony in 1977.

Chronological Table

1964	October	General Election. Labour elected (Wilson). Majority 4 seats.
1965	March	Prices and Incomes Board established.
	April	Donovan Commission on industrial relations started work.
1966	April	General Election. Labour re-elected. Majority 96 seats.
	June	Seamen's strike. Wilson described Communist Party's industrial apparatus in Commons debate.
	September	Car production disrupted by small-scale strikes. Layoffs and short-time working.
1967	January	Unemployment rose to more than 600,000.
	September	Exports hit by unofficial dock strikes at most ports.
	November	Sterling devalued from $2·80 to $2·40.
1968	April	Conservative proposals for industrial relations published in *A Fair Deal at Work.*
	May	Public opinion polls showed 28 per cent Conservative lead.
	June	Donovan Report published.
1969	January	Government's industrial relations proposals published in Draft White Paper, *In Place of Strife*, based on Donovan Report.
	March	*In Place of Strife* rejected by TUC and Labour Party NEC.
	June	Government withdrew *In Place of Strife.*
	August	Army took over responsibility from RUC for public order in Northern Ireland.

1970	June	General Election. Conservatives elected (Heath). Majority 30 seats.
	October	Economic policy announced. No statutory incomes policy but target of 8 per cent wage rise maximum in 12 months. Prices and Incomes Board to be abolished.
	December	Electricity work-to-rule. Blackouts. Wilberforce Inquiry awarded rise of 15 per cent.
		Industrial Relations Bill presented in Parliament. 'Kill the Bill' demonstrations widespread but orderly.
1971	January	Postal workers' strike began. Demanded 15–20 per cent rise.
	February	Rolls-Royce bankrupt. Government took over 100 per cent holding.
	March	Postal workers settled for 9 per cent rise.
	August	Industrial Relations Act became law.
	September	TUC Annual Congress instructed trade unions not to register under the Act (vote 5,625,000 to 4,500,000).
	October	House of Commons voted by 356 to 244 to join EEC.
	November	Miners refused to accept Government's 8 per cent wage rise target and began overtime ban to run down coal stocks.
1972	January	Miners' strike began. First national coal strike since 1926.
	February	Mass pickets closed Saltley Coke Depot, 30 injured, 76 arrested.
		Wilberforce Inquiry awarded miners 27 per cent pay rise.
	March	TGWU fined £5,000 and later £50,000 for contempt of NIRC order to stop dockers picketing container depots.
		Northern Ireland Parliament prorogued. Britain assumed direct rule from Westminster.
	April	Railway unions demanded 16 per cent rise. Work-to-rule.
	May	Government ordered compulsory ballot of

	May	railwaymen under provision of Industrial Relations Act before strike action.
	June	Railwaymen voted 5 to 1 to support strike. Government settled for 13 per cent rise.
		Pound allowed to float freely instead of being tied to dollar.
		Three dockers facing imprisonment for defying NIRC order to cease picketing. Released on intervention of Official Solicitor.
	July	Five shop stewards (dockers) imprisoned. Later released as result of House of Lords reinterpretation of law in a ruling on another case.
	August	National dock strike. State of Emergency. Settled 15 August.
	September	Violent picketing at Shrewsbury during national building strike (26 June–6 September). Two of leaders later served 3-year and 2-year prison sentences.
	November	Stage 1 of Incomes Policy—90-day prices and wages freeze.
	December	23,909,000 working days lost in strikes in 1972.
1973	January	Britain joined EEC.
	March	Provisional IRA bombs in London; 1 killed, 243 injured.
	April	Stage 2 of Incomes Policy. Annual rises not to exceed £1 per week plus 4 per cent on current pay bill.
		Pay Board and Prices Commission established.
		Miners voted 2 to 1 to settle wage claim within Stage 2.
	June	Election of Northern Ireland Assembly with 2 to 1 majority in favour of power-sharing.
	October	Most unions had settled within Stage 2. In its first seven months, Pay Board approved 6,544 settlements and refused 44.
		Arab-Israeli War began.
		Government announced Stage 3 of Incomes

October   Policy to come into effect on 7 November.
             Norm to be £2·25 a week or 7 per cent,
             plus flexibility margin. Provision for un-
             social hours and threshold payments.

             NCB offered miners wage rise of 7 per cent
             with extras for unsocial hours, etc., which
             brought it up to 16½ per cent.

             Middle East oil price raised by 70 per cent
             and deliveries cut by 25 per cent owing to
             Arab–Israeli War.

             Electrical power engineers ban on out-of-
             hours working.

November   Miners rejected NCB offer.

             NUM launched overtime ban to reduce coal
             stocks.

             State of Emergency to conserve coal, oil and
             electricity.

             Heath met NUM executive at 10 Downing
             Street.

December   William Whitelaw became Employment
             Secretary.

             Sunningdale talks between London, Dublin
             and Stormont representatives agree on
             power-sharing Constitution for Northern
             Ireland.

             Train drivers (ASLEF) start work-to-rule.

             Three-day working week to save electricity.

             Public expenditure cuts of £1,200 million
             announced.

1974 January   OPEC oil prices quadrupled from pre-
             October price.

             Power-sharing executive (Brian Faulkner)
             took office in Northern Ireland.

             Pay Board published Relativities Report.

             NUM executive voted 16–10 to call ballot
             for strike.

             Heath offered to refer miners' case to
             Relativities Board if they resumed normal
             working. NUM refused (ballot already set
             in motion).

February   Miners' ballot voted 81 per cent for strike.

IRA bomb killed 12 in coach on M62 motorway.

Heath announced General Election for 28 February.

Miners' strike began.

Relativities Board released evidence suggesting that miners were entitled to at least 8 per cent more than NCB offer (making 24–25 per cent).

General Election. Indecisive. Wilson formed Government with 4 seats more than Conservatives but 31 short of overall majority. All Unionist candidates elected in Northern Ireland opposed power-sharing.

March   Miners' strike ended with wage rises of up to 32 per cent. Coal prices raised by 48 per cent, electricity by 30 per cent and steel by 25 per cent.

May   Protestant strike (UWC) brought down power-sharing executive in Northern Ireland. Faulkner resigned. Britain resumed direct rule from London.

June   Kevin Gately killed in Red Lion Square when IMG demonstrators charged police cordon in attempt to block National Front meeting; 54 injured including 46 police. 51 arrested.

July   Pay Board abolished. Statutory Incomes Policy replaced by voluntary Social Contract between Government and unions. Diamond Commission on Incomes and Wealth set up.

Trade Union and Labour Relations Act, 1974, supplanted Industrial Relations Act.

August   Violence at Windsor Park Free Festival. 116 injured, including 70 police; 584 arrested —296 for drug offences and 220 in connection with violent resistance to police clearing the site.

	October	IRA bombs killed 5 and injured 65 in pubs in Guildford.
		General Election. Labour re-elected. Overall majority 3 seats.
	November	IRA bomb killed 21 and injured 162 in pubs in Birmingham.
		Prevention of Terrorism (Temporary Provisions) Act passed quickly through Parliament and became law.
1975	January	FT Index fell to 146 (from 313 in March 1974).
		National Enterprise Board set up with initial capital of £1,000 million. Later took over 95 per cent holding in British Leyland.
	March	FT Index recovered to 292.
	July	Government White Paper introduced Stage 1 of Pay Policy, limiting wage rises to £6 per week. Later endorsed by miners (3 to 2) and TUC Annual Congress (2 to 1).
	August	Inflation over past 12 months reached 27 per cent (RPI).
		Unemployment reached 1 million (from 577,000 in March 1974).
		Government introduced Employment Protection Bill (came into force as EPA in 1976).
	October	New IRA bombing campaign in London. Attacks mainly on West End restaurants.
	December	Four IRA men arrested after 5-day siege with two hostages in Balcombe Street, London.
1976	January	Unemployment reached 1,403,369 (6·1 per cent).
	March	Unemployment fell to 1,284,915 (5·5 per cent).
		'Right to Work' marchers, organized by International Socialists, injured 41 policemen at West Hendon. 43 arrested.
	April	James Callaghan became Prime Minister.
		Inflation over past 12 months reduced to 12·6 per cent.

May		Stage 2 of Pay Policy announced. Maximum rise £4 per week.
June		TUC Special Congress approved Stage 2 with 95 per cent in favour (9,202,000 to 531,000).
July		Government announced public expenditure cuts of £1,012 million.
August		Strike began at Grunwick film processing laboratory.
		Unemployment total 1½ million. Highest since 1930s.
		Notting Hill Carnival; 250 injured (120 of them police).
September		Labour Party NEC published proposals to nationalize banks and insurance companies. Repudiated by Prime Minister.
		Government applied for IMF loan of £2,300 million.
October		Sterling fell to $1·57, then began slow recovery.
November		Government lost its overall majority in Parliament after several by-election defeats, one with a swing of 27·3 per cent to the Conservatives.
December		Government announced public expenditure cuts of £2,500 million to meet terms for IMF loan.
1977	March	Government, faced with defeat in vote of confidence, made Parliamentary pact with Liberal Party.
	April	Strikes over differentials by skilled workers at British Leyland and in British Airways.
	June	Mass picketing at Grunwick Factory. By 11 July 243 policemen had been injured and 377 people arrested. Court of Inquiry under Lord Scarman ordered into causes of dispute.
	July	Stage 3 of Incomes Policy (Social Contract) abandoned. Government called on industry

K

July   and unions to keep rise in earnings below 10 per cent in next 12 months.

August   SWP demonstrators attacked NF march in Lewisham and later switched attack to police. Police used riot shields for first time.

SWP demonstrators attacked police guarding NF by-election meeting in Ladywood, Birmingham. Of 400 police on duty, 58 were injured.

Scarman Report on Grunwick dispute published.

Notting Hill Carnival; 170 police injured.

Notes

Introduction

1 On BBC Television *The Age of Uncertainty*, published in *The Listener*, 7 April 1977. This view seemed to be confirmed by a remarkable survey, published in *New Society*, 28 April 1977, entitled 'Do the British sincerely want to be rich?' A representative quota sample of 1,081 adults was interviewed, and nearly twice as many considered it better to work only as much as was needed in order to live a pleasant life than to work as hard as they could for as much money as they could get. This preference was consistent amongst all socio-economic classes. Most seemed relatively content with their incomes, and over half considered that a rise of £10 a week or less was all that they needed to live without money worries. On the other hand, asked to choose on which three of eight objectives the country should concentrate, two-thirds chose a 'stable economy'—by far the most popular choice.

2 Michael Moran, *The Politics of Industrial Relations* (Macmillan, London 1977), p. 156.

Chapter 1

1 Figures from *Department of Employment Gazette*.
2 Moran, *op. cit.*, p. 6.
3

	Average No. of strikes	Workers involved (000)	Man-days lost (000) per year
1933–9	735	295	1,694
1945–54	1,491	495	1,816
1955–64	2,521	545	2,073

Figures from *Department of Employment Gazette*.

4 Eric Wigham, *Strikes and the Government 1893–1974* (Macmillan, London 1976), p. 126.
5 Gallup recorded that trade unions were considered a 'bad thing' by 12 per cent in a 1954 poll and by 23 per cent in 1959.

6   See Eric Heffer, *The Class Struggle in Parliament* (Gollancz, London 1973), p. 26. This book admirably expresses a left-wing Labour view of industrial relations over this period and through 1972. A right-wing Conservative view, setting out the proposed reforms, can be found in a publication by the Inns of Court Conservative and Unionist Society, *A Giant's Strength* (1958), while Eric Wigham gives a middle-of-the-road analysis in *What is Wrong with the Unions?* (Penguin, Harmondsworth 1961).

7   This technique has been most lucidly described by a mixed Trotskyist–Anarchist group called 'Solidarity' in their Pamphlet No. 37, *Strategy for Industrial Struggle* (undated, about 1970). Advising on how to disrupt production by stopping a different shop in turn, on any pretext, the authors describe an effective example in Italy, claiming that 'Alfa Romeo produced 10,000 fewer cars than its planned programme, which would hit its whole ambitious expansion programme in the impoverished South.' The cynicism of this strategy, in relation to relieving poverty, speaks for itself.

8   The members of the Donovan Commission were Lord Donovan (a Lord of Appeal), Lord Robens (Chairman of the National Coal Board and a former Minister of Labour), Lord Tangley, Lord Collison, Sir George Pollock QC, George Woodcock (General Secretary of the TUC), Hugh Clegg (Professor of Industrial Relations and a member of the Prices and Incomes Board), Mary Green, Otto Kahn-Freund, Andrew Shonfield, John Thomson and Eric Wigham.

9   Donovan's research director commented that there was not much room for movement either way, and that any attempt to be more definite would have led to 'half a dozen minority reports'. W. E. J. McCarthy in the *Guardian*, 3 September 1970, cited by Moran, *op. cit.*, p. 150.

10 Lord Donovan, *Royal Commission on Trade Unions and Employers' Associations 1965–68*, Report (Cmnd. 3623, HMSO, London June 1968).

11 Moran, *op. cit.*, p. 27, suggests that there were, in fact, three systems: first, an established and effective *national* system of industrial relations which did in fact, largely determine conditions of work, especially in nationalized industries; secondly, Donovan's 'formal' system of official negotiation at factory or plant level; and thirdly, the 'informal' system, in which action was unofficial and unconstitutional.

12 Donovan, *op. cit.*, p. 129.

13 *Ibid.*, p. 136.

14 *Ibid.*, pp. 138–9.

15 Wigham, *op. cit.*, pp. 134–5.

16 *Hansard*, 20 June 1966, Cols. 42–3.

17 *Hansard*, 28 June 1966, Col. 1613.

18 *Hansard*, 28 June 1966, Col. 1616.

19 National Opinion Polls (NOP), July 1966, 'Communists and Trade Unions'.

20 NOP, 1–6 November 1967.

21 Conservative Central Office, *A Fair Deal at Work* (1968).

22 In a Gallup Poll in December 1976 only 26 per cent thought the incomes policy to be a 'good thing'.

23 Rodney Cowton in *The Times*, 10 October 1968. In the event, the total for 1968 reached nearly 4·7 million, and in 1969 rose to 6·8 million, cited in David Butler and Michael Pinto-Duschinsky, *The British General Election of 1970* (Macmillan, London 1971), p. 38.

24 Butler, *op. cit.*, p. 174.

25 Cmnd. 3888 (HMSO, London 1969).

26 In November 1968, for example, twenty-two machine setters downed tools over a 'who-does-what' dispute at the Girling brake factory in Cheshire. Their strike lasted four weeks and affected over 5,000 other car workers. And in February 1969, during the public discussion of *In Place of Strife*, a national strike began at Fords, partly over a no-strike clause in their collective agreements. This strike lasted until 20 March and the Ford workers were severely criticized by Harold Wilson.

27 The apparent contradiction between these figures and the views of trade union members is not as great as it appears. The Congress vote is a card vote. The representative of a large union may record a million votes though he is in fact reflecting the views of his Union's Executive Council. These views will certainly not reflect the opinion of a million members and may not even reflect the opinions of the majority of them. This problem is further discussed on pages 230–1.

28 Leo Panitch, *Social Democracy and Industrial Militancy: the Labour Party, the Trade Unions and Incomes Policy 1945–1974* (Cambridge University Press, 1976), pp. 201–5.

29 Reproduced in Butler, *op. cit.*, p. 45.

30 Panitch, *op. cit.*, pp. 213–20.

31 The *DEP Gazette* records 6·8 million days lost in 1969 and 11 million in 1970, of which half were before the June election.

32 Panitch, *op. cit.*, p. 218.

33 Butler, *op. cit.*, pp. 128–9.

34 *Ibid.*, p. 178.

35 *Ibid.*, p. 165.

36   The Conservative share of the vote, in the event, exceeded
     Labour's by 2·4 per cent. ORC forecast a Conservative lead of
     1 per cent. All others forecast a Labour lead of between 2 per
     cent (Harris) and 9·6 per cent (Marplan). The scatter of these
     forecasts (11·6 per cent) was far in excess of the normally assumed
     3 per cent statistical error either way, which could give a scatter
     of 6 per cent. This did much to shake confidence in public opinion
     polls. No convincing explanation has ever been given for their
     failure. See Butler, *op. cit.*, p. 181.

Chapter 2

1   Eric Wigham, *Strikes and the Government 1893–1974* (Mac-
     millan, London 1976), p. 167.
2   *The Economist*, 13 February 1971.
3   Wigham, *op. cit.*, p. 168.
4   *Ibid.*, p. 168.
5   A. W. J. Thomson and S. R. Engleman, *The Industrial Relations
     Act. A Review and Analysis* (Martin Robertson, London 1975),
     p. 26.
6   They had technically 'deregistered' because, on the passing of
     the Act, all recognized unions were deemed to be registered and
     therefore enjoyed the legal immunities and other privileges
     thereof, though they were required to confirm their registration.
7   Thomson and Engleman, *op. cit.*, p. 30.
8   Moran, *op. cit.*, p. 132.
9   *TUC Annual Report*, 1972, p. 428, cited by Moran, *op. cit.*, p.
     126.
10   Wigham, *op. cit.*, p. 161.
11   *Financial Times*, 15 June 1972, cited by Moran, *op. cit.*, p. 141.
12   Eric Heffer, in *The Class Struggle in Parliament* (Gollancz,
     London 1973), p. 317, suggests that the intervention of the
     Official Solicitor was proposed by Lord Denning, whose Appeal
     Court ruling that the individual shop stewards, not the union,
     must be held responsible, had precipitated the crisis.
13   Heffer, *op. cit.*, p. 322.
14   Moran, *op. cit.*, p. 142.
15   Thomson and Engleman, *op. cit.*, pp. 53–4.
16   Moran, *op. cit.*, p. 145.
17   Thomson and Engleman, *op. cit.*, pp. 59–60.
18   Moran, *op. cit.*, p. 146.
19   *Hansard*, 30 May 1911, Col. 1022, cited by Heffer, *op. cit.*, p. 9.
20   Thomson and Engleman, *op. cit.*, pp. 10–11.
21   Wigham, *op. cit.*, p. 160.

22 In its two and a half years of life, the NIRC received 1,102 applications (not to mention the many thousands of cases resolved at industrial tribunals), of which 408 were withdrawn or settled in court, and judgements were given on 694; of these judgements, only 83 concerned collective bargaining. Thomson and Engleman, *op. cit.*, p. 40.

Chapter 3

1 Wigham, *op. cit.*, p. 161.
2 See, for example, pp. 58 and 59.
3 This view was strongly expressed to the author by, amongst others, a senior official of the National Coal Board in an interview in 1973.
4 See Alfred Robens, *Ten-Year Stint* (Cassell, London 1972).
5 They could, in fact, have described the cut as greater than this, in that any rise was taxable (since most miners would be paying the basic rate of tax on at least the top end of their income) so that the 8 per cent rise would, in fact, bring them a 'take-home' rise of less than 6 per cent.
6 The author became interested in Arthur Scargill, as a remarkably effective leader, as soon as he began his research into this subject in 1973. They had a three-hour interview in December 1976, and these impressions are based on this, on his writings and television appearances, and in a five-hour interview Scargill had with Robin Blackburn, later published in *New Left Review* in June 1975.
7 *New Left Review*, September 1975. Their italics.
8 *Ibid.*
9 Wigham, *op. cit.*, p. 169.

Chapter 4

1 This account is based upon interviews with officials of the National Coal Board and the National Union of Mineworkers, including Arthur Scargill; with officers of the West Midlands Police including Sir Derrick Capper; shop stewards of other unions which reinforced the picket; members of the Communist Party who assisted in accommodating the miners in Birmingham; and journalists of the BBC, the *Birmingham Post* and the *Birmingham Mail*. It will be evident to the reader that their views conflicted and none of them will agree wholly with the assessment. With the exception of those mentioned in the text and above, their names have therefore not been given. The interviews

were supplemented by studying material generously made available by those two newspapers; and reports and interviews in the national press and in the *New Left Review* and *The Miner*.

2   Police records show that there were never more than 800 police on duty at the gates, facing a peak of 15,000 pickets. Arthur Scargill claims that there were 3,000 police, and that they relieved each other in shifts every hour. The total number of police available, including reserves nearby, was probably between 1,500 and 2,000. For comparison, there were 9,000 police in the vicinity of Grosvenor Square in October 1968, though less than one-third were ever used.

3   Interview with *New Left Review*, June 1975.

4   Alan Law, 'The Miners are Coming', *The Miner*, April 1972.

5   Interview with the author, 10 December 1976.

Chapter 5

1   This account of the 1972 building strike, the Shrewsbury picketing incidents and the trial are based largely on interviews by the author and his research assistant with those involved. These included twelve building trade employees, fourteen trade union officials and shop stewards (four of them members of the CPGB), three police officers, two victims of violence or intimidation and a number of journalists and other witnesses. As almost all were extremely frank, and because some of the scars could easily be reopened, none of their names will be mentioned. All sides gave conflicting views, and none can be expected to agree wholly with the account or the assessment. In addition, the author and his assistant attended part of the Appeal Court proceedings on the Shrewsbury pickets. They were also given the most generous assistance by the editor and staff of *The Shropshire Star*, who made available all their reports and photographs throughout the strike and the trial. Supplementary sources included *The Times*, *Guardian*, *Daily Telegraph*, *Sunday Times*, *Observer*, *Sunday Telegraph*, *Morning Star*, *Charter*, *The Economist*, *Red Weekly*, *Socialist Worker* and *Up Against the Law*; also J. Arnison, *Shrewsbury Three, Strikes, Pickets and Conspiracy* (Lawrence and Wishart, London 1974).

Chapter 6

1   The pattern had similarities with the period after the defeat of the postal workers' strike in the first quarter of 1971.

Working days lost in strikes (000)

1971	1st quarter	9,497 (postal workers' strike)
	2nd quarter	1,469
	3rd quarter	1,282
	4th quarter	1,304
1972	1st quarter	12,552 (miners' strike)
	2nd quarter	2,992
	3rd quarter	6,833 (docks and building strikes)
	4th quarter	1,562
1973	1st quarter	2,256
	2nd quarter	1,884
	3rd quarter	1,353
	4th quarter	1,680

Source: *Department of Employment Gazette.*

2   On these less abrasive and more individual problems, the Industrial Relations Act was a substantial improvement on previous legislation. There were over a hundred applications dealing with bargaining structures and these were generally resolved successfully except where two rival and viable organizations were competing for bargaining rights. The use of the Act was also successful in dealing with appeals against unfair dismissals, of which there were 14,547. Of these the majority were settled by conciliation or withdrawn. The remaining 5,791 were heard by Industrial Tribunals under the Act and of these 36 per cent were settled in favour of the applicant. The provisions for unfair dismissals were amongst those retained when the Act was repealed by the 1974 Labour Government. Thomson and Engleman, *op. cit.*, pp. 40–7.

3   See Chapter 2.

4   David Butler and Dennis Kavanagh, *The British General Election of February 1974* (Macmillan, London 1974), pp. 12–13. Official figures were:

	Weekly Earnings Index (1970 = 100)	Retail Price Index (1970 = 100)	Gross Domestic Product at 1970 prices (1970 = 100)	World commodity prices (1968–70 = 100)
1971 1st quarter	107	106	100	101
2nd quarter	110	109	101	102
3rd quarter	113	111	102	101
4th quarter	115	112	102	102
1972 1st quarter	118	114	101	111
2nd quarter	122	116	104	113
3rd quarter	127	118	104	114
4th quarter	133	121	106	121

5   Wigham, *Strikes*, p. 173.
6   *Ibid.*, p. 173.
7   Report by the Pay Board, 8 November 1973.
8   *The Economist*, 20 January 1973.
9   See Note 4.
10 *The Economist*, 17 November 1973. The rise in prices, however, was uneven, and the food element in the Retail Price Index had risen by 18·7 per cent between October 1972 and October 1973.
11 See Note 4.
12 These points were made, in retrospect, by two Oxford University economists, R. W. Bacon and E. W. Ellis, in an article in the *Sunday Times*, 9 November 1975.
13 *The Economist*, 13 October 1973.
14 Stephen Fay and Hugo Young, *The Fall of Heath* (p. 6), reprinted from articles published in the *Sunday Times*, 22 and 29 February and 7 March 1976.

Chapter 8

1   Fay and Young, *op. cit.*, pp. 6–8.
2   *Keesing's Contemporary Archives.*
3   Fay and Young, *op. cit.*, p. 14.
4   Wigham, *Strikes*, pp. 161, 172.
5   Fay and Young, *op. cit.*, p. 14.
6   Butler and Kavanagh, *February 1974*, p. 30.
7   Wigham, *Strikes*, pp. 175–6.
8   *Keesing's Contemporary Archives.*
9   *New Left Review*, interview, June 1975.
10 Butler and Kavanagh, *February 1974*, pp. 31–2.
11 Fay and Young, *op. cit.*, p. 16.
12 *Ibid.*, p. 18.
13 *Ibid.*, p. 15.
14 *Ibid.*, p. 19.
15 *Ibid.*, p. 17.
16 Wigham, *Strikes*, p. 176.
17 *Sunday Times*, 23 December 1973.
18 Labour Research Department figures:

		Take-home pay at *Jan. 1974 prices*	Index of real take-home pay
1973	October	£37·67	105
	November	37·79	106
	December	37·69	106
1974	January*	35·71	100

* Three-day week period.

		Take-home pay at Jan. 1974 pribes	Index of real take-home pay
1974	February*	35·53	99
	March	37·00	104
	April	35·82	100
	May	36·08	101

* Three-day week period.

19 *The Economist*, 2 February 1974.
20 Wigham, *Strikes*, pp. 177–8.
21 Fay and Young, *op. cit.*, p. 22.
22 *Ibid.*, p. 29.
23 Butler and Kavanagh, *February 1974*, p. 43.
24 *Guardian*, 2, 9 and 11 February 1974.
25 J. E. Trice, 'Methods of and Attitudes to Picketing', *Criminal Law Review*, May 1975.
26 *Guardian*, 9 February 1974. Arthur Scargill, in his interview with the *New Left Review* on 15 June 1975, supported this view. He also claimed that a decisive factor in forcing the election was the closure of the Scunthorpe Steel Works. This, however, is not borne out by other evidence. The three-day week alone, regardless of the strike, was expected to reduce steel production to 50 per cent, but in fact output remained at approximately 70 per cent, throughout January and February. See *The Economist*, 2 March 1974.
27 *Guardian*, 28 January 1974.
28 Butler and Kavanagh, *February 1974*, p. 44.

Chapter 9

1 Butler and Kavanagh, *February 1974*, p. 28.
2 Fay and Young, *op. cit.*, p. 24.
3 *Ibid.*, p. 7.
4 Butler and Kavanagh, *February 1974*, p. 42.
5 *Ibid.*, p. 43.
6 Fay and Young, *op. cit.*, p. 29.
7 Wigham, *Strikes*, p. 180.
8 For fuller details see Butler and Kavanagh, *February 1974*, pp. 275 ff.
9 *Ibid.*, p. 260.
10 See Chapter 11.
11 Heath remarked in January 1974: 'This country sorely misses Vic Feather.' Fay and Young, *op. cit.*, p. 20.

Chapter 10

1   D. Butler and D. Kavanagh, *The Britsih General Election of October 1974* (Macmillan, London 1975), p. 18.
2   Wigham, *Strikes*, p. 182.
3   *The Economist*, 9 March 1977.
4   Butler and Kavanagh, *October 1974*, p. 19.
5   *Ibid.*, p. 25.
6   Wigham, *Strikes*, p. 182.
7   Butler and Kavanagh, *October 1974*, p. 18.
8   Wigham, *Strikes*, pp. 183–4.

9

1974	Days lost in strikes 000s	Retail Price Index	Average Earnings Index	Industrial output	FT Index
March	2,200*	103	168	106	313
April	664	106	166	107	263
May	844	108	171	108	302
June	862	109	180	109	276
July	499	110	184	110	254
August	520	110	185	109	235
September	999	111	190	108	216
October	1,632	113	193	108	197

* Mainly the continued strike by 258,000 miners until 11 March, after Labour had taken power.

All figures from Butler and Kavanagh, *October 1974*, p. 25.

10 During the period March–October, exports (visible and invisible) exceeded imports by about £1,750 million but Britain's gold and dollar reserves rose by £300 million. What this meant, in effect, was that the oil states were willing to leave a large proportion of the increased prices paid for oil invested or on deposit in Britain. Butler and Kavanagh, *October 1974*, p. 26.
11 Wigham, *Strikes*, p. 184. The Pay Board had thus been very successful—as had the Prices and Incomes Board during the previous Labour Government. It was characteristic of one of the scourges of British politics that in each case—in 1970 and 1974— the incoming Government was committed by its election manifesto to abolish a useful body which had got through its teething troubles and was operating effectively.
12 The 'Certification Officer' was to be appointed by the Employment Secretary in consultation with ACAS. He took the place of the Chief Registrar of Friendly Societies. EPA Clause 7.

Chapter 11

1 In Londonderry, for example, two-thirds of the population were Catholic and voted for nationalist candidates, but they only held one-third of the twelve seats. This was done by the simple expedient of drawing the boundaries to encompass the majority of Catholic voters in four wards, which they won with overkill, while the Protestants were spread so as to win the other eight wards by a small but comfortable majority. When those responsible refused to change the boundaries, O'Neill disbanded the Council and appointed a Commission to run the city.

2 The main sources of this account, especially for facts and dates, were the daily reports in *The Times*; the book by Robert Fisk (*Times* correspondent in Northern Ireland), *The Point of No Return* (André Deutsch, London 1975); and interviews (mainly in 1976) with people who took part, including both strikers and victims of intimidation, 'loyalist', Unionist and SDLP politicians, and members of the Royal Ulster Constabulary, the Army, the Northern Ireland Office and the UWC executive. Because of the circumstances prevailing in Northern Ireland they have not been quoted by name.

3 Numbers of victims of sectarian and factional murders recorded by the RUC between 1972 and 1975 were as follows ('factional' meaning killed by rivals of their own side):

Year	1972	1973	1974	1975	Total	(Of whom)
Protestant victims	40	32	37	49	158	(34 killed by own side 1973–5)
Catholic victims	82	53	58	64	257	(32 killed by own side 1973–5)
Total	122	85	95	113	415	

There were correspondingly more murder charges against Protestants than Catholics—162 to 119 in 1973–5.

4 The Red Hand Commando was a particularly tough group, consisting mainly of Protestant boys led by John McKeague, a middle-aged man who, as leader of the Shankill Defence Association, had led the communal rioting in Belfast in August 1969.

5 Quoted more fully by Fisk, *op. cit.*, p. 49.

6 See Fisk, *op. cit.*, pp. 79–81.

7 By the end of the strike 862 road blockages had been recorded but only seventy-one people were ever charged—and of these thirty-one were concerned with the rampage in Ballymena on 24 May (see page 141). Of the other forty some were discharged

and some fined but none were sent to prison. See Fisk, *op. cit.*,
pp. 99–100.

Chapter 12

1   See, for example, 'Solidarity with the IRA' in *Red Weekly*, 26
    October 1974, published just after five people were killed by
    bombs in a pub in Guildford and shortly before 21 more were
    killed by the bombs in Birmingham. Thereafter, open propaganda
    for the IRA was restricted by the Prevention of Terrorism Act.
    The October article recognized that the struggle 'inevitably means
    the use of arms' and added: 'We also have to see that the Irish
    may wish to extend the war to Britain.'
2   The best technical account of bombing can be found in *Bombs
    Have No Pity* (Luscombe, London 1975) by Colonel George
    Styles, who won the George Cross for disarming bombs in
    Northern Ireland.
3   The IRA often used girls, like Judith Ward, to place bombs, as
    they aroused less suspicion. A boy and girlfriend team was used
    in some of the pub bombings to dump a shopping bag under a
    seat while they canoodled in a corner.
4   There is an excellent account of the formation and operation of
    this cell in *The Birmingham Bombs* (Barry Rose, London 1976)
    by Brian Gibson, a television producer who at the time was pro-
    ducing a BBC series in Birmingham, *Day and Night*, about the
    police. He had close relations with the West Midlands police
    and attended the whole of the trial of the Birmingham bombers.
5   For a fuller discussion of the public reaction to terrorism and of
    legislation against it, see Richard Clutterbuck, *Guerrillas and
    Terrorists* (Faber and Faber, London 1977), pp. 106–16.

Chapter 13

1   *The Times*, 18 June 1974.
2   Sir Robert Mark, 'The Metropolitan Police and Political Demon-
    strations' in the *Police Journal*, July–September 1975 (transcript
    of a lecture at the Police College, Bramshill).
3   Lord Justice Scarman, *The Red Lion Square Disorders of 15 June
    1974* (Cmnd. 5919, HMSO, London, February 1975).
4   Mark, *op. cit.*
5   This account is based mainly on a comparison of three conflicting
    reports on the incident—the Scarman Report (see Note 3), *Only
    One Died* (K. Beauchamp, London 1975) by Tony Gilbert, who
    led the Liberation march from which the IMG contingent broke

away, and the National Front's *Report to the Home Secretary* (National Front, 1974); also the lecture by Sir Robert Mark (see Note 2). This documentary evidence was supplemented by interviews with a number of those who took part in or witnessed the incident, including police officers and demonstrators. The author's research assistant attended part of the Scarman inquiry. Further details and comments were also obtained from the national press and from the journals of IMG (*Red Weekly*) and the National Front (*Spearhead*); also from *Time Out*, *Socialist Worker* and *The Criminal Law Review*.

6 Scarman, *op. cit.*, p. 42.

7 *Ibid.*, p. 4.

8 *Ibid.*, pp. 4–5. Scarman uses quotes for 'pickets' in this context to differentiate them from lawful pickets in a trade dispute.

9 The Communist Party of *England*, Marxist–Leninist (CPEML) which was a very small movement, mainly university based, had a record of physical attacks on visiting speakers at universities. CPEML is not to be confused with Reg Birch's CPBML (see page 237) or the CPGB.

10 The term 'left-wing demonstrators' is used to refer to those who had broken away from the Liberation march. They included members of IMG and other movements.

11 *Guardian*, 17 June 1977.

12 *The Times*, 27 June 1974.

13 Scarman, *op. cit.*, p. 7.

14 Scarman, *op. cit.*, p. 7. Tony Gilbert, in *Only One Died*, commented about Bailey's evidence: '. . . it is doubtful if there has ever been such an open declaration by an organization that they had come to a demonstration with plans to divert it in the direction they desired and at a moment they chose. All Farquharson (counsel for the Metropolitan Police) had to do was to get him to talk, for with almost every sentence (even if the witness was less wordy than Heron) he could later claim justification for police action. (p. 132).

15 Scarman, *op. cit.*, p. 7.

16 *Ibid.*, p. 7.

17 Gilbert, *op. cit.*, p. 94.

18 Scarman, *op. cit.*, pp. 33–8.

19 Mark, *op. cit.*

20 Scarman, *op. cit.*, p. 42.

21 *Windsor Freek Press*, August 1974.

22 *The New Society: A Report on the Development of Pop and 'Free' Festivals in the Thames Valley Police Area 1972–75*, by the Chief Constable, Thames Valley Police, 1975.

23   *Ibid.* Note that Windsor is not in the Metropolitan Police area, so
     these figures are separate from those on page 153, which were
     for the London area only.

Chapter 14

1   Figures from Butler and Kavanagh, *October 1974*, pp. 293–4,
     with the breakdown between Northern Ireland and 'others' based
     on *The Times*, 14 October 1972.
2   Figures from Central Statistical Office, *Economic Trends*, January
     1977, pp. 18–36.

Quarter	RPI % rise over previous 12 months	Production Index (1970 = 100)	Investment in Manufacturing Industry—% change over previous 12 months	Unemployment
1973 3rd	10	111·5	+17	578,800
4th	12	111·3	+21	524,700
1974 1st	15	107·0*	+19	577,100
2nd	17	110·1	+14	577,400
3rd	17	109·9	− 1	613,700
4th	20	106·0	+ 7	
1975 1st	22	106·1	− 4	737,900
2nd	26	100·5	−10	847,400
3rd	27	99·7	−17	1,000,000
4th	25	100·4	−28	1,132,100

     * Three-day week.

3   *Financial Times*, 17 January 1976.
4   Royal Commission on the Distribution of Incomes and Wealth,
     Report No. 2 (Cmnd. 6172, HMSO, London, July 1975),
     Table 11.
5   Cited by Butler and Kavanagh, *October 1974*, p. 10.
6   'It is an undertaking by the TUC to restrain workers from using
     their bargaining strength to achieve wage and salary increases
     which they feel necessary, justifiable and attainable.' Bert Ramel-
     son (CPGB industrial organizer), *Social Contract or Social Con-
     Trick?* (Communist Party Pamphlet), 1975.
7   *The Economist*, 7 September 1974.
8   *The Times*, 'Annual Financial and Economic Review', 26 Sep-
     tember 1974.
9   HMSO, London, August 1975.
10   *Bank of England Bulletin*, December 1976, quoted in Labour
     Research Department *Fact Service*, 5 February 1977.
11   Labour Research Department, *Guide to the Employment Protec-*

tion Act 1975 and to the Trade Union and Labour Relations Act 1974 (LRD Publication, London 1976), p. 9.

Chapter 15

1   CSO, *Economic Trends*, January 1977.
2   *The Economist*, 4 September 1976.
3   *The Times*, 21 June 1977.
4   Cmnd. 6171 and 6172 of 1975 and Cmnd. 6388 and 6626 of 1976 (HMSO, London).
5   See Diamond, *Report No. 4*, pp. 47–8.
6   *Ibid.*, p. 47.
7   *Ibid.*, Table 29, p. 57.
8   *Ibid.*, p. 49.
9   Diamond does not attempt this precise breakdown, but figures of the number of people with specified assets (e.g. over £50,000) are in his *Report No. 4*, Table 22, p. 50.
10 Diamond makes the approximate assumption that 53 per cent of the 39·2 million have NIL (i.e. negligible) marketable assets. This will be true for many, especially some women and young people. If so, the remaining 27 per cent would average over £2,151 each.
11 The figures for income distribution in 1976 (page 184) were derived from Diamond, *Report No. 4*, Tables 5 and 6, pp. 14 and 15. These tables in both cases gave the lower limit of income for each quantile group, so the first adjustment (calculated graphically) was to interpolate average incomes for each group. Diamond's most recent figures were for the tax year 1973–4 so the second adjustment was for inflation of earnings during the 2¼ years up to July 1976. This was estimated at 10 per cent for those with incomes above £8,500, 20 per cent for those with incomes of £5,000 to £8,000, 30 per cent for those between £3,500 and £5,000 and 40 per cent for those with less than £3,500. Most of this wage inflation was, of course, during the first year (1974–5) before Stage 1 began.
    Diamond gives the numbers of the highest incomes in 1973–4 as: 300 incomes of £100,000 or over (£20,500 after tax) and 1,600 incomes of £50,000 or over (£13,900 after tax).
12 Labour Research Department, *Fact Service*, 25 June 1977.
13 Diamond, *Report No. 4*, Table 11, p. 24.
14 The net income of the average married man with two children after deduction of tax and national insurance and after addition of family allowances, fell in real terms (that is, adjusted to April

L

1977 prices) from £64·44 in July 1976 to £60·39 in April 1977. Labour Research Department, *Fact Service*, 25 June 1977.

15 Labour Research, *op. cit.*, June 1977.

16 From information obtained on a visit by the author to China in August 1975. At that time, the eight-grade system started at £2·50 a week, with a maximum of £7. The average was £4. The manager of an average-sized factory got £16. The Japanese also run a system whereby wages rise with the length of service, a man of fifty getting 2½ times as much as one of twenty doing the same job in the same firm. Socially there is much to be said for this—though it would mean a drastic cut in young people's wages if it were attempted in Britain.

17 *Daily Telegraph*, 29 June 1977, quoting *Employment Conditions Abroad* (ECA).

18 Diamond, *Report No. 3*, Table 49.

19 *Department of Employment Gazette*, October 1975, cited in TUC Pamphlet *The Distribution of Income and Wealth*, December 1976.

20 Diamond, *Report No. 4*, Table 19.

21 Labour Research, *op. cit.*, June 1977.

22 See Dominic Harrod, *The Listener*, 14 July 1977, pp. 34–5.

Chapter 16

1 Roy Grantham, in evidence to the Scarman Inquiry, reported in *The Times* Law Report, 27 July 1977.

2 *Sunday Times*, 26 June 1977.

3 *Observer*, 26 June 1977.

4 Lord Justice Scarman, *Report of Inquiry into Dispute between Grunwick Processing Laboratories and members of APEX*, Cmnd. 6922, HMSO, August 1977.

5 *The Times* Law Report (Grunwick *v.* ACAS), 13 July 1977.

6 Scarman, *Grunwick*.

7 *The Times* Law Report (Grunwick *v.* ACAS), 13 July 1977.

8 *Sunday Telegraph*, 26 June 1977.

9 *The Times* Law Report (Grunwick *v.* ACAS), 5 July 1977.

10 *Observer*, 26 June 1977.

11 *Sunday Telegraph*, 26 June 1977.

12 They were, respectively, the Ministers of Education, Defence and Sport and, since the departure of Roy Jenkins to head the EEC Commission in Brussels, Shirley Williams had become the leading spokesman of the moderate wing of the Labour Party.

13 *Observer*, 26 June 1977.

14 Six pickets had earlier been convicted of obstruction during the peaceful phase, but the convictions were quashed by the Appeal Court during May. *Sunday Times*, 26 June 1977.

15 *The Times*, 15 June 1977.
16 *Socialist Worker*, 23 May 1977. This issue also derides the visit of Shirley Williams and the others: 'Enough to make you want to throw up ... stayed just long enough to have their picture taken.'
17 *Socialist Worker*, 11 June 1977.
18 *The Times*, 14 June 1977.
19 *Observer*, 26 June 1977.
20 *The Times*, 15 June 1977.
21 *The Times*, 17 June 1977.
22 *Observer*, 26 June 1977.
23 *The Times* Law Report, 19 July 1977.
24 *The Times*, 18 June 1977. This is a situation not to be confused with a demand for an injunction against an *anticipated* breach of the law, in the public interest. That, as was ruled by the House of Lords in a different case concerning a planned boycott of mail and telephone calls to South Africa, can only be instituted by the Attorney General. *The Times* Law Report, 27 July 1977.
25 *The Times*, 29 June 1977.
26 *Socialist Worker*, 25 June 1977.
27 *Socialist Press*, 22 June 1977.
28 *Worker*, 4 July 1977.
29 *Socialist Worker*, 2 July 1977.
30 The students were quickly spotted by reporters and others. They chanted their slogans ('the workers—united—will never be defeated') in voices reflecting what has been described as the '*proletkult*'—the attempt by middle-class students to adopt working-class accents. The hybrid result—familiar in University demonstrations—is characteristic and easily recognized.
31 *Sunday Times*, 26 June 1977.
32 *The Times*, 21 June 1977.
33 *The Times*, 22 June 1977.
34 *The Times*, 23 June 1977.
35 There was later some criticism by other Yorkshire miners of the cost of this picketing, which was estimated at £2,000 on 23 June and a further £23,000 on 11 July. This included travel and a payment from Yorkshire NUM funds of £15 to each man for loss of pay and £8 subsistence. This was contrasted with 30p per day paid to the flying pickets in 1974. *The Times*, 28 June 1974.
36 *The Times*, 25 July 1977.
37 *Listener*, 30 June 1977.
38 *The Times*, 24 June 1977.
39 *Socialist Worker*, 2, 9 and 16 July 1977.
40 *Militant*, 1 July 1977.

41   *The Times*, 12 July 1977.
42   *The Times*, 15 July 1977. Most of these were minor injuries. The
     police take note of all their injuries, but there is no similar record
     of injuries to the demonstrators and pickets, since many of those
     with light injuries may not report them.
43   *The Times* Parliamentary Report, 15 July 1977.
44   *Daily Telegraph*, 23 July 1977.
45   *The Times*, 9 August 1977.
46   *Free Nation*, 21 July 1977.
47   *The Times* Law Report, 19 July 1977.
48   *The Times* Law Report, 13 July 1977.
49   Scarman, *Grunwick*.
50   *The Times*, 1 September 1977.
51   See Chapter 9.
52   *The Times*, 2 September 1977.
53   *Daily Telegraph*, 7 September 1977.
54   The police also had occasion to warn the strike organizers that,
     by following the bus when it went round picking up workers from
     their homes during an industrial dispute, they were committing a
     criminal offence. *The Times*, 14 July 1977.

Chapter 17

1   For an account of the earlier developments of IS, see pages 234
    to 236.
2   This account is based on the issues of *Socialist Worker* over the
    period before and after the march; on interviews with witnesses;
    on evidence given at the court hearings; on reports of the march
    and of the hearings by the *Hendon Times*, and in *The Times* and
    other papers; and on the *Report of an Inquiry* published by the
    Brent Borough Trades Council in June 1976 (hereafter referred
    to as the Brent Report).
3   The Brent Report noted 466 'sponsoring bodies', and *Socialist
    Worker* gave some details of contributions. Before the march Paul
    Foot, Editor of *Socialist Worker*, toured universities to raise funds;
    speaking to an audience of over 200 at Exeter University, he said
    that if everyone in the room contributed £1, this would finance
    one marcher for the whole period. That would have worked out
    at about £200 per head. Some of this would have been spent on
    food and accommodation, though *Socialist Worker* reported much
    free hospitality *en route*. Whether any of the money was spent
    on supplementing the dole for the unemployed marchers is not
    recorded, though there were inevitably accusations of 'rent-a-
    mob'.

4 *Socialist Worker*, 20 March 1976.
5 Brent Report; see also *Socialist Worker*, 6, 13 and 20 March 1976, and also Emergency Edition published 20 March.
6 *The Times*, 7, 8 and 9 September 1976.
7 *Sunday Times*, 14 August 1977.
8 *Sunday Telegraph*, 14 August 1977.
9 *Socialist Worker*, 11 June 1977.
10 Butler and Kavanagh, *October 1974* (p. 328), record that Lewisham and Deptford was twenty-second out of the 635 seats in the October election in its percentage of coloured immigrants.
11 *Sunday Times*, 14 August 1977.
12 *The Times*, 20 August 1977.
13 See page 153. In 1972–4, of 1,321 demonstrations in London, only 54 involved disorder.
14 *Socialist Worker*, 20 August 1977.
15 *The Times*, 15 August 1977.
16 *Daily Mail*, 15 August 1977.
17 *Sunday Times*, 14 August 1977.
18 *Daily Mirror*, 15 August 1977.
19 See Butler and Kavanagh, *op. cit.*, p. 328. In the General Election of October 1974, 29·7 per cent of the *population* in Ladywood were born in, or had a parent born in a New Commonwealth country—the highest in any of the 635 constituencies. As most of these were of voting age, the proportion of coloured voters was higher still.
20 *Daily Mail*, 16 August 1977.
21 *Socialist Worker*, 27 August 1977.

Chapter 18

1 *The British Road to Socialism*, Communist Party Programme, Draft for Discussion, published by the Communist Party, 16 King Street, London, 1977, lines 5–6.
2 *Ibid.*, lines 1480–5.
3 *Ibid.*, lines 1457–66.
4 Frank Chapple, General Secretary of the Electrical, Electronic and Plumbers Trade Union, writing in the *Reader's Digest* in February 1976. Chapple was himself once a CPGB member and was a leading figure in the unmasking of the Communist attempt to gain control of the Electrical Trades Union by ballot-rigging in 1961.
5 As pointed out in Chapter 3, their strength in the miners' union in 1972 (and continuing so) was even larger. Out of twenty-

seven, six (22 per cent) were CPGB members and five (18 per cent) Labour Party Marxists—a total of 40 per cent.

6 Chapple, *op. cit.*

7 Lenin's tactics were masterly. As the time for the key vote approached, he made a calculatedly insulting remark to five Jewish delegates, knowing that this would make them walk out. They did, and he sprung the vote. He also cleverly gained a by-product; for just this moment his minority (revolutionary) faction was in a majority, in the room, over their normally more numerous (constitutional) rivals. He thereafter always referred to his faction as the *Bolshevik* ('majority') and the others as the *Menshevik* ('minority') faction. The names stuck—despite the fact that the Mensheviks remained in an actual majority right through from 1903 to 1917.

8 He told a story of a convenor on a big building site who was a Trotskyist. The men were getting really angry about the refusal of the management to provide decent toilets—nothing more than a 'pole and a hole'. The Trotskyist, sensing their anger, saw it as a chance to advance the collapse of capitalism by calling a strike. He summoned the men to a mass meeting. He talked with passion about the opportunities for world revolution; about the situation in Ethiopia; in Portugal; in Angola; in Cambodia; but not a word about the iniquities of the 'pole and a hole'. Then he called for a show of hands for a strike. They voted against it, and as they broke up one man's muttering reflected the mood: 'If we have to go through all that to get a decent shit, he can keep it.'

9 SWP also rejects the system in Russia, Eastern Europe and China as 'state capitalist'.

10 SWP's plan, under the heading 'Where we stand' can be found in most issues of *Socialist Worker*.

11 This printing works also played a significant role in the Right to Work march and confrontation at West Hendon, as described in Chapter 17.

12 See Chapter 5.

13 The Rastafarians subscribe to a religion which quotes a prophecy that one day a black god will be crowned king and lead the black people to dominate the world. That black god was Ras Tafari—or Haile Selassie—but his deposition and death does not seem to have affected the movement, which now has its own momentum.

14 These and most other figures quoted are from *The National Front* (Fontana, London 1977) by Martin Walker, The *Guardian* journalist whose report on Red Lion Square was quoted on page 159.

15 *Daily Telegraph*, 11 March 1977.

16 This point was put to the author in an interview with a NAFF
    member during the Grunwick dispute in 1977.
17 The oldest, at the time of writing, is the Soviet Union, whose
    sixtieth birthday was in November 1977. She is having to learn,
    very slowly, to live with dissent, though so far only in a very small
    way. Would we ever have heard of a Solzhenitsyn or a Bukovsky
    in 1936? Nevertheless, there is some doubt whether Russia will
    survive for another 10 years without revolution. See Bernard
    Levin in *The Times*, 5 August 1977. Spain, after thirty-eight years
    under Franco, saw the danger and carefully opened the door to
    dissent. Portugal had its revolution but, before the Communist
    Party had consolidated control, its people seized their liberties
    against all the odds. If pluralism does survive in either or both of
    these, it will be immensely encouraging for the world.

Chapter 19

1   For reference see the Table of Contents for appropriate headings
    in Chapters 2, 4, 5, 8, 10, 12, 13, 14, 16 and 17.
2   In an interview with the author in New York, 1974.
3   See Richard Clutterbuck, *Living with Terrorism* (Faber and
    Faber, London 1975), pp. 117–20.
4   *Ibid.*, pp. 136–9.
5   Public Order Act 1936, Section 3(i).
6   *Ibid.*, S. 3(2) and (3).
7   Scarman, *Red Lion Square*, para. 131.
8   *Ibid.*, paras. 126–8.
9   They were also, of course, helped by the ALCARAF march in
    the morning, which ended nearby two hours earlier. They par-
    ticipated in organizing that march and advised their members to
    attend it.
10 *Socialist Worker*, 13 August 1977 and *Observer* 14 August 1977.
11 Smith and Hogan, *Criminal Law* (3rd Edition, Butterworth,
    London 1973).
12 *Ibid.*
13 Scarman, *op. cit.*, paras. 154 and 155. See also page 162.
14 See the Home Secretary's comment on Grunwick, page 204.
15 *The Times*, 2 July 1977.
16 TULRA 1974, S.30(1), as amended by TULR(A)A 1976,
    S.3(3).
17 TULRA 1974, S.5, as amended by TULR(A)A 1976, S.1(a).
18 Walker, *op. cit.*, pp. 73–4.

Chapter 20

1   See page 225.
2   In one well-known marginal seat, the Labour and Conservative
    agents know each other well and occasionally split a pint in a pub.
    They are to be seen, metaphorically shedding tears into each
    other's beer, bewailing their reliance on political activists for
    canvassing and addressing the envelopes; the Labour man on his
    Trots and the Tory on his 'hangers-and-floggers'. But each knows
    that the voters who decide which candidate will get in are in the
    middle ground; the Trots drive them to vote Tory and the
    hangers-and-floggers drive them to vote Labour.
3   See Peter Walker, *The Ascent of Britain* (Sidgwick and Jackson,
    London 1977).
4   Because of the well-publicized contacts between Government,
    the TUC and the CBI, the media tend to overlook the importance
    of the City in this equation—especially that of the merchant
    banks and the insurance market (including Lloyds). The mer-
    chant banks handle not only an immense amount of the money
    invested in Britain by Arab oil states and others, but also a large
    proportion of the £27,000 million Britain has invested overseas,
    second only to that of the USA. Return on these investments,
    with earnings from insurance, transport services (like the Baltic
    Exchange) and other agencies amount to invisible exports
    totalling £12,800 million a year—one-third of our total foreign
    income. The handling of this money by the City of London,
    inwards and outwards, has a major effect not only on the balance
    of payments, but also on the pattern of investment and therefore
    of employment inside Britain. See letter from the Director-
    General of the Committee on Invisible Exports, *The Times*, 9
    August 1977.
5   Japan's post war economic miracle was based on a remarkable
    degree of co-operation between the government, the banks, the
    big companies (the Zaibatzu) and the trade unions. The Zaibatzu
    (Mitsui, Mitzubishi, etc.) have two fingers in the pie because
    they hold a major share in the big banks. The banks, in turn,
    owned (at the time of the author's visit to Japan in 1971) 83
    per cent of industrial stock, only 17 per cent being owned in
    equity shares. Much of this 83 per cent was made up of workers'
    savings—the average wage-earner in 1971 was putting 25 per
    cent of his earnings every week into savings accounts—in other
    words he was investing it in Japanese industry. So trade unionists
    had a vested interest in industry making a profit. All were thus

pulling in the same direction. The American who coined the phrase 'Japan Inc.' had a point.

6 This philosophy was lucidly expressed by Margaret Thatcher in an interview on BBC *Panorama*, 11 July 1977.

7 Though occasionally, as in the Lib–Lab pacts of 1923 and 1977, a minority Labour Government has had to do a deal with the Liberals.

8 It can be argued in theory that Mr Callaghan's Government in 1977 enjoyed the support of those who voted Labour and Liberal in October 1974, that is of 39·2 per cent + 18·3 per cent = 57·5 per cent of the electorate. In practice, however, by-elections and public opinion polls showed that their combined support had by 1977 fallen well below 50 per cent of the electorate.

9 Figures from Butler and Kavanagh, *October 1974*, p. 294.

10 R. H. S. Crossman, *Diaries of a Cabinet Minister, Vol. I* (Hamish Hamilton and Cape, London 1975).

11 In the USA a Congressman *does* have an office and a staff. On the other hand, Congressmen do not have any firm expectation of Cabinet office. The President picks his Secretary of State and other members of Cabinet wherever he likes, by no means usually from Congress. Kennedy picked his Secretary of State from the Rockefeller Foundation (Rusk) and his Defence Secretary from Ford Motors (McNamara). Nixon took a Professor of International Relations (Kissinger) as Secretary of State. This has obvious advantages but it does reduce the incentives for standing for Congress—or rather it drives Congressmen to seek other and not always so honourable incentives. On average, Congressmen seem to be of lower calibre and enjoy less respect than MPs.

12 In practice, a large proportion of list seats would go to the Liberals so that a majority of Labour and Conservative MPs (nearly two-thirds of them) *would* represent constituencies. It is also worth noting that, in Germany, the fear that non-constituency members would feel second-rate does not seem to have been realized.

Chapter 21

1 Harold Wilson's 1975 referendum on remaining in the EEC would appear to have been conducted largely for internal Labour Party political reasons. Having himself in the past been critical of Britain joining, he had to justify his own position. He also wanted to call the bluff of his own left wing (it was Tony Benn who called for a referendum, presumably not believing that Wilson would take up the challenge) to discredit their claim to represent the

majority of British public opinion. The vote was two to one in favour of remaining in the EEC—almost exactly as predicted in the public opinion polls.

2 Richard Hodder-Williams, *Public Opinion Polls and British Politics* (Routledge and Kegan Paul, London 1970), p. 17. This book gives a lucid account of sampling systems. 'Random' sampling aims scientifically to eliminate any bias or human error by the interviewer in selecting his victims. 'Stratified random' sampling adds an insurance that if there are, say, known percentages of blue- and white-collar workers, or of people between certain ages, or of men and women in a district, these percentages are accurately reflected in the sample. 'Quota' sampling carries this idea further. The author gives examples of accuracy and consistency, and also examples of inconsistency, and of isolated 'maverick' polls. In particular he records the remarkable inconsistencies in the polls before the General Election of June 1970. He establishes, that, while no poll can be perfect, it is possible to make the probable error very low, and (by multiple polls) to eliminate or at least identify the maverick poll.

3 Milton Shulman, in *The Ravenous Eye* (Cassell, London 1973) contends that this has damaged the political process by cutting down the leader to the size of those he leads, and removing his mystique. But whether Shulman is right or wrong, the problem is here to stay unless we introduce state control of television, which would be a disastrous decision.

4 The 'high conspiracy' theory is passionately put by the Glasgow Media Group in *Bad News* (Routledge and Kegan Paul, London 1976) and by largely the same team, Peter Beharrell and Greg Philo (eds.) in *Trade Unions and the Media* ('Critical Social Studies Series', Macmillan, London 1977). The 'high conspiracy' theory is, in fact, effectively discredited by Professor Richard Hoggart in an interesting forward to *Bad News*.

5 See, for example, the interview with Arthur Scargill in the *New Left Review* in June 1975. See also the comments on the Bullock Report (*Report of the Committee of Inquiry on Industrial Democracy*, Cmnd. 6706, HMSO, London 1976). The far Left press unanimously condemned it for the same reasons.

6 George Goyden, *The Responsible Worker* (Hutchinson, London 1975).

7 Walker, *op. cit.*, pp. 72–80.

8 This account is based on an interview by the author with Sir Bernard Miller, then Chairman of the John Lewis Partnership. By contrast, the co-operative movement pays low managerial salaries and their performance reflects this.

9 Dr Johnson remarked that man is never more innocent than when he is trying to make money.
10 Mark, *op. cit.* See also pages 165 to 166.
11 These convictions were all by magistrates. None were tried in the Crown Court except those who appealed to that Court against the magistrate's conviction or sentence. One was tried at the Old Bailey, and he was acquitted.
12 William Belson, *The Public and the Police* (Harper and Row, London 1975).
13 Jeremy Bentham, the author of this famous phrase, was not only a radical reformer but one who believed that the best results came from allowing people to pursue their own interests unhindered by restrictive legislation.
14 *Listener*, 4 August 1977. See also the comment of Lord Scarman on page 166.

Bibliography

Arnison, J., *Shrewsbury Three: Strikes, Pickets and Conspiracy* (Lawrence and Wishart, London 1974).

Balfour, C., *Unions and the Law* (Saxon House, Farnborough 1973).

Beharrell, Peter and Philo, Greg, *Trade Unions and the Media* ('Critical Social Studies Series', Macmillan, London 1977).

Belson, William, *The Public and the Police* (Harper Row, London 1975).

Bullock Report, *Report of the Committee of Inquiry on Industrial Democracy* (Cmd 6706, HMSO, London 1976).

Butler, David and Pinto-Duschinsky, Michael, *The British General Election of 1970* (Macmillan, London 1971).

Butler, David and Kavanagh, Denis, *The British General Election of February 1974* (Macmillan, London 1974).

Butler, David and Kavanagh, Denis, *The British General Election of October 1974* (Macmillan, London 1975).

Central Statistical Office, *Economic Trends*, January 1977.

Chapple, Frank, 'The Marxist Battle for Britain: Trade Unions', *Rreader's Digest*, February 1976.

Chief Constable, Thames Valley, *The New Society: A Report on the Development of Pop and 'Free' Festivals in the Thames Valley Police Area, 1972–75.*

Cliff, T., *The Crisis: Social Contract or Socialism* (Pluto Press (Socialist Worker), London 1975).

Clutterbuck, Richard, *Living with Terrorism* (Faber and Faber, London 1975).

Clutterbuck, Richard, *Guerrillas and Terrorists* (Faber and Faber, London 1977).

Communist Party, *The British Road to Socialism* (Communist Party Programme, Draft for Discussion, Communist Party, 16 King Street, London 1977).

Communist Party, *Social Contract or Social Con-trick?* (Pamphlet) 1975.

Conservative Central Office, *A Fair Deal at Work*, 1968.

Critchley, T. A., *The Conquest of Violence* (Constable, London 1970).

Crossman, R. H. S., *Diaries of a Cabinet Minister, Vol. 1* (Hamish-Hamilton and Cape, London 1975).

Diamond Commission, *Royal Commission on the Distribution of Incomes and Wealth, Report* (Cmnd 6172, 1975; Cmnd 6171, 1975; Cmnd 6388, 1976; Cmnd 6626, 1976; HMSO, London).

Donovan, Lord, *Royal Commission on Trade Unions and Employers' Associations 1965-68, Report* (Cmnd 3623, HMSO, London 1968).

Employment Protection Act, 1975.

Fay, Stephen and Young, Hugo, *The Fall of Heath* (*Sunday Times*, London 1976).

Fisk, Robert, *The Point of No Return*, (André Deutsch, London 1975).

Gibson, Brian, *The Birmingham Bombs* (Barry Rose, London 1976).

Gilbert, Tony, *Only One Died* (K. Beauchamp, London 1975).

Glasgow Media Group, *Bad News* (Routledge and Kegan Paul, London 1976).

Goyden, George, *The Responsible Worker* (Hutchinson, London 1975).

Haseler, Stephen, *The Death of British Democracy* (Paul Elek, London 1976).

Heffer, Eric, *The Class Struggle in Parliament* (Gollancz, London 1973).

Hodder-Williams, Richard, *Public Opinion Polls and British Policy* (Routledge & Kegan Paul, London 1970).

Hooberman, Ben, *An Introduction to British Trade Unions* (Penguin, Harmondsworth 1974).

Inns of Court Conservative and Unionist Society, *A Giant's Strength*, 1958.

Keesing's Contemporary Archives.

King, Anthony (ed.), *Why is Britain Becoming Harder to Govern?* (BBC Publications, London, 1976).

Law, Alan, 'The Miners are Coming', *The Miner*, April 1972.

Longmate, Norman, *Milestones in Working Class History* (BBC Publications, London, 1975).

Mackenzie, W. J. M., *Power, Violence, Decision* (Penguin, Harmondsworth 1975).

Mark, Sir Robert, 'The Metropolitan Police and Political Demonstrations', *Police Journal,* July–September 1975.

Moss, Robert, *The Collapse of Democracy* (Temple Smith, London 1975).

National Front, *Report to the Home Secretary* (National Front, 1974).

Panitch, Leo, *Social Democracy and Industrial Militancy: the Labour Party, the Trade Unions and Incomes Policy 1945–1974* (Cambridge University Press, 1976).

Robens, Lord Alfred, *Ten Year Stint* (Cassell, London 1972).

Scarman, Lord Justice, *The Red Lion Square Disorders of 15 June 1974* (Cmnd. 5919, HMSO, London 1975).

Scarman, Lord Justice, *Report of Inquiry into Dispute between Grunwick Processing Laboratories and members of APEX* (Cmnd 6922, HMSO, London 1977).

Shipley, Peter, *Revolutionaries in Modern Britain* (The Bodley Head, London 1976).

Shulman, Milton, *The Ravenous Eye* (Cassell, London 1973).

Smith and Hogan, *Criminal Law* (3rd Edition, Butterworth, London 1974).

Stewart, Michael, *The Jekyll and Hyde Years: Politics and Economic Policy since 1964* (London, Dent, London 1977).

Styles, George, *Bombs Have No Pity* (Luscombe, London 1975).

Terr, F. and Spence, J. D., *Political Opinion Polls* (Hutchinson, London 1973).

Thomson, A. W. and Engleman, S. R., *The Industrial Relations Act: A Review and Analysis* (Martin Robertson, London 1975).

Trade Union and Labour Relations Act, 1974.

Trade Union and Labour Relations (Amendment) Act, 1976.

Trice, J. E., 'Methods of and Attitudes to Picketing', *Criminal Law Review,* May 1975.

Urry, John and Wakeford, John (eds), *Power in Britain* (Heinemann, London 1973).

Walker, Martin, *The National Front* (Fontana, London 1977).

Walker, Peter, *The Ascent of Britain* (Sidgwick and Jackson, London 1977).

Wigham, Eric, *What is Wrong with the Unions?* (Penguin, Harmondsworth 1971).

Wigham, Eric, *Strikes and the Government 1893–1974* (Macmillan London 1976).

ADDENDA

Rogaly, Joe, *Grunwick* (Penguin, Harmondsworth 1977).
Ward, George, *Fort Grunwick* (Temple Smith, London 1977).

Index